Advance Praise for

The Healing Heart ~ Communities

There is an infinite well of meaning in story. Here are storytellers plumbing and sharing that meaning in an amazing array of settings. *The Healing Heart* gives us the opportunity to dip into the well, coming up with stories, exercises, and inspiration that strengthen our connections to heritage and community, to personal, social and planetary health.

— GAIL ROSEN, storyteller and bereavement facilitator, founder of the
Healing Story Alliance (a Special Interest Group of the National Storytelling Network)

This potent collection of wisdom stories sparkles with insight into the healing of emotional, social and environmental wounds. The tales and the tellers, who are themselves healers, entreat, encourage, and entice us to care for ourselves, each other, and our precious planet as if life depended on it, which it surely does!

— ERICA HELM MEADE, psychotherapist, and author, *The Moon in the Well: Wisdom Tales to Transform Your Life, Family and Community*

"The Healing Heart" is one of those rare books that awaken, startle and delight. It's fiery and completely alive. It lets you see your story more clearly. This book is full of stories that go to the heart of life. It's marvelous.

— JAY O'CALLAHAN, Winter Olympic Bard, NEA Recipient, writer, teacher, storyteller.

Deep wisdom is inherent in our stories, the bedrock and heart of who we are as a culture. This book feeds our organic hunger for meaning and community, so important in these chaotic times.

— MICHAEL TOMS, Co-founder and principal host of New Dimensions Radio, author of *A Time For Choices: Deep Dialogues for Deep Democracy* and co-author of *True Work*

The Healing Heart

~ Communities

The Healing Heart

~ Communities

Storytelling to Build Strong and Healthy Communities

Edited by Allison M. Cox and David H. Albert
Foreword by Margaret Read MacDonald

NEW SOCIETY PUBLISHERS

Cataloguing in Publication Data:
A catalog record for this publication is available from the National Library of Canada.

Cover design by Diane McIntosh. Image: Artville, illustrator: Lisa Zador.

Printed in Canada by Friesens.

Paperback ISBN: 0-86571-468-1
Library Binding ISBN: 0-86571-469-X

*Some of the authors of this book have offered their stories for other tellers' oral use. These stories are indicated by an asterisk in the table of contents. Please credit the author when you use these stories.

If this symbol(*) does not appear with a story, please contact the author to request permission before telling his or her story (contact information is given with the author biographies at the back of the book). Audio recording or reprinting of any material in this book requires permission from the authors.

Inquiries regarding requests to reprint all or part of *The Healing Heart* should be addressed to New Society Publishers at the address below.

To order directly from the publishers, please add $4.50 shipping to the price of the first copy, and $1.00 for each additional copy (plus GST in Canada). Send check or money order to:

New Society Publishers
P.O. Box 189, Gabriola Island, BC V0R 1X0, Canada
1-800-567-6772

New Society Publishers' mission is to publish books that contribute in fundamental ways to building an ecologically sustainable and just society, and to do so with the least possible impact on the environment, in a manner that models this vision. We are committed to doing this not just through education, but through action. We are acting on our commitment to the world's remaining ancient forests by phasing out our paper supply from ancient forests worldwide. This book is one step towards ending global deforestation and climate change. It is printed on acid-free paper that is **100% old growth forest-free** (100% post-consumer recycled), processed chlorine free, and printed with vegetable based, low VOC inks. For further information, or to browse our full list of books and purchase securely, visit our website at: www.newsociety.com

NEW SOCIETY PUBLISHERS   www.newsociety.com

Dedication

To my family, who waited forever for me to finish writing and always applauded from the back of the room — Mark, who listened to half-baked tales in the wee hours of the night; Shanon, who insisted that I can do whatever I want; and Breean, who pushed me to search for the deeper meaning. And for all the stories yet to come… — A.M.C.

To family, fish, flowers, and bedbugs (among others) who have goaded me into telling, and are still working heroically to make sure I get it right. — D.H.A.

Contents

*Authors have offered their stories for other tellers' oral use. Please credit the author when you use these stories.

See copyright page (vi) for more details.

Foreword

MARGARET READ MACDONALD

PARENTS, GRANDPARENTS, AND community and spiritual leaders have always used story as a path to guide the thoughts of those for whom they feel responsible. Today's religious and educational leaders still make good use of story. But taking story into the social health and medical professions can be challenging. Allison Cox and David Albert have drawn together in two volumes the work of 66 individuals who have found ways to use story effectively in their work. We hear from folks who work with children, dysfunctional teens, at-risk families, and elders. We see tellers at work in hospitals, schools, shelters, detention facilities, community centers. And we hear from those who work one-on-one with troubled individuals, using story as a way in. This book and its companion volume, *The Healing Heart: Storytelling to Encourage Caring and Healthy Families*, will do much to encourage the use of story in human services.

No one can pass through this book without coming out the other side full of ideas and encouragements. Joseph Andrejchak Galata leads the way for work with endangered teens. He begins by asking them to stand absolutely still on stage in full spotlight for several minutes. Until they have emptied themselves and learned to just stand and listen, how can they refill themselves with story and begin to tell? What an amazing technique! Steve Otto shows us the danger of letting our elders' stories go untold. And he gives us

clear steps for helping them share. Cathryn Wellner gives us much encouragement for our sharing of stories in her "Seven Lessons." Telling to disdainful junior high students, she felt she had failed and that the stories she offered were of no account. Returning a year later, she found that one of those stories had lodged like a burning coal in the student's minds. You will find in this book many techniques and remarkable stories chosen for hopeful success with target audiences.

But let me add my own notions to this book by suggesting that any story shared is a good thing. The very act of telling bonds our hearts together. Story shared from the heart is always understood to be a gift. As the one who offers this gift, you may never know whether or not it was accepted. But rest assured that the story will have made its way into many hearts and that the act of giving will have been appreciated. And one more enormous value of storytelling: the story event bonds the listening group. In this sharing of emotion and idea, the group becomes one. The teachers with whom I work always express amazement at the almost magical effect the act of sharing story has on their classes. Story takes us to another place. And when we return from this moment of shared experience, the individuals and the group are changed just a little.

May you enjoy *The Healing Heart: Storytelling to Build Strong and Healthy Communities* and take from it many gifts to further your own work. For health care and social services providers, I wish you great success in adapting these techniques. Using story does not require great expertise. Don't stress out over the "performance" of the story. Just find a tale that speaks to you and share it from your heart. That is all that is required. It is the caring with which you share, that makes the tale effective. Educators, religious leaders, and environmentalists, please look carefully at the tales and suggestions in this book. Think of ways to incorporate this use of story in your own lives. For those professional storytellers reading these pages, I challenge you to look beyond your usual work and help with some of the desperately needed storywork revealed here.

Acknowledgments

THE FOLLOWING PEOPLE championed the birthing of this book:

The Healing Heart finally got rolling when community members of Tacoma, Washington, planned a conference: Storytelling For Prevention, Building Wellness In Our Communities. Many thanks for the hours dedicated by the planning committee, above all Gene Uno, Sheri Badger, and N.C. Griffith, and to Louie Thadie for asking the question "Who wants to learn more about storytelling?"

My appreciation goes to fellow workers at the Tacoma Pierce County Health Department who encouraged and validated my work in storytelling — especially Merle Hemphill and Sue Winskill. And particular recognition must be given to the "Odyssey Ladies," Willie Goble and Ruth Jeynes, as well as the wonderful teachers and students who welcomed us into their lives every week.

Kudos to my professors at the University of Washington's Public Health Graduate Certificate Program, who expressed interest in my efforts to apply storytelling to health promotion/disease prevention and allowed me to begin compiling the *Healing Heart* books as my practicum project.

My heartfelt thanks to the storytelling organizations of western Washington that have repeatedly welcomed me to their stages, allowing me to delve into new story frontiers: the Mount Tahoma Storytelling Guild, Seattle Storytelling Guild, Olympia Storytelling Guild, Story People of Port Angeles, and Storytellers Network of Longview. I am grateful for the friendships that have been forged through these alliances and all the encouragement that was offered.

The storytellers of the Vancouver Society of Storytelling and the Vancouver Storytelling Festival gave me vital feedback while offering endless enthusiasm and inspiration — special thanks to Nan Gregory, Melanie Ray, Kira Van Deusen, and Catherine Racine for opening up their homes and hearts to me. And my gratitude to Merle Harris, Sandy Byer, Barb Gale, Nancy Duncan, Gail Catlin, Joan Stockbridge, Josephine Pedersen, Frances Feist, and all the others who believed strongly enough in my work to invite me to travel across Canada and the United States to share these tales and speak of the healing applications of story.

The members of Texas Women's University's Storytell listserv offered guidance on countless occasions during my search for tellers and stories to include in these pages. The Healing Story Alliance listserv and board members rallied to help, especially Cristy West, who kept urging me on, and Gail Rosen, who acted as my patient sounding board on all those late-night phone calls. Kind words from Steve Sanfield and Merle Davis gave me courage. I am grateful for all the storytellers, health workers, teachers, and other community members who told me they were eager to read this book and cheered me on along the way.

I could not have completed the work without Madonna Sturmer, who washed dishes and cooked meals while I typed. And Allan Sturmer, who planted, weeded, and watered the gardens while I typed. And Mark Bassett, who built the fire, kept the computer running, and rubbed my shoulders — sore from all that typing.

I am grateful to the Brimstone Foundation for a grant that supported my work on this book, and to the staff at New Society Publishers for sharing the vision. The credit goes to my co-editor, David Albert, for suggesting this book in the first place and for keeping the dream alive.

And finally, I offer my deepest thanks for all those marvelous listening faces in the audience, hugs in the grocery aisles and school hallways (Look, Momma, it's the storyteller!), and parting smiles in the detention centers, shelters, recovery clinics, community centers and at the elder meal sites. Each time you ask "Will you please come back again?" — I want to tell these tales all night long and would be willing to start this book from scratch. This book, above all else, was inspired by you.

— *Allison M. Cox*
Storytelling crosses over all boundaries
for it speaks the language of the heart.

Thanks —

- to the members of Olympia Friends Meeting, who have taught me to find stories in silence;
- to the people of Bread & Roses, who have taught me to find stories in service, and to seek out the particulars;
- to all my wondrous friends in India, who first taught me — confirmed city dweller that I am — to find stories in the earth;
- and to my family — Ellen, Aliyah, and Meera — who've put up with the fact that I am often a notoriously slow learner.

— *David H. Albert*

STORIES 'R' US

New Beginnings

DAVID H. ALBERT*

Shiva and Parvati lived together in a house off in a far-off corner of the world that only the gods could inhabit. All would have been well, perhaps, except Shiva would often go away for eons at a time to dance his destruction of the world — from whence all creation springs — leaving poor Parvati alone in the house.

Parvati was very lonely. Then she came up with an idea to deal with her loneliness. She took a ball of mud, combined it with dirt from her own body, and with her own hands fashioned the loveliest little boy to keep her company. And he did — laughing and playing ball and doing all the little things that mothers adore about their little boys.

One day, Parvati decided to take a bath. She asked the little boy to stand guard while she was bathing. Suddenly Shiva came home, having danced himself out for a while, and barged in through the door. Seeing the boy angered him, and in a jealous rage he cut the boy's head off.

"What have you done?" cried Parvati, still shaking. "This boy you have killed is your son!"

Shiva, now calming down and seeing what he had wrought, said to Parvati, "I will make amends. I will take the head of the next person who comes along and fashion it to the body of the boy, and he'll be as good as new."

Just then they looked out the window. And lo and behold, the first person who came along was an elephant.

And that is why Lord Ganesh, the Bringer of Boons and Destroyer of Obstacles — the firstborn of Shiva and Parvati his consort — has the head of an elephant and the body of a boy. And, I am told, like an elephant, Ganesh never forgets. 🐚

At the beginning of any new venture or of a long journey, or at the birth of a child, Hindus offer a prayer to Lord Ganesha, the god of new beginnings and of second chances. Ganesha, in his strange, hyphenated body, is also seen as the deity who is a connector between the world of the divine — symbolized by the head — and that of phenomenal existence — the body of the little boy.

As lord of wisdom, learning, and, most of all, memory, Ganesha is the god of storytelling. For every story is a new beginning, a bringing forth of memory, whether by a telling gesture that with a sweep of the hand gathers the pebbles of an almost forgotten past, or by a turn of phrase that brings forth the bittersweet of a childhood long gone, or by a narrative that stings the locus of love and loss and brings with it renewal.

Every well-turned story, or so it can be said, is a hymn of praise to Ganesha. For in the remembrance of things past, real or imagined, is the promise of a second chance. Ganesha is the lord of linkages and the guardian of entrances. As I look through the stories contained in the two volumes of *The Healing Heart*, each links the exigencies of the phenomenal world — whether physical injury, chronic conditions, sickness, and even death, or the emotional pain born of domestic violence, alcohol or other drug addiction, homelessness, child abuse, environmental degradation, the disappearance of cultures, and community disintegration — with an entrance into a new or perhaps *re-membered* awareness, born of grace, the new, wiser head grafted to the older body.

Stories are the *re-collection* of parts of ourselves in the process of becoming who we are or were truly meant to be. The knight sets forth on his journey, discovers himself in a barren wasteland, is confronted by his personal dragons, and makes his way to the other side, having rescued his damsel in distress, unearthed the golden chalice (itself a metaphor for the heart of humankind), or simply stumbled his way, bloodied and bedraggled, perhaps, but newly made whole, back to his own bed. But Ganesha is also the lord of categories and of multitudes — each of our journeys, and our stories, is our own, but the re-collection and re-membrance of them collectively is the multitudinous storehouse of culture and community, the fruits and sugared rice and sesame cakes Ganesha holds in his four hands.

Ganesha is always depicted with a large belly, an emblem of the fact that we can learn to consume and digest whatever experiences life throws in our path. (This book, and its companion — *The Healing Heart ~ Families: Storytelling to Encourage Caring and Healthy Families* — is certainly large enough, and filled with enough morsels of experience, to warrant a lengthy digestion!) One foot touches the ground, and the other is tucked up under him, providing a balance between the grounding of our experience and our imaginative selves. And Ganesha rides around on the back of a rat — I guess one could call that a commitment to basic transportation. It would be interesting to do a survey of the make, model, and especially the age of automobiles that storytellers included in *The Healing Heart* use these days, but we haven't availed ourselves of the opportunity! (I'm sure there are stories about these vehicles, too!)

Hindus look upon the image of Ganesha as timeless. He doesn't exist in history and doesn't make demands upon us other than to be aware of his presence. In Western traditions, in contrast, God intervenes in human history. But the idea of the new beginning is equally embodied not only in the New Testament Jesus, but also in one of the most miraculous stories of the Old, the declaration of Jubilee.

Every 50th year, or so it says in Leviticus, the soil of the land is to be allowed to lie fallow. All landed property outside the walls of towns reverts to its original owner, who may have been driven by poverty to sell it. And Israelites, reduced to slavery for similar reasons, are to go free.

I call Jubilee a story, although none is attached to it in the Old Testament, because no one knows for sure if it was ever observed. But it has all the makings of a story, for consider:

In the year before Jubilee,

- Interest rates soared, for no one would take property as surety on loans.

- The price of food rose steeply, for there wouldn't be a harvest, and the speculators had a field day, for no one could predict what would happen to the food supply.

- Slaves began to disobey their masters, knowing that their days of servitude were numbered.

- Birthrates skyrocketed, as farmers had nothing to do.

- The number of marriages fell, for who could afford a dowry? With it went the market for wedding garments and good wine.

- The value of land dropped precipitously.

- Real estate developers worked feverishly to convince town authorities to annex outlying areas.

- Banks foundered, and gold rose in the international currency exchanges.

- The cities overflowed and the poor went begging for work and for food, for no one would take them in servitude.

- The slave market for Israelites dried up.

- Moving and storage companies had all the business they could handle, and yard sales were outstanding!

And then on the first day of Jubilee, the ram's horn sounding its utter astonishment, the Lord God Almighty, Fashioner of All Things Great and Especially Small, stroking His beard and wiping His perspiring hands upon His blue workingman's smock, looked down from His workshop in heaven and saw that it was indeed all worth it. For He saw, if but for a moment, that the earth was at peace, and even in the midst of a world scarlet-draped in greed, cunning, and just plain indifference, the poorest of the poor, their debts forgiven, would, if just once in 50 years, be provided a second chance. ❧

In the world of storytelling — as I hope you will find in *The Healing Heart* —
there is a little touch of Jubilee all year round.

The Goats Know the Way

A Jewish folktale retold by Erica Lann-Clark

"The Goats Know the Way" is a story about many things, one of which is daring to follow the promptings of intuition, the unexpected signs that come our way. Sometimes we're too busy or too distracted by our doings in the world to listen to the inner prompting, even when it is calling loudly at the gate. What good is a sign if no one notices? Embedded in each story, in the universal language of metaphor, there are signs aplenty, and they can take years to explore. Like underground passages, they only reveal themselves step by step, and in this way they lead us ever deeper toward an unknown destination.

I choose to tell a story because something in me resonates to the characters, the images, the often hidden symbolism. When I first discovered this story, it stopped me cold. "Retell me as I ought to be told," the story seemed to cry, and so I did. As I have lived with this story and told it time and again, it has led me ever deeper toward a place in my own soul that was wounded and needed to be healed. My people say sometimes we need a story more than food. Certainly there are times we need to hear a story to heal our souls. But there are also times we need to tell one. Here, then, is "The Goats Know the Way," my feminized retelling of a Jewish folktale, "The She-Goats of Shebreshin."

The story begins in a little village in Yugoslavia, but it has deep roots that travel back in time 2,000 years to when the Jews were thrown out of their homeland and had to run for their lives (a typical Jewish theme). As they left, they took what anyone fleeing death would take — the bare essentials — and the Book, the Torah.

North, south, east, and west they went, looking for any halfway hospitable place to stay. Though they wanted to be welcomed in their new countries, they were at the same time filled with a longing for a homeland they would never see again. They dreaded being changed and becoming strangers to themselves. So when they read their Torah, they were comforted. Here was their story, and theirs alone: how their ancestors had wandered homeless for 40 years with Moses in the desert; how even Abraham, the Patriarch, had been forced to leave his homeland of Ur to look for G-D. Now they could see this exile as just the latest chapter of their destiny.

Certainly the book was a recipe for homesickness, but it also contained, embedded in code, a secret labyrinthine passage leading all the way back to Gan Eden, Paradise, the original home of all human beings. That was why they took the Book. The first duty of every tribe in exile is to find the way home, no matter how perilous the journey. But how should one parse the path, when the Torah was written in the cunning, many-layered Hebrew alphabet, whose every letter carried a lifetime of meaning? Worse yet, each letter also doubled as a number, and each number carried altogether different layers of meaning. Each word could be read as language or numbers. Only a truly inspired reader could hope to uncover the mysterious path to Paradise.

You had to *daven* the Torah, read with your whole soul, drink in the music of each syllable. Surrendering in ecstasy, you had to *daven* day and night. Then perhaps the heavens would open and the Master of the Universe would hear you asking to go home. That is why the first thing the Jews did, wherever they settled, was build a house of study. It was a remarkable effort. There, day or night, everyone — the men, the women, even the children— could *daven* nonstop. But the women were always being called out of the house of study. A child was sick, a woman in labor, an elder dying; without question, that was woman's work. Even an animal in labor, how could a woman turn her back? And if the grain needed threshing, everyone knew whose work it was. Who else should heal the children, catch the babies, cut the cords, comfort the dying, or lay out the dead? Certainly not the men! Thus it was the men did not object when the women were called away from their *davenning* in the house of study. They were very understanding. "Go," they said. "We understand. You have permission because this we also need — it is survival."

Over the centuries, what had once been permission to leave transformed into prohibition from entering. The men continued to *daven*, but the women stopped, and not just *davenning*, but reading and writing, too. By the Middle Ages, in Europe, no ordinary self-respecting Jewish woman ever set foot in a house of study. "Let the men *daven*," said the women, "it's men's work. After all, don't we do practically everything else?"

Perhaps in a few Jewish enclaves in the great cities there were women who learned to read and write, who even became scholars, but in the villages and towns? Definitely not. And this is where everything that is about to happen, happened. Middle-aged Moishe and middle-aged Tsetse, the hero and heroine of my story, and their two milking goats, also middle-aged, lived in just such a little pinsky village in the heart of Yugoslavia, a land riddled with tunnels.

Now, Moishe was no ordinary *davenning* Jew. He had a fire in his heart! He knew from earliest childhood that he had been chosen to lead his people back. He could remember lying on his back in his swaddling clothes, his *wimple*, scarcely three months old, when suddenly the unnameable Master of the Universe looked down from the heavens and, seeing Moishe, pinched his cheeks and crooned, "*Daven* well, little Moishe, because you could do it. You could be the one to lead them home to me, Moishele. I'm counting on you." Little Moishe reached up with his pudgy arms and crooned back, "Gaaaa." It was a solemn promise.

From that moment on, a fire burned in Moishe's soul and to *daven* became his whole life. Well, of course, he had a little side job, and naturally he was married — to Tsetse — but only till the moment the heavens opened and showed him the path to bring his people home, home to Gan Eden, Paradise.

Now, Tsetse was no ordinary woman, for she also had a fire in her heart, or, as Moishe called it, "a little wild hair." What exactly was this wild hair? Tsetse wanted someday to *daven* herself. There was power in those letters. Why should women be kept from them? If she dared, others would, and she would bring the women back to their rightful place in the house of study. To that end, she was teaching herself to read and to write, but only on the side and between her real jobs: going to the market, cleaning the house, baking the bread, making the bed, cooking the chicken (and everything else), and milking the middle-aged goats, who were, to tell the truth, no trouble at all.

In the morning, she only had to open the gate and let them out. There they went, slowly enough, looking for good things to eat. They never went too far. They weren't adventurous. They were middle-aged. As the sun went down, they came home. They were no fools. They wanted to be warm and safe at night, like everybody else. Tsetse milked them. Then she made dinner. That was her job. Meanwhile, Moishe helped. He *davenned* at home, so Tsetse could easily call him to dinner.

So, nu, what do middle-aged goats give for milk? Maybe a quarter of a pail between them. Enough for two middle-aged people, and maybe a little left over to trade at market. One evening, as Tsetse let in the goats, they looked … different. Their fur seemed shinier. Their eyes were clearer. When she milked them, they gave half a pail — more than they had given in years! Astonished, she looked at the frothy milk bubbling in the pail and, redirecting the next squirt to her open mouth, Tsetse tasted. The milk was delicious. She poured herself a glass and drank it down. It was divine! How could she not at once bring Moishe a taste?

There he stood in the central room of their little house, rocking back and forth on his heels, eyes cast upward as if he could see right through the ceiling. He was making little crooning sighs in counterpoint to the rhythms of the sacred words that he half-sung and half-spoke to himself.

Tsetse looked him over and thought he was just doing his usual, daily, pre-dinner *davenning*, for so it seemed to her, but if she had asked him, Moishe would have answered without hesitation that, actually, *he* wasn't even in the room. *He* was poised halfway down a remarkably elastic spider web of thought that led from their little pinsky village all the way to Paradise. He could practically smell the Garden of Eden. In spite of his growing excitement, Moishe reined in his feelings and, with his mind, raised his mental right foot like a trained acrobat to take another carefully balanced mental step toward Paradise. It wasn't easy. He had to think his way through the jungle of meanings and counter-meanings, the forest of insinuations and the swamp-like bog of connotations, but he was doing it, inching forward, closer and closer, when, out of the ether, Tsetse appeared, holding out a giant glass of milk. It wobbled before him like a devilish mirage, diverting his mental gaze. Her voice boomed and roared like the waves of the ocean. "Taste, Moishe, it's divine!"

Stunned, Moishe emptied the glass. As he drank, the path to Paradise disappeared. With his thick eyebrows drawing together in anguish and disbelief, he shouted, " I don't believe it! A man can't even *daven* in his own home? How could you, Tsetse? I was so close to the secret of our return to Gan Eden — it was such a beautiful thought, so clear. And you just broke it! How many times have I told you, don't interrupt me when I'm *davenning*!"

"But the milk, Moishe, how did it taste? Wasn't it delicious?"

"Tsetse, it was only a glass of milk from a middle-aged goat. Good, not good, delicious. What is that compared to the return of our people to their original home?"

"But, Moishele —"

"Tsetse, you know from milk, and that's it.

You didn't know, but I wasn't even in the room. What you saw was the hard shell of flesh that imprisons the divine radiance, not me. How should you understand these things of which I speak? You're just a woman. Have some respect, beloved wife, for those who do the deep work of *davenning* our way out of exile."

Tsetse's face fell, Moishe turned away, and they spoke not another word that evening. Clearly, what was a wonderment to Tsetse was beside the point to Moishe.

The next evening, when the goats came home and frolicked at the gate instead of standing there like sedate, middle-aged goats, Tsetse kept silent. When they rose on their hind legs and began knocking their horns together as if they were a couple of kids and no longer had stiff joints, she said nothing. When they gave her almost a full pail of milk, she didn't mention it But she drank and it was delicious and extraordinary, and she said not a word to Moishe.

The extra milk Tsetse took to the market, and when the women at the market tasted it, they were very curious. "Such wonderful milk from two old goats? Where are they feeding? What are they eating? Show us so we can take our goats there." To all their questions Tsetse gave the same answer. With a toss of her head and a shrug of her shoulders, she said, "How should I know?"

In private, to herself, she thought, "In fact, I should know. Look what's happening to the goats; they're growing younger every day. Imagine, if we ate what they are eating, maybe the same would happen to us." What was beside the point to Moishe had become a consuming wonderment to Tsetse. She decided to find out.

The next morning when she let the goats out of the gate, she followed. The goats led her through one field, then another. They seemed to have a destination in mind. From time to time they looked at a few flowers or a clump of particularly fresh greens, but they didn't eat. They kept moving farther from the village and higher into the surrounding hills until suddenly they stopped at the entrance to a cave. Glancing back at her briefly, as if inviting her to follow, they walked into the dark cave. Stepping in, she saw only the whitish undersides of their tails as the goats disappeared. Instinctively, Tsetse shrank back, but then she thought, "Those goats are not much smaller than me. Where they can fit, I can, too."

The cave opening led to a tunnel that plunged downward. Quickly, Tsetse and the goats were engulfed in total darkness. The goats slowed down. Tsetse followed the sound of their hooves and used her hands to feel her way. The tunnel walls were warm and moist, and all was dark — as it must be while we are inside our mothers, before we're born, thought Tsetse. For a long time she followed along in this way. Then the tunnel seemed to turn this way and that and the goats started moving faster. Tsetse hurried after. The tunnel began to climb upward. It was a steep slope and slippery. The goats clambered up the incline easily, but Tsetse had to work hard to follow. Suddenly, she saw a speck of light. It grew and grew till it became a large, round, blue hole. The goats leaped through the blue hole. Tsetse raced to catch up.

At last she reached the mouth of the cave. What she saw took her breath away. Her goats were gamboling and frolicking in a garden more beautiful than any she had ever seen. Flowers taller than Tsetse bent their heads toward the little woman and spoke. "Hello," they murmured. When at last Tsetse remembered to breathe in, the aromas — first lilac, then orange blossom, frangipani, rose, jasmine, ginger — filled her with childish delight. She took a bold step into the garden. The sky was turquoise blue and filled with towering white clouds. The garden was surrounded by ancient giant trees. Each tree was a tree of trees, for on the broad horizontal branches of each giant there grew small trees, rising straight upward like candles, and each looked like the tree of life itself.

Filled with an unsettling physic, a confusing mix of delight and disbelief, astonishment and happiness, fear and relief, Tsetse began to dance wildly around the meadow, laughing and shouting songs of praise she'd forgotten she knew, and all the while her tears flowed freely down her cheeks. Then she saw it. From head to foot she began trembling. There, before her, loomed an immense figure of light. She tried to hide, but the figure looked right at her. Then it spoke. "Tsetsele," it boomed.

Her teeth began chattering, but she couldn't move or look away.

"Do you know who I am?"

"No," she answered, and then, in a flash, she knew. "Maybe," she said coyly. "Are you the God of my Fathers?"

"Very good, Tsetsele. Now, do you know where you are?"

She tried to make sense of it, but flowers that speak, trees that bear new trees on their branches — it was too much for the woman.

"I have no idea," she sighed. "Can I stay anyway?"

"You're home, Tsetsele. Of course you can stay. As a matter of fact, the Goddess of your Mothers is waiting to see you."

Tsetse echoed in astonishment, "The Goddess of my Mothers?"

"She's in the gazebo at the head of the garden. Come, give me your hand and I'll take you there."

Emboldened by her adventures, Tsetse held out her tiny human hand. The immense figure of light touched her with one finger. Instantly, she was aloft, weightless as a feather, flying effortlessly. They alighted at the head of the garden beside a gazebo made of light where, resplendent and radiant, the Goddess of our Mothers, the divine Shekinah, sat pouring tea.

"Tsetsele," she crooned. Her voice was like honey, golden, thick with love. "You had a long trip, you must be thirsty. You want a little tea?"

Wordless with astonishment and admiration, Tsetse nodded.

"You want a little sugar? One lump or two?"

With great effort, Tsetse managed to answer. She heard herself say, "Just plain," and something about her own voice reminded her of the bleating of her goats. She watched herself reach for the cup and saucer. Raising the cup between forefinger and thumb, Tsetse drank thirstily, and as that ambrosia passed her lips, she went into ecstasy. For as long as she remained in rapture, time stood still; but, in the end, a thought entered — the uncooked chicken at home — and paved the way for more thoughts — the unbaked bread, the unmade bed, Moishe! Tsetse leaped to her feet.

"My jobs!" she cried. "I have to go do them now, right now."

But the God of our Fathers and the Goddess of our Mothers replied, as in one voice, "Don't look a gift horse in the mouth, Tsetsele. Send a note. The goats know the way."

"Send a note?" Of course, that's what she should do. Finally, her "reckless reading and writing" was coming in handy! All her life, Tsetse had told everyone that women should learn how to read and write, just like the men, because it was useful. But never in her wildest dreams did she dream of this. Reaching into her deep apron pockets, she found something to write with and a little something to write on.

"Moishe," she wrote, "Come quick. I'm in Paradise. We're all invited. Bring everyone. Tsetse. P.S. The goats know the way." She folded the bit of paper, tied string around it, and, wrapping the string around the neck of one of the goats, she attached her note. The goats left. Tsetse stayed.

Moishe came home from his side job, ready to *daven* till dinner. When he entered the house he saw the uncooked chicken, the unbaked bread, the unmade bed.

"Tsetse," he called. There was no answer. He looked out the door. The goats were at the gate. He called Tsetse. The goats bleated. Moise ignored them and went to the neighbors. No one had seen Tsetse all day. Soon the whole village was looking for her, shouting and running back and forth. Each time a person passed by the gate of Moishe and Tsetse's house, the goats bleated eagerly. Their udders were full. They wanted to be milked. But no one had time for them.

Taking lanterns to light the night, the villagers helped Moishe search deep into the dark, but they found no clue, not a shred of an apron, nothing. At last, Moishe came home. He was exhausted, but there were those goats, bleating piteously. He had to milk them. So he milked and he milked and he milked. They gave him a pail brimming over!

"My God!" he cried. "What's the matter with you goats? You're middle-aged. What are you, late bloomers?" But the goats only looked at him with their golden eyes and licked his salty hands with their rough tongues.

The next morning, there was no time for *davenning*. He had milk to sell. Day after day it was the same. Moishe had to let the goats out, take the last night's milk to market, and stand there, selling milk like a woman. And when he finally finished with that, he had to go looking for his disappeared wife, of course. By the time darkness fell and he finally came home, again there was no time for *davenning* because guess who was at the gate, waiting to be milked? His life had become a living hell! Moishe was explaining this to his best friend, Feivel.

"Moishe, my friend," said Feivel, "let's face it. Maybe you have to look for your lost wife, but a man like you — born to *daven* — it's one in a million! You, of all men, should be *davenning*, not milking goats or marketing. Get rid of the goats. They're a nuisance. Give them to me."

"No, I can't. They remind me of Tsetse."

And Moishe was adamant for another 10 days. But one night as he was milking the relentlessly fruitful goats, Moishe knew, with a flash of certainty, he would never find Tsetse again. He had to do what he was born to do. He had to *daven*! The next day, he took the goats to Feivel.

Now, Feivel was a butcher. He did what a butcher does. He slaughtered the first goat and hung her up to drain. As he hung her up, something fell from her neck and landed on the ground near the growing pool of blood. Feivel bent over to see what it was. It looked like a little bit of folded paper. Instinctively, Feivel kicked the little folded packet out of the way of the blood. He wanted to open the bit of paper. He was curious. But Feivel was an orderly man. His hands were bloody. He wasn't wearing his spectacles.

"Finish the job first," he told himself, and so he slaughtered the second goat and hung her up to drain. Then he washed his hands, got his spectacles, and opened the bit of paper. It just fit in the palm of his hand. There was writing on it. "Moishe," he read, "Come quick. I'm in Paradise. We're all invited. Bring everyone. Tsetse. P.S. The goats know the way."

Feivel looked up at those slaughtered goats. No one will ever know the recriminations, the self-blame, the grief that flooded his heart as he stared at them. But some say that Feivel, ashamed of what he had done, squeezed the incriminating little paper into a ball, then put it in his mouth and swallowed it. Impossible. We have the story.

Everyone with an ounce of common sense will realize that if Feivel had done that, the story of the goats who found Paradise would never have reached our ears. 🙚

Seven lessons

Cathryn Wellner

Eavesdropping in a café, poring through old tomes, listening to other storytellers, I am drawn to stories that reflect the chaos or peace of my life at that moment, the questions whose answers elude me, the wisdom for which I hunger. It feels as if the story chooses me, calling out to be told.

In performance, my motives are sometimes less worthy. Faced with a rowdy group of middle schoolers, I pull out a story with enough strange or violent elements to still the savage beasts. Sensing indifference from an audience unaccustomed to stories, I search my mental filing cabinet for something entertaining, not enlightening. Nobility of purpose is not on the agenda. The issue is survival.

These are times when the mantle of storyteller feels like a hair shirt. Bringing stories to the great unwashed is not the noble calling I once envisioned. It is a search for the lowest common denominator, for the key to the laugh track. Sometimes the sense of failure dogs the entire performance and whips me all the way home.

Yet I am sometimes reminded, weeks or even years later, that as a teller I am only a vessel from which stories pour. Someone will approach me or write a note, grateful for a story they now carry like a talisman, sometimes from an event I have tried hard to scrub from memory.

What happens to stories when they leave my mouth, told with whatever assurance I can muster at the time, is not within my control. The stories refuse my efforts to turn them to my own purpose. They escape my intent, striking chords of their own, resonating in ways that elude my puny attempts at orchestrating the score.

In the same way, the people who have passed through my workshops in the course of nearly two decades set their own goals for the work. They take ownership of their stories and their reasons for telling them in ways that often have little to do with the objectives I so carefully craft before beginning the process.

Story listeners and budding tellers have become my mentors. They, as much as the extraordinary tellers I have met on the circuit, have taught me the emotional reality of the landscape of stories. From them I have learned these lessons.

1. Embracing the mystery is as invigorating as finding solutions

In the tale, in the telling, we are all one blood. Take the tale in your teeth, then, and bite till the blood runs, hoping it's not poison; and we will all come to the end together, and even to the beginning: living, as we do, in the middle.

—Ursula LeGuin,
Dancing at the Edge of the World (1997)

For two seasons I traveled the American school route in Germany and England, telling stories to military offspring. The principal approached me before a performance in one of the German schools. It was a tough group, he told me. "Better you than me," he said, in a voice that intimated he was throwing me to the lions.

They filed in with all the chaos that accompanies a school on the edge of out-of-control. One boy in particular stood out. He slouched into the room with that boneless walk only a teenager can muster. Second row from the back, third seat in, he planted his lanky form. Feet stretched across the narrow aisle, arms crossed, face set, he sat poised to retaliate against the students who would inevitably graze him while trying to clamber over his legs.

He also set the tone for the next 45 minutes. Others would cast side glances his way, to see if it was acceptable to listen or if verbal tomatoes were called for. The first story had to work. Two minutes in they would accept my offering or eat me for lunch.

Doing a last-minute set shuffle, I chose a short tale guaranteed to settle and center a middle-school audience. I don't remember what it was now, only that the group was stretched tense as a rubber band aimed in my direction. The story worked. They didn't fire.

The second story had to keep them hooked, so I chose one that had never failed, "Tayzanne," from Diane Wolkstein's extraordinary collection of Haitian tales *The Magic Orange Tree*. There was nothing noble in the choice. The story is disturbing, haunting, dark enough to calm even a roomful of adolescents. I used it as a club, to dash any troublemakers into silence so I could finish the program and get out of there intact. I'm not proud of the motivation, but it worked.

The lanky boy sat forward and listened, to "Tayzanne" and every story that followed. His compatriots took their cue from him, and the session ended without mishap. I had no illusions that the group was transformed by the stories, but we had all survived without undue injury to their spirits or mine.

A year later I returned to the school. The students showed no recognition of the middle-aged woman who had spun tales for them the year before. Once again, the boy with long legs and an attitude slouched in and posted his challenge across the aisle.

When I began the first story, he looked up, his eyes fixed and calculating. He leaned forward and stared. At the end of the story, he shouted, "You the lady that was here last year?"

"Yes," I replied, expecting the worst.

"Tell that fish story," he said. "Yeah," the others chimed in. "We've been talking about it for a year. We still don't get it. We want to hear it again."

It was the only story they wanted to hear, the only story they would allow me to tell. When it ended, they peppered me with questions I didn't even try to answer. Instead, we shared the mystery, the possibilities, the strangeness of the tale and what it revealed about us and about the culture from which it comes.

I left that school with an exhilaration that returns to me as I write. The long-legged boy and his friends reminded me to love the questions. The answers are never clear. They change with each telling of a story, with each hearing of a tale. They change when the events of today mix with the experiences of yesterday.

I have learned to embrace the mystery. I have not found answers, which are as elusive now as when I first understood that the spiritual certainty of my childhood stumbled in the face of a growing appreciation for the questions. What I have found are companions who are as invigorated by the questions as I am, who find as much joy in exploration as in discovery.

2. We are strangers only until we hear each other's stories

As long as we look out at each other only through the masks of our composure, we are looking through hard eyes. But as the masks drop and we see the suffering and courage and brokenness and deeper dignity underneath, we truly start to respect each other as fellow human beings.
—F. Scott Peck, *The Different Drum* (1993)

Here in British Columbia we are embroiled in tense First Nations treaty negotiations, a tug-of-war that threatens to last for decades. Patience on both sides is frayed. First Nations communities watch resources being extracted at a fast clip from lands they consider traditional territories. The descendants of colonizers see their livelihoods threatened by negotiations that drag on through years of uncertainty.

We look at each other across an invisible line. Our shadows are cast larger and more threatening than they would be if we knew each other's stories.

A young Native woman in a workshop on Vancouver Island brought that home to me. She was a shy participant in a storytelling class. It took the first three sessions of group work, participatory exercises, and modeling to give her courage to tell her own autobiographical story.

In a voice barely audible, yet with quiet assurance, she showed us the six-year-old child ripped from her family. She drew word pictures of the stern man who came for her, the bullied family who gave her up, the cold unfamiliarity of a drab institution, the isolation from those she loved.

Up until that evening she had been a blank slate to the group, participating hesitantly yet always returning for the next session. She was like a shy deer, gazing at us with round, curious eyes, her body poised for flight.

In the moment of telling, she changed for us, and the group changed with her. We felt her anguish, remembered our own, and saw her as a full and complex human being. She was no longer Other, no longer the quiet stranger from a culture different from the mainstream most of the others represented. She was Woman Who Overcomes.

Her willingness to share one of her defining stories opened a floodgate. Her risk became permission for others to tell stories that cut close to the bone. Sitting in a circle, listening to her words, the others understood that whatever stories they told would be accepted, would be held in the open heart of the group.

Listening to this young woman, watching the reaction of others in the circle, I saw living proof of the way in which sharing our stories is essential to community. Her story became ours. No longer Other, she took us across the boundary of strangeness into the land where, for a time, we could all walk the same path.

I have learned to recognize kindred spirits through stories. In performances and workshops, rooms full of strangers have become companies of friends. Ours is only a stop on the journey. We leave and take up our separate paths. But for a while we see each other with some of the ease of old friends.

3. Healing begins with speaking the pain

Isak Dinesen said, "All sorrows can be borne if you put them into a story."
—Sam Keen, *The Passionate Life: Stages of Loving* (1983)

Inge (not her real name) was in her 60s, her soft accent still colored by a Dutch childhood. At the end of World War II, she had married her foreign soldier and moved with him to his native Canada. She was pregnant and isolated from family, friends, and mother tongue for the first time.

Canada prides itself on being a civil nation, but the war had taken a heavy toll on tolerance. Inge's limited vocabulary of English words probably had a German edge to ears unaccustomed to the difference between German and Dutch accents.

When Inge went into hospital to deliver her first child, she could not communicate easily with the staff, but she could understand. She did not need a translator to tell her what the nurse meant when she referred to Inge as a "dirty DP" (displaced person).

That offhand remark silenced Inge for 40 years. Though her English was impeccable, her accent slight, she could not open her mouth without hearing the words. All through the years of rearing children, she held onto the shame, the sense of unworthiness as a "dirty DP."

Now she had grandchildren who wanted her to tell them stories. They would not accept her reluctance. She could not break past it. So she signed up for the storytelling workshop, hoping it would break the spell of silence cast on her in a hospital nearly 50 years earlier.

The first three weeks she said little, but she was always there, absorbing, participating in exercises but not telling stories. The fourth and last session she broke her silence. She said she had not prepared a story, but she wanted us to hear the experience that had thrown a hedge of thorns around her. She wanted us to know that she was ready now, that she realized the importance of her own voice, the legacy only she could

give to her grandchildren. She would go home now and tell them stories. The healing had begun.

I have learned that storytelling can help heal old wounds. Of course, painful stories can be told too soon, while the wound is so raw that it rubs salt into the listeners' sore places. The time for the telling, the time for the healing, is when the pain has been replaced by understanding, forgiveness, and acceptance. That is the time when the telling spreads balm on the souls of both teller and listener.

4. Stories can even the playing field

Memories are stories our lives tell us.
—Ivan Doig, *Ride With Me, Mariah Montana* (1991)

One man sat quietly in his wheelchair during the personal stories workshop I taught at a storytelling festival in Tulsa, Oklahoma. He participated in the small-group exercises but contributed nothing memorable or unusual or even particularly personal to the group as a whole.

I thought nothing more about him during the rest of the day's workshops and performances. It was not until an open-mike session that I understood his motivation in coming to the workshop. He was one of the first to come to the front, where he told a funny, detail-rich story of his childhood.

In the break after open-mike, he took me aside. He wanted badly to be a storyteller, he said, but his short-term memory had disappeared along with the condition that had stolen his ability to walk. He thought being a storyteller meant memorizing stories. He couldn't do that.

The workshop planted a seed. The open-mike audience watered it. "Now I know I can be a storyteller," he said. "I still remember my childhood."

He not only remembered it, but he also had an instinctive skill for shaping it. The audience responded with delight, giving him permission to go on, to identify himself as a storyteller.

Before then, I had given little thought to the therapeutic value of storytelling. Articles about storytelling in prisons or nursing homes had intrigued me but were outside my experience. The man in the wheelchair confirmed that storytelling can level the playing field, can admit anyone to its ranks who is willing to speak from experience, to make the personal universal. We have only to widen the circle, to find ways that stories can be shared.

The man in the wheelchair is only one of many who have taught me that storytelling is an equal opportunity art, whatever the means of sharing the stories. The human spirit shines through stories given freely and openly, stories that allow us for a time to set aside our otherness, to accept our own flaws, and to celebrate those things that bring us closer to understanding life.

5. The act of storytelling can change our lives

Our very deepest sense of our own identity — the deeply familiar flavor in our mouths when we use the word "I" — is more a matter of conviction than a matter of fact. If we believe we are kind or smart or good or bad, competent or incompetent, mean or dumb, valuable or worthless, on the strength of our convictions, we are likely to become so.

—Elizabeth Stone, *Black Sheep and Kissing Cousins: How Our Families Stories Shape Us* (1989)

The oldest children in the up-state New York school where I was paid to bring children and books together were in Grade 3. I would have preferred a Grade 6 storytelling troupe, but you work with what you have.

Earlier, I had committed the social gaffe of asking for a transfer from the top of the heap (as a high-school librarian) to the bottom, hoping the move would rejuvenate my flagging enthusiasm for working within a bureaucratic system. It worked, though not as I had anticipated. Not having a degree or experience in early childhood education, I quickly learned that first graders are not just small adolescents. Hugs in the supermarket helped ease the sense of inadequacy that threatened to overwhelm me at times.

The children fanned the storytelling spark in me. They reflected what they heard in eager faces, bodies leaning forward, and the long silence when a story resonated for them. A storytelling troupe seemed a natural step, so I put out a call for ten volunteers.

There were only two requirements, besides desire. Parents had to agree to allow the children to stay late once a week. Teachers had to assess whether the children could afford to miss an hour of class each week.

Robbie was among the first to bring in his volunteer sheet, signed by his parents and his teacher. He was one of those children who are easily overlooked. Neither a problem child nor a stellar student, he was simply there. He was a good but not inspired student, with a personality kept in shadow by shyness.

Robbie's teacher was cautious in her approval. Missing class was not a problem. Lack of spark was. She wondered about the wisdom of trying to change a shrinking violet into a showy sunflower.

I confess I was not convinced he would shine as a storyteller, but his mother was my best volunteer. I wanted to keep her happy. Nepotism crept into what should have been an objective process. Robbie joined the troupe.

The children were paired as story buddies to coach and encourage. The partners learned two sets of stories, their own and their buddy's. In performance, the buddy was prepared to coach from the sideline in case of a memory lapse. The buddy was also the performer's best audience, giving encouragement through subtle body language that said, "Way to go! You're terrific!"

A month into the training, Robbie knew everyone's stories, not just his buddy's. He became troupe leader, giving encouragement where it was needed, suggesting words or gestures to enhance a story, volunteering to work with troupe members who were struggling.

In performance, it was toward Robbie's open face that nervous storytellers turned. When he stepped center stage, all eyes were on him. He was lively and confident, telling stories in an easy, natural manner.

After the last performance, his mother confided that she had been skeptical when Robbie asked her to sign his permission sheet. "Robbie," she asked, "why do you want to be a storyteller? You're too shy."

His answer was simple. "Mom, I think it's about time I stopped being so shy."

Robbie was the first of many I have seen in the intervening years. The act of stepping out, of declaring oneself as a storyteller, can have a profound effect. Part of that is the discovery that people will listen. For a normally shy boy, that deep listening was liberating, acknowledgment that his words had value. No longer content to sit at the edge, Robbie took center stage, the strength he found in performing spilling over to the rest of his life.

And so I have learned to celebrate the spirit-freeing power of telling stories. We are silenced by so many things in our lives, by disapproval and uncertainty, by past mistakes and more confident colleagues, by interruptions and unresponsive listeners. The deep listening of a group gathered to hear and tell stories, to honor and attend, can lift us out of the disappointments we carry. We can set down our pack of troubles, open our hearts to our own and others' stories, and walk on refreshed.

6. When we find our stories, we find our path

Stories are valuable precisely to the degree that they are for the moment useful in our ongoing task of finding coherency in the world.
—William Kittredge, *Owning It All*
(1988)

When I left Rochester, New York, to move back to Seattle, one of my last storytelling events was an evening of stories with the Genesee Storytellers. Each teller was to bring a story she had never told before to share at a potluck for storytellers and their friends.

My choice was a folktale about a little hen who defeats a giant who has been taking her eggs. I had shared the picture-book version with children in the school where I was a librarian. They always dissolved in giggles when the hen shouted her salty challenges from behind a rock.

The step from reading to telling was easy, but the performance fell flat. This was the last story I told in Rochester, and I left feeling disappointed that it hadn't been a stunner.

Four years later I returned for a storytelling conference. After one of the workshops, Paula Ziegelstein walked over to introduce herself. She had been at the potluck and had hoped to say thanks one day. "You told a story there that changed my life."

My face must have betrayed skepticism, so she told me she would bring something to show me. The next day she unwrapped a small sculpture she had commissioned for her 40th birthday. It was a large-boned woman dressed in a low-cut, high-slit evening dress, looking confident and sexy — with the head of a chicken.

Paula had not noticed my flat performance. What she heard was the story of a hen whose eggs were being stolen every day. No eggs, no chicks. Paula thought of her own life, of the giants who were stealing her eggs, of the ideas and talents that would never hatch if she allowed the thefts to continue. Armed with the vision of the little hen who took on a giant, Paula set about slaying her giants. Four years later she had a new confidence, thanks not to me but to the story of a little chicken.

Paula taught me the truth behind something shared by nearly every storytelling workshop leader: the storyteller is the conduit for, not the focus of, the story. I liked the story of the hen, though not my telling of it. The deeper levels of the simple tale eluded me. I told it for delight, not illumination. It was not my story.

It was Paula's story. Her response rings in me now as I search for stories to take me through the middle years. There are giants in my life, and they are stealing my eggs. The story of the hen and the giant is still not my story, still gives me no clue as to how to slay the giants. What it does give me is the memory of Paula, the re-affirmation that when I find the stories for this period of my life, I will also find the key to slaying my giants.

Whenever a story heard or read says emphatically "Tell me!" or "Don't tell me!" it contains lessons we need to learn. Some speak to our joys and successes. Those are the stories we tell to celebrate who we are and what life has taught us. Others speak to our uncertainties.

7. We cannot predict how people will react to our stories

Language is the light that comes out of us.
—Ivan Doig, *Ride With Me, Mariah Montana* (1991)

The children from the Seattle hospital's burn unit were brought in on stretchers and in wheelchairs. Some were ambulatory and pushed IV poles. The youngest was 5, the oldest 15. The 15-year-old was burned over most of his body. He faced years of skin grafts and a lifetime of unwanted attention from people who would not know how to react.

I was having the same trouble people outside the hospital would have with these children, wondering where to put my eyes, how to reach beyond the disfigured surface to the spirit within. The stories I had chosen seemed puny in the face of their overwhelming needs.

I decided to tell them a story I had learned from Bill Harley called "The Freedom Bird." It is the story of a hunter who shoots a magnificent golden bird, only to find that he cannot kill it, no matter what he does. It is the Freedom Bird, irrepressible, rising from any adversity. The violence often makes adults uncomfortable, but children love it.

Halfway into the story, I looked at the 15-year-old. In my mouth was a story of hacking, boiling, and burying. In front of me was a boy who had lived the bird's fate, through fire, surgeries, and pain. I wanted the floor to open and swallow me.

The floor refused. I finished the story, tucked my tail between my legs, and slunk home. For the next week I practiced mental flagellation, knowing I should call the burn unit and apologize, putting it off until tomorrow.

The burn unit called first. One of the staff members wanted to tell me about the 15-year-old boy. He had been despondent, wishing he could die. The story changed his mind. Each time the hunter shot or hacked or buried the bird, the creature rose like the phoenix, until at last the hunter realized that he was trying to destroy an indomitable spirit. The boy decided he was the Freedom Bird. No fire or surgery or pain, no insensitive staring or comment would destroy his spirit. He would rise and rise again.

That boy taught me to trust the stories that call to me, to give them truly, knowing that they may heal or harm, but that I cannot predict how anyone hearing them will react. Life is in control, not me. A burned child may see the Freedom Bird as a reflection of the years of agony and reversals he faces. Or he may see in it the soaring of his own brave spirit.

I continue to learn to let go of the need to control. If we believe we can always choose the right stories and tell them at the right time, we are fooling ourselves. Everyone who hears our stories filters them through the lens of experience. We cannot know the hearts and lives of all our listeners. What we can do is tell with care and love, sharing the stories that touch our own lives, that make us laugh or cry or ponder. Release stories like butterflies, knowing they will fly their own crooked paths and land wherever they will.

To walk a crooked path

Storytelling is a peculiar calling, more like a maze than a straight path. My companions are tellers, listeners, and the stories themselves. None of them is predictable. Struggle as I might to pick out the right stories for a given audience, the right story exercises for a particular workshop, I arrive to find that my traveling companions may have taken a different turn. I shift directions, round a bend, run up against a barrier, shift directions again, and try to trust that wherever we end up is where we should be.

YOUTH ON THE EDGE

Not angels — just champions

JOSEPH ANDREJCHAK GALATA

*The child who makes up stories and comes to
believe them himself is not a liar but a poet. He
is answering that eternal demand of man's soul.*
                                        —Felix Maril Ibanez

IN MY CAREER AS A THERAPIST, teacher, administrator, counselor, and creative artist, I have
worked with well over 18,000 students, multiracial/ethnic adolescents, and young adults from
socioeconomically deprived environments. They
include kids from street gangs, often addicted to
alcohol or other drugs; kids with sexual promiscuity problems; kids who have grown up in foster
homes; kids who dropped out of high school in
Grade 7 or 8; kids who have known sexual, physical, emotional, or mental abuse firsthand.

I am a faculty member in the Continuing
Education Department at University of Nevada
at Reno, working at the Alcohol and Other Drug
Abuse (AODA) Medical Clinic in the U.S. government's Department of Labor, Sierra Nevada
Job Corps Center. I train doctors, nurses, teachers, counselors, therapists, and administrators in
multicultural counseling. I design counseling
programs in the AODA department using storytelling and other creative arts to reshape the
behaviors and value systems of young adults
affected by guilt, self-recrimination, resentment,
anger, hatred, fear, shame, jealousy, loneliness,
pain, and powerlessness.

I have found that traditional approaches to
therapy and education are not effective in working with this population. You cannot take a 23-
year-old who has been homeless since the age of
eight, who has survived on the streets and
dropped out of school in Grade 7, and expect an
hour's worth of therapy each week to have a significant impact. These kids are still in survival
mode and are not able or willing to sit at a desk
and be taught what seems to have no relevance to
their world. An additional result is that doctors,
nurses, teachers, counselors, therapists, and
administrators working with these youth burn
out quickly, as they are surrounded by all the negative energy these youth bring with them. I have
discovered that storytelling — successfully combined with drama, music, dance, theater, poetry,
and puppetry — is a powerful and passionate
force that both assists these adolescents and overcomes the burnout of professional staff in the
healing profession.

I worked with a group of youths — ages 16
to 24, high-school dropouts from the streets of
Los Angeles, Oakland, San Diego, Las Vegas,
and elsewhere — living at the Job Corps school
in Reno, Nevada. Our goal was for students to
compete in the National History Day Program.
The program brings together students from all
50 states who work to create ten-minute videos
and theatrical performances. Teams initially

compete in state competitions. The winners of these competitions represent their state in the National History Day competition in Washington, DC.

For an hour and a half, five days a week, we gathered in the theater. The students engaged in a series of exercises. First, the students stood still on stage in a darkened theater, with a spotlight shining on their faces, without laughing, giggling, sneezing, belching, or moving. The object was just to stand still (which is not easy if you have never done it). This was to prepare them to listen to another person's stories. Just as it takes cultivation, talent, and skill to tell a story, so it requires a similar talent to really listen to a story. How do you listen to a story if you've got a thousand voices and noises rattling around in your head? It's not easy, and for some it was the hardest thing they learned to do, listening to that silence within themselves.

Next, we went through a series of breathing techniques and vocal exercises. They learned to breathe like a baby again. They studied diction and how to use their voices. They learned to speak eloquently, rather than in vulgarities and shouted put-downs. They learned how to recite lines from various poems. They practiced accents: Swedish, German, Yiddish, Russian, Romanian. Why? Not because they are likely to ever go to Romania or Australia, but because when they go to tell their stories, I want them to forget who they are for that brief moment and become a different character — to talk differently, to speak in a way they don't speak themselves.

I taught them exercises in dance and movement to learn the beauty of their bodies. Some of these kids were obese. I had one student in the group who weighed 400 pounds. These are kids who had abused their bodies with alcohol, cocaine, and heroin. They learned that their gen-

italia are good for getting money or to ward off worse abuse. They've learned that their bodies are ugly and that they have no control over them. I taught them through music and dance to see the power and the beauty of each part of their body and how they own it, so when they tell a story, they will tell it with their entire physical selves.

I led them in a meditation class. The students lay on stage in the dark and learned to visualize. I used *The Wizard of Oz*. In their visualization, they were dancing down the yellow brick road to the Emerald Palace to see the Wizard of Oz and get their wishes fulfilled. What were their wishes? A reunion with their families? Purity again? A job? A career? Self-esteem? To get rid of self-hatred? To conquer that horrible disease of loneliness? They found that they had the creative power of imagination. And now they were ready to begin storytelling.

J.M. Barrie, the author of *Peter Pan*, wrote at the beginning of his famous story, "When the first baby laughed for the first time, the laugh broke into a thousand pieces and they all went skipping about and that was the beginning of fairies." These teenagers and young adults have never been given much of a chance or an opportunity to run or laugh or skip about like Tinkerbell. They were too busy learning and cultivating the techniques of survival and dodging the slings and arrows of abuse. They were too busy learning how to shield themselves from bullets, fists, and knives. They have spent their lives weaving in and out of mass arrays of social and personal disorganization. But, through storytelling, these same adolescents began to discover new ways to redesign themselves and their views of the world around them. For, as Marcel Proust wrote, "The real voyage of discovery consists not in seeking new lands but in seeing with new eyes."

As they each became immersed in story, the students learned new symbols to help meet life's challenges. For many of the adolescents with whom I work, their magical symbols have been guns, bottles of booze, crack pipes, needles, or sexual paraphernalia. Now they were looking at fairytales and folktales and learning about objects that become magical symbols of transformation: Cinderella's glass slipper or Jack's magic beans. With storytelling, these teenagers exchanged their horrific instruments of expression for new magical symbols.

I encouraged the students to become involved in historical stories to help them shape their own identity. Most of these youth have no conscious identity or, if they do possess one, it is negative and self-destructive. I told all the kids that they could not be creative and destructive at the same time. Most of these kids have learned how to be destructive because they have not had opportunities to be otherwise. The historical stories gave the students a sense of belonging, a connection to the past. By using history stories, I gave them healthier choices for identities. The students could relate to the historical characters and took on their identities while telling these characters' stories.

I tried to match historical characters/historical settings and situations with the circumstances of the youth's lives. One student, a 19-year-old girl who was a midget and born with rickets, had multiple physical deformities and had undergone 13 surgeries. Most of her life she had been homeless, living in the back of a bus. Her family sexually abused her. But she also has such a creative mind! She played Florence Nightingale, a nurse who healed other people despite her own infirmities.

Stories from various racial and ethnic backgrounds also helped bestow a sense of identity on the students. I had a group of African-American students from Las Vegas. They kept getting into big fights with each other as to whether they were Black or Black African-American or African-American. I asked them all if their ancestors were from Kenya, Uganda, Trinidad, Tobago, Tunisia, or the Bahamas — they didn't know. The kids whose parents were from Mexico or El Salvador wondered whether to call themselves Latino or Hispanic. Then the government sent me young adults from the Marshall Islands. Some of these islands were used for atomic weapons testing during World War II. The poverty there is severe. But these students were the most spiritually creative human beings I have ever met in my life. They knew their people's stories. I told the youths that it was important to understand how their forebears came to America and where they came from. I encouraged the students to seek out those stories of their own ancestry to build a sense of their ethnic identity.

I also suggested the class find holiday stories about Halloween, Christmas, or Thanksgiving, since holidays evoke a sense of enchantment in which they could creatively participate. In their pasts, this had seemed impossible for many of them because of the hard reality of their lives, but through story they could create a world of beauty and learn to shape it into reality. Stories have the power to awaken the innate traits of, and the desire for, honesty, faithfulness, obedience, love, generosity, forgiveness, perseverance, contentment, and kindness that these teens might perhaps have known and felt only once upon a time during their rare days of childhood innocence.

I broke the students up into small groups, and they chose projects for the competition, including the following:

- The migration of African-American storytelling, from Africa to the United States, through the slave era to the present day;

- The untold story of the suffering Chinese prostitutes in Virginia City during the Gold Rush era in the 1800s;

- Christmas stories from various countries and how Santa Claus and the Christmas tree are still traditional today (It was a wonderful surprise for them to discover that the first story of Santa Claus actually came from Turkey);

- The lives of Queen Victoria and Dr. Joseph Lister, who is known as the father of antiseptic surgery;

- The story of AIDS as seen through movies and television.

The students worked hard on this special project. They had to struggle to research, write, direct, and perform in their videos and stage programs. This was NOT an easy project! Many students joined and stayed from the beginning to the end. Some students came, dropped out after a week, but rejoined three weeks later. Throughout this program, each participant was required to share his or her learning process. They talked of the challenges and triumphs involved as they changed individual and group communication patterns, such as personal feelings, behaviors, beliefs, value systems, and rationales.

When these kids went to Carson City to enter the Nevada History Day Competition, they knew that the prize would be college scholarships. These drop-out, alcoholic, drug-addicted kids won first place in all of their categories, not once, but two years in a row! Each time, they won the right to represent the state at the National History Day Competition, sponsored by the National Endowment of the Arts, National Endowment of History, National Endowment of Humanities, The History Channel, and the McArthur and Ford Foundations.

In Washington, DC, the students competed against thousands of high schools from every state in the country. For two years in a row they won gold medals. They came back to Nevada no longer failures. As one kid said, "We're not angels, we're just champions!"

This was possible because the power of storytelling is non-threatening and helped them to see themselves as creative human beings. Their minds became focused on overcoming adversity through exploration and adventure. The shepherd boy becomes a king; the ugly duckling beautiful; the beggar a great hero; the ragged suitor a wealthy man; the weakling becomes strong and independent; the frog turns into Prince Charming.

Swiss psychologist Jean Piaget stated, "The mind needs an explanation of how the world operates." Storytelling was the medium that helped these adolescents overcome their justified fears, self-protective delusions, and socially imposed misconceptions of human behavior. The stories allowed them a safe and healthy environment to experience the components of passion, commitment, and self-intimacy, the foundations of genuine love for oneself, others, and life itself.

Leonna, The Ugly Girl

JOSEPH ANDREJCHAK GALATA*

The following is a story from my own Gypsy roots that I share with my students to encourage them to find the beauty they each carry inside.

> *Everyone has a different concept of what beauty may be. For many people, beauty is in the eye of the beholder, and I, growing up the son of a junkman, find junk to be very beautiful.*

But there are different types of beauty, and I'd like to share with you the story about the beauty of a young girl. In Frank, Pennsylvania, a train would rush by every evening — summer, fall, winter, and spring. All of us kids, except for one, would rush out to the train tracks every evening as we heard the train and stand along the train tracks as it whooshed by. As soon as it had passed, we would jump on the tracks and we could feel the vibration of the train disappearing in the distance. That was our entertainment seven days a week. I say it was all of us kids but one, because there was one child who never came out to jump on the railroad tracks because none of us would play with her. Her name was Leonna.

Now, Leonna was ugly. Leonna's hair was like the silk on the cobs of corn you would find out in the field after months in the sun, the cobs that nobody picked in autumn. Her long, stringy, corn silk hair just hung there. She was three times taller than any child should be, and her nose seemed as long as her legs. Her teeth, well, her teeth went straight out. She was what us children

thought of as ugly, and none of us would play with her. Every morning as we walked up the path through my father's junkyard to school, we'd all walk together, carrying on, playing games, telling jokes. Except for Leonna. She would walk through the junkyard all by herself. At school, she would sit in the corner by herself because none of us wanted to sit by her because she was so ugly. After school, when we needed to take out the day's frustrations for having to sit still all day and listen to Mrs. Mulligan teach, we'd take them out on Leonna. We'd call her horrible names. Then we'd go home, eat, play, and run to the railroad tracks for the 7:10 train.

One night, I remember running home after the 7:10 train and my grandma was sitting on the porch. I noticed she was sitting there talking to Leonna. Leonna had been walking down the little cobblestone alleyway by herself, and she stopped to say hello to my grandmother and my grandmother waved to her and they talked. I really had never heard Leonna speak because I had never spoken to her because I was one of

26

those rotten kids who thought Leonna was really too ugly to talk to. But when I went in the house, my grandmother called to me. Leonna was gone.

"Oh, I had a wonderful conversation with that pretty girl Leonna." And I thought my grandma had been drunk. She referred to Leonna as pretty!

I said, "Oh ...?"

"Such a beautiful young girl, you should be so blessed to grow up and marry such a beautiful girl."

And I thought, "Grandma is insane! We are already the laughingstock of Frank because my father is the junkman; what if I grew up to marry Leonna, the ugliest girl in Frank?"

I said to my grandma, "How can you think she is pretty?"

My grandma looked at me and said, "You don't think Leonna is beautiful?"

"No, she is the ugliest girl in the whole of Frank!"

And my grandmother said, "She is the most beautiful girl in the whole town. Let me tell you a story ..."

A long time ago, in the Old Country, there was a handsome Gypsy boy, so handsome the birds would sing to him and the flowers would bow to him as he walked by. He thought that God, "Alako," had created him so beautiful that of course he deserved to marry the most beautiful Gypsy girl in the country. As he was getting older, the people would say, "He must marry the most beautiful Gypsy girl in the country, he is so handsome."

So one day his mother and his father said to him, "You must go talk to the Bello Rom, the Gypsy chief. You must ask him, 'Where is the most beautiful Gypsy girl in the land, for that is who I deserve to marry, since I am the most handsome Gypsy boy in all of the country.'"

So he went to the Bello Rom and he said, "Oh, Gypsy chief, where may I find the most beautiful Gypsy girl in the country, that I may give her myself in marriage?"

The Bello Rom said, "Ah ... to find her you must walk seven days and nights without stopping. You must walk over this hill, around this mountain, over the river, and through this forest. But you must do it wearing a blindfold, and on the seventh day you will walk straight into a tree. And sitting there under the tree will be the most beautiful Gypsy girl in the country and you must ask her to marry you."

The boy said, "How will she refuse? I am the most beautiful Gypsy boy in the land." So the Bello Rom put a scarf around his eyes and pushed him in the right direction. For seven days and nights the Gypsy boy walked, over the hill, around the mountain, across the river, and through the forest. And after seven days and nights without stopping, he finally walked straight into a tree. He said to himself, "I have found her at last."

Before he took the scarf from his eyes, he said, "Gypsy woman, oh, the most beautiful Gypsy woman in the world, I, the most beautiful Gypsy man in the land, have come to take you as my bride." He whipped the scarf off his eyes, and sitting there beneath the tree was the ugliest woman he had ever seen. Her skin was like a lizard a thousand years old. Her eyes were the eyes of a frog a million years old. Her teeth were the rotting like the teeth of a wolf who was ten million years old. The Gypsy boy's eyes opened wide, as he said, "You are not the most beautiful Gypsy girl in the world; who are you? You are the ugliest woman I have ever seen."

With a voice that pierced his ears, with a voice that sounded like caterpillars sucking on sour lemons, she said, "But I am so beautiful … marry me, marry me."

The Gypsy boy said, "Oh, you are the ugliest woman I have ever seen. I would rather live all by myself in a cave with nothing to look at but myself and nothing to hear but my own voice than to ever listen to that voice or ever have to lay eyes on that ugly face again!"

And he ran. He ran for seven days and nights back through the forest, across the river, around the mountain, and over the hill, back into the village, panting. He said to the Bello Rom, "How could you do this to me? I am the most handsome Gypsy boy in the world and you send me to meet the most beautiful girl and an old hag is sitting there beneath the tree."

"What would you have me do?" asked the Gypsy chief.

"I would rather live all by myself in a cave with nothing to look at but myself and nothing to hear but my own voice than to ever listen to that voice or ever have to lay eyes on that ugly face again!"

And the Bello Rom said, "So be it!"

The boy found himself in a cave surrounded by mirrors, and everywhere he looked, all he saw was his own reflection.

He screamed, "Help! Help! Is anybody here?" And all he heard was his echo, "Here, here, here …" But nobody answered him. The days went on, the weeks went on, the months went on, and the year went on. All the Gypsy boy had to do was look and talk to himself until he was about to go insane. The Gypsy boy said, "O Devel [Oh God], get me out of here. I would rather marry that old ugly woman with the lizard skin and frog eyes and voice that sounds like caterpillars sucking on sour lemons than listen to myself once more or see my face once more."

The minute he said that, the mirrors cracked and the cave opened up and the sun was shinning. The Gypsy boy jumped out. He was still as handsome as ever, and the birds began to circle him, serenading of his beauty, and the flowers began to bow to him as he walked through the gardens.

He approached the Bello Rom. "I have learned my lesson. I will now go and marry that ugly old Gypsy woman, for it is better for me to marry her than for me to be alone. I will do her the favor for she must be as lonely as I am."

The Gypsy boy put the scarf over his eyes and he walked the same path for seven days and nights and he came to the tree and said, "Are you here?"

The voice said, "Yes, yes, I've been waiting for you." The voice pierced his soul and he took off the scarf. He saw the same green ugly lizard skin hanging from her jowls, and the big bulging eyes of a million-year-old frog, and the teeth of a zillion-million-year-old wolf.

The Gypsy boy said, "Oh Gypsy woman, ugly Gypsy woman, I graciously shall marry you. For it is better to marry you than for me to live in that cave by myself."

The old Gypsy woman thought and said, "You are not worthy of my beauty."

"Beauty? What are you talking about? You are the ugliest woman I have ever seen." And that moment the tree split in half and the Gypsy woman's skin fell off, her hair grew into a beautiful bouffant hairdo that the birds began to weave because it was so beautiful. Her voice was lovely and her teeth sparkled like pearls. Her eyes were a dazzling rainbow of blue, green, and violet. Standing there before him was the most beautiful Gypsy woman in the world.

The Gypsy boy said, "Marry me!"

"Go away, I was this same woman all along, but you did not recognize this beauty because you were so in love with your own beauty." And the beautiful Gypsy woman turned and walked away.

The young man followed her on his hands and knees begging, "Marry me, marry me ..."

She turned and said, "Go back to your village. You are not worthy of my beauty."

To this day the most beautiful Gypsy woman in the country walks through the forest, across the river, around the mountain, up the hill, and begins her path again as the birds serenade her and the flowers bow for her. The Gypsy man crawls on his hands and knees behind her, begging, "Will you marry me?" And still to this day, beauty is in the eye of the beholder.

My grandmother told me that story on the day she thought Leonna was the most beautiful girl in Frank. I never knew what happened to Leonna after I moved away. My father died and was no longer the junkman. Years later I was on a bus going home to visit my grandmother, and there in the back of the bus sat Leonna, 20 years older, same as I. She remembered me and I remembered her. I wanted to apologize for being such a cruel child and making her childhood so lonely and horrendous.

She asked me about myself, "How are you doing?" I asked her how she was, thinking certainly she's as lonely as she was as a child. But she said she had married a wonderful man and they had three lovely children. She asked me if I would like to see pictures of them and I said yes. So she showed me a picture of her husband, and I must tell you, as shamed as I am, he was as ugly as she was — the ugliest man I have ever seen. And I thought, how ugly will these children be? But when she showed me the pictures, I lie not, they were the three most beautiful children I have ever seen.

I invited Leonna to my grandmother's house that night because I wanted my grandma to see that she was right. For when I looked into Leonna's eyes as she showed me those pictures, there was great beauty there. 🐾

Sharing stories at Compass House: Offering direction for runaway and homeless teens

Lorna Czarnota

WHEN I FIRST BEGAN telling stories at Compass House, I didn't know much about these teens other than the fact that they had problems at home and were staying in a "safe house." I originally contacted Compass House because of its teen population and my own need to find peace of mind. Working with these youth helped me deal with the trouble my family was having with my teenage niece. I found that sometimes the messenger cannot come from too close, and I was too close to my niece to be of help. Maybe I could do some good with kids I didn't know as well? My first impression was of chaos. I still get flutters in my stomach before I visit.

As time went on, I was able to gain the trust of the staff members and shelter director. This trust has been extremely valuable because now I can call before my visits and find out how many youth will be there and generally the issues they are dealing with.

I don't ask about specific kids, but rather the group as a whole. I don't want to be hindered by prejudice or personal safety concerns when dealing with the teens. And the staff can't tell me specifics due to confidentiality issues. The only rule I follow for my personal safety is to be on a first-name basis. I never give them my last name or my address. But I do share plenty of personal stories with them. If I want them to open up and talk about themselves, then I have to be willing to talk about myself.

One challenge of working in this setting is the nomadic quality of the listeners. These adolescents don't always accept the storyteller right away, and they are prone to moving around and not listening well. More importantly, I may only see them once and never again. I need to be real and gain their trust and interest in the first ten minutes.

The teens I work with are both girls and boys, ranging in age from 12 to 21, and from a variety of cultures and backgrounds: Black, white, Hispanic, even Russian. How they get there and why they are there varies just as much. Sometimes parents, who just don't know what else to do, drop them off at Compass House's door. They are often kids who have run away and need to get off the street for a while. They may have committed crimes, and their choice in court was Compass House or a placement in a halfway house or detention center. One girl beat her grandmother. One was recently arrested when the police showed up with a warrant at Compass House's door because she was ready to give herself up. Sometimes these kids are about to become parents and need help when nobody else will provide it.

On the whole, the teens in this program are tough, loud, sometimes violent, but always needy. What they need most are love, truth, compassion, and tools for coping and survival. That's why I tell them stories. I believe that through story they learn they can trust me and, I hope, other adults. In story they may find the tools they need to cope, they may discover other possibilities for choice, and they may be enfolded, if only for the moment, in a place that is safe and compassionate. Through story, they may come face to face with the truth, something they so deeply desire.

Compass House also runs a resource center, and I do a monthly story program there. The resource center helps kids get the social services they may require: apartments, jobs, and the everyday needs that we take for granted, like refrigerators and clothing.

My story "Bleeding Heart" is just one of the many stories I tell. I use "Bleeding Heart" when I need a story that speaks about the nature of unconditional love. I share the story when I know there are teens dealing with confused feelings regarding their families, or who are in difficult relationships of their own. Many times, girls have told me that their biggest hope is to strengthen a relationship with their boyfriends. We talk about when to keep trying and when to give up, in the context of the story. Some of the girls may have children of their own and may need the comforting support of knowing they are part of a cycle. "Bleeding Heart" speaks to this as well. And if nothing else, "Bleeding Heart" is a story of hope. The teens at the shelter need hope. Many of them have at one time or another attempted suicide.

⧼Bleeding Heart⧽

LORNA CZARNOTA*

I've learned a lot about love. Real love. I'm not talking about physical attraction. I'm talking about the kind of love a mother can have for her child. The love that just won't quit no matter how hard you try to sabotage it. I've learned about the love a mother has for her child even after the child has been imprisoned for some unthinkable crime. Even when the child claims not to love the mother. The love that we call "unconditional." And, I've tried very hard to make sense of it, even though it seems impossible.

One day, after talking to my sister, I called a friend to discuss my niece. It's been up and down with her for over two years. She ran away from home, dropped out of school, was beaten by her boyfriend, and now her mother said she was pregnant by that same boy. I had just brought a bouquet of bleeding hearts in from the garden and was looking at them while I spoke.

"I just don't know how much more I can take," I said. "My heart is breaking. No," I corrected myself. "My heart is bleeding." That was when the metaphor hit me and the story began ....

*Once there was an old mother who had three grown sons.
One day, her daughter-in-law, wife to the middle son and very much
with child, sought her advice.*

"Old Mother, I wonder what is a mother's love? A never-ending love?" The young woman eased herself into a chair.

The old woman thought for a moment. "I still remember the day my oldest son was born. He had a handful of dark hair that stood straight up on the top of his head and I thought, "He will be a thinker." My middle son, your husband, was not so gentle. He was a warrior. He kicked me from within, and when he was born, he kicked from without. He was a difficult child. But my youngest son, his head was made of stone. Where it took his brothers but a short time to learn their lessons, it took him years. If he was told that

something was not good for him, he still had to try it out for himself. Wear his own mistakes. He was stubborn, but I loved him just the same."

"That is what I mean, Old Mother. How can a mother love a child who is unworthy?"

The old woman motioned toward a flower in a vase on the table. "Daughter-in-law, do you know this flower?"

"Yes. It is the bleeding heart."

"A mother's love is like a bleeding heart. If her child skins his knee, her heart bleeds for him. If he does something wrong, her heart bleeds. If he does harm to himself or others, a mother's heart bleeds for her son."

"I do not understand," said the younger woman. "How can a mother love even then?"

"Look closely at the flower, Daughter-in-law. What do you see?"

The young woman leaned forward. "Where each petal is split, a new white blossom emerges."

"And what else do you see?"

"Ah," sighed the young woman. "A seed. I see a seed."

"That is the seed of hope, and the secret of a mother's love. A mother must have hope for her children even if her heart is broken. That is a never-ending love."

The young woman smiled. "Now I understand. Give me your hand, Old Mother." And she placed the old woman's wrinkled hand on her belly. The child kicked.

"Ah," smiled the old woman. "It begins." 🐚

After the story is over, I sometimes ask if anyone would like to comment on it or if anyone has had that experience. "Bleeding Heart" was met with quiet respect and contemplation. Then I say, "Perhaps there is someone out there whose heart bleeds for you, or perhaps you love someone the way this mother loved her child. Just remember, sometimes we have to learn to let go as well. It's give and take." Then we close the circle in our usual way. We visualize that we take energy from the person on our left and pass it to our right with the reminder that what we take we must return.

CROSSROADS: *Stories of Choice and Empowerment* is an audiotape recorded by Lorna Czarnota that contains stories she has used in her work with youth. Lorna has also written a study guide to accompany this tape of stories about making difficult choices. This collection includes stories drawn from African, Celtic, and Native American traditions, as well as some original tales written by Lorna herself. Order a copy by phone (716-837-0551) or by e-mail (Lczarnota@aol.com).

The following two stories are from two different cultures and environments — Africa and Siberia. Yet both these folktales run parallel in content, form, and purpose. Sometimes parents of all cultures must go out after their children or youth, who may be living on the edge, and do their best to guide them back to safety again. In both tales, community members recognize this need and offer help. These two tales can be told to unite a community as it creates safe havens for our children.

— *Allison M. Cox*

The Girl Who Crunched Bones

A FOLKTALE FROM ZAMBIA RETOLD BY MARGARET READ MACDONALD*

There was this girl.
Every day she went into the bush.
Every evening she returned.

Her mother called her.
"Here, come and eat.
Here is good food for you."

The girl replied, "No.
I am not hungry."

Each day it was this way.
The mother worried.
"How can my daughter refuse to eat?
How can she live like this?"

The mother went to a person for aid.
"Here is a magic herb.
Put this in your mouth.

When you call ...
your daughter must answer.
This way you can discover her.
In the day she does something.
You must find out."

Next day the girl left her home.
The mother waited.
Then she put the herb in her mouth.
She walked into the bush and began to call.

"Kambilocho! Kambilocho! Tuuu!
The daughter answered from over there.
"Kukutu ... kukutu ... kukutu ...
I am crunching bones.

Retold from "The Child Who Puzzled Her Mother" by Mr. F.D. Sakala, a Nyanja folktale in *Folktales From Zambia* by Dorothea Lehman (Berlin: Verlag von Dietrich Reimer, 1983).

Kukutu ... kukutu ... kukutu ...
Crunching peoples' bones."
The mother ran home in terror.
They said, "What happened! What
happened!"
"My daughter, she made sounds like
crunching bones!
Her voice came from that place ...
that place where graves are made."

They said, "We will go with you."
All walked to that place.
They said, "Keep calling.
You are her mother.
She will know your voice."

"Kambilocho! Kambilocho! Tuuuu!"

"Kukutu ... kukutu ... kukutu ... pm!
I am crunching bones.
Kukutu ... kukutu ... kukutu ... pm!
Crunching peoples' bones."

They said, "That's her.
Call her.
You are her mother."

"Kambilocho! Kambilocho! Tuuu!"

"Kukutu ... kukutu ... kukutu ... pm!
I am crunching bones.
Kukutu ... kukutu ... kukutu ... pm!
Crunching peoples' bones."

Now they were very close, those people.
That girl was busy crunching.
They crept all around her.
Strong women.
They grabbed her.
Her mother touched her hand.
They carried that girl home.
Everywhere they surrounded her.
All good things they brought for her.
After a while she began to take porridge.
A little.
Then more.
They kept her in the village.
They surrounded her and comforted her
Until she was able to eat porridge
like all other people.
This mother saved her child
With the help of her village. 🖋

How Old Woman Kytna Brought Her Daughter Home:
A Koryak Story from Kamchatka Peninsula

A FOLKTALE FROM RUSSIA RETOLD BY KIRA VAN DEUSEN*

This tale describes a shamanic healing journey like those often undertaken to find parts of a human soul that have either been stolen or shocked out of the body. Shamans may go to other worlds themselves, or they may send their spirit helpers. Shape-shifting illustrates the shaman's intimate relationship with animals, her special strength, agility, wisdom, and the ability to go beyond oneself to help others. Drumming, singing, and poetry traditionally help a shaman like Kytna seek out lost souls and bring them home.

Old woman Kytna lived in Kichiga village with her old man.
They had a daughter named Ralinavut, a grown-up daughter.
Not far from their village lived a wolf pack, 28 wolves.

One time Ralinavut went for a walk and got lost. She did not return home.

They looked for her everywhere, in all the surrounding settlements, but no one had seen her. Then they decided that she must have lost her way, frozen to death, and been covered with snow. No one realized that on the same day Ralinavut got lost, the wolf pack had gone away from that place. And no one guessed that the wolf pack had taken her away as one of them.

Only Kytna did not believe that her daughter had died and kept waiting for her to return. Three years went by, but Ralinavut did not come back.

Then Kytna took up her shaman's drum. She played and sang all night, and in the morning she said to her husband, "Our daughter is alive. She is in a wolf pack, far away in the north. The place is called Talkap. Three years ago, this wolf pack was living in our area, 28 wolves there were. Those are the ones who took our daughter away."

"That is very far away," said the old man. "It's too far for you to go. You'll get lost in the tundra."

"I won't get lost," said Kytna, "I know how to get there."

"Then prepare supplies for the road," said the old man.

They prepared supplies for the road, and the next morning, just as it was getting light, Kytna set off on her way. She went on foot along the snow. And as soon as she had gone a hundred paces, she turned into a wolf. Wolves go very quickly on the snow.

Towards evening a reindeer-herders' nomad camp appeared. Kytna took her own form and went up to the camp. One reindeer-herder greeted her.

"Greetings! Where have you come from and where are you going, old woman on foot?"

"I'm going north, to Talkap," said Kytna. "My daughter is living there among the wolves. The wolves took her away."

"That's a long way to go!" said the reindeer-herder. "On foot it is very difficult. I will give you reindeer. Good reindeer!"

"I feel more at ease on foot. I'll continue on foot," said Kytna.

"You know best," said the reindeer-herder. "But we have good reindeer and you are welcome to them."

The next morning, just as it got light, Kytna went on her way. As soon as she had gone a hundred paces, she turned into a wolf. The reindeer-herder watched her go.

"So that's why she refused our reindeer!" he said.

Along the way, Kytna met a wolf and questioned him.

"Tell me, brother, have you met an unusual wolf anywhere in a pack in the north? The kind of wolf who is at the same time a wolf and a human?"

The wolf told this tale: "Far away in the north, beyond Talkap, lives a big pack, 29 wolves. I was once their guest. I noticed that there was one unusual wolf among them. In my opinion this was not a real wolf but a person."

"Most likely that was my daughter, Ralinavut," said Kytna.

"She's called Ralinavut?" said the wolf. "I have heard that name. In that pack there was one female wolf with that name."

Kytna kept running north. She came to a settlement of Chukchi reindeer-herders. The Chukchi were glad to have a guest. She was treated to meat and fat and then they asked her, "Where do you come from and where are you going, old woman on foot?"

"I come from far away in the south, a place called Kichiga," said Kytna.

"That is a long way," said the Chukchi. "I was there once."

"Tell me," said Kytna, "is there a large wolf pack living in this vicinity? Don't the wolves prey on your herds?"

"Yes, there is a big pack, 29 wolves. And oh, how sick I am of them! They do prey on our herds."

"Those wolves took away my daughter," said Kytna. "Now she lives in their pack. Three years have gone by. I don't know if I will be able to take her home."

"It is time to sleep," said her host.

"I need to get up early," said Kytna.

In the morning they ate and they drank tea. Kytna went on her way. She came to a place where wolves were eating reindeer that they had killed in the night. Kytna turned herself into a wolf and circled around the wolves, singing.

Many wolves here eat their food,
Among them must be Ralinavut.

YOUTH ON THE EDGE 37

The wolf Ralinavut shivered and stopped eating. "Who is looking for me here in the tundra?" she thought.

Kytna came closer; she circled one more time and sang:

These wolves are thieves,
Here daughter Ralinavut lives.

The wolf Ralinavut thought, "It's my mother looking for me. Who else would it be? Of course, it's mother." Quietly she moved toward the voice and sang:

Mama, how did you find me?
Oh, mama, I wish you hadn't come.
I've been a wolf so long now,
Taken in by the wolves.

Kytna made a third circle and sang her answer:

Ralinavut, you are human.
Like us you have a human name.

Ralinavut could not contain herself. She ran to her mother. "Mama, why are you here?"

"My heart was frozen," answered Kytna. "I've come for you and without you I will not leave. I am your mother. Let us run away while the wolves are not looking. Not far from here is a village of reindeer-herders. We'll rest there. I am very tired. I came the whole way on foot."

"All right, let's go," answered the wolf Ralinavut. They came to the village, turned into people, and went into the tent.

"Oho, what a brave old woman!" said the Chukchi. "Not only has she come back, but she has taken her daughter away from the wolves!"

Kytna and Ralinavut rested. They rested and then Kytna said, "It's time to go home."

"Your Kichiga is very far away," said the Chukchi. "Let me take you on my reindeer."

"We don't need reindeer," Kytna replied. "We'll go on foot. We'll leave early in the morning."

Early the next morning Kytna and her daughter left. The Chukchi watched them go. When the two women had gone a hundred paces they were no longer there — and in their places ran two wolves. They were moving very quickly.

"So that's why they refused our reindeer!" said the Chukchi. "Wolves will get there much faster."

Kytna and her daughter ran all day. Kytna's husband looked out and saw two wolves running side by side into the village. He thought, "That must be my wife and daughter."

People rushed out, calling, "Wolves are coming! Wolves!"

But the old man calmed them. "They are not wolves," he said. "They are human. Why would wolves be running straight into the village in broad daylight?" And suddenly there were no more wolves. Kytna and her daughter were walking along the snow.

They came home. 🐾

Suggested reading

Shamanic Worlds: Rituals and Lore of Siberia and Central Asia, edited by Marjorie Mandelstam Balzer (Armonk, NY: North Castle Books, 1997) is a collection of articles written by indigenous Siberian scholars.

For more sources of Siberian tales, read these other books by Kira Van Deusen:

- *Shyaan Am! Tuvan Folk Tales* (Bellingham, WA: Udagan Books, 1996).
- *Raven and the Rock: Storytelling in Chukotka* (Seattle: University of Washington Press, 1999).
- *Woman of Steel: A Tuvan Epic* (Bellingham, WA: Udagan Books, 2000).

- *The Flying Tiger: Women Shamans and Storytellers of the Amur* (Montreal/Kingston: McGill-Queens University Press, 2001).

And on CD:

- *Tales of Tuva* (Scientific Consulting Services, 2000). This compact disc includes four stories from *Shyaan am! Tuvan Folk Tales* and is accompanied by Tuvan musicians.

Tell down the walls

BOB KANEGIS

TOMORROW IS THE BIG PERFORMANCE. It will be the first ever student storytelling assembly at the Springer Boy's School, a juvenile correctional facility in northern New Mexico. We've learned a few lessons from previous projects in similar settings; among the most useful is the lesson that we should be prepared for the unexpected. So that's what we're doing. There is a good chance that Manuel, who has been preparing to narrate a story called "The Difference between Heaven and Hell," will be transferred tomorrow to a county jail to wait for a reconsideration hearing. No one can say with certainty whether this will happen or not. When we last saw Manuel at our final class session he was in the middle of rewriting his part of the story in his own words and had promised to try and find a stand-in if it should prove necessary.

While we are at Manuel's lodge, trying to assess where things stand, Jack, one of our students who we don't know too well, steps up to the plate and volunteers to be Manuel's replacement. We are delighted. But the curve ball is

coming. Nathan, another resident and perhaps the brightest student in this class, begins to pester Jack with predictions that he will fail. Nathan assures us, "I'll be in the audience so I can take his place if Jack screws up!" Nathan has turned down several entreaties to perform before, and now he seems to be having second thoughts about missing an opportunity. It doesn't take much to activate someone's fear of failure and ridicule, so we are curious to see what will happen next. Manuel witnesses this whole interaction and turns to the new volunteer to say, "Hey, Jack, go for it, Nathan is just trying to turn your shoes around!" We don't always know whether a story has reached someone, but Manuel has just referenced the key phrase in a Yiddish story about the fools of Chelm he heard a few days earlier, and he used it at exactly the right place and time. Best of all, Jack got it!

No, Jack will not be like the fool from Chelm. In the story, a man starts out on a journey to see something new, gets sleepy, and points his shoes in the direction of his destination before dozing off. When he awakes, unaware that a rogue has turned his shoes in the night, the fool proceeds haplessly home, marveling at how all places are alike, and travel and adventure useless. We strive to help our young offenders see their lives as an unfolding story over which they hold the key to possibilities. During this journey, will the hero take up the challenge of changed circumstances or "go back to sleep" and stay "at home"? Our students have very strong worldviews and often very limited experience beyond the "hood." Their peers tell them that they cannot or should not change, and adults often re-enforce the idea that they can't. These are the people who, if our students "fall asleep," will turn their shoes around to hold them back.

We call our program for incarcerated teens "The Hero's Journey," using the term Joseph Campbell coined to define a universal pattern found in world mythology and folklore. Simply expressed, the hero's journey describes the movement of the hero from his or her normal world, through crisis and a call to adventure. During the journey, allies and mentors appear, there is a series of tests and trials, and finally the hero is victorious and brings home a prize or elixir. We begin by telling hero's journey stories, move through a series of games and exercises, and have students retell stories. We bring in huge stacks of folktales. We guide students as they write original hero's journey stories. A final performance event is always an important part of the process. Our hope is that our students will begin to see connections between the stories and their own lives. If one's life is indeed a story, then the choices one makes each day help to determine which way the story goes. Manuel's warning to Jack about not getting his shoes turned around is the kind of moment that gives us heart that we are on the right track.

Our next stop is Cedar Lodge. We check in on Perry, a 17-year-old Navaho who has been preparing to tell "Jumping Mouse" from the book *Seven Arrows* by Hyemeyohsts Storm. "Jumping Mouse" contains all the elements of the hero's journey. A little mouse lives in the grassy normal world of mice, but is called to adventure with the guidance of his mentor Magic Frog. The mouse sees the far-off mountains for the first time and determines to reach their top. His journey is fraught with peril from the hawks above. The little mouse meets other allies and is tested in many ways along the journey. He must resist the efforts of friends, family, and strangers to deter him. Jumping Mouse even offers his own eyes to others before he earns the object of his quest in an unexpected way — for his acts of selflessness he is rewarded and transformed into an eagle.

Perry sat through our first sessions, hunched in his chair, fists clenched, arms over his head. Something about this story reached him, though, but his fear of telling has been palpable. In practice sessions, his legs shake violently, but in the Lodge, Perry, who has always been seen as an outsider, has been getting continuous encouragement and coaching from his peers. He tells the story for the first time from beginning to end in front of the group and announces that he will make his decision about whether to tell on the morning of the performance.

The Possibles Bag

To get to the Boy's Ranch, we drive north on Interstate 25, which follows part of the Old Santa Fe Trail for many miles. Along the way we pass landmarks that the pioneer traders used as guideposts to mark their progress, places like Wagon Mound and Glorieta Pass. At Wagon Mound there is a geologic formation that looks uncannily like the prairie schooners used by the settlers. I think about what it must have been like to embark on such an epic journey, a trail to adventure fraught with risks and danger. The mountain men found their way before the traders. They were a rugged breed of trailblazers, each one carrying a "Possibles Bag." A Possibles Bag! Just the phrase stirs a storyteller's imagination! How can we help our students set out with a Possibles Bag of perspectives and tools that will equip them for the difficult journey they must make from broken homes, losses, deaths, drugs, and alcohol towards wholeness?

The one indispensable item in the mountain man's Possibles Bag was a fire starter, usually flint and steel. Here is a place for us to start. I have a little ritual with which I often begin a storytelling encounter. I tell folks that my favorite setting for telling is around the campfire, but with fire codes being what they are, an open flame might not be a good idea in the library (or auditorium, school, or wherever we are). But I must have my fire! So I ask everybody to help with the creation of an imaginary fire. In our mind's eye, I ask the youngest to find tinder to spark the fire, older kids to get the kindling that will catch the flame, adults to find larger wood, and the elders to find the larger logs that will sustain a steady blaze. We place our contributions at the hearth site. To light the fire, we must rely on an ancient technique. No matches allowed! I ask everyone to rub their hands together vigorously until they can feel the heat. When hands are sufficiently warm, we send the heat to the wood. Soon we watch the spark catch, the flames leap up, and the smoke and red embers drift upward to the stars. We look for the familiar constellations. Then we rub hands for a second time. This time, when hands are warm, we take a deep breath, place our right hand on our hearts, and feel the warmth to remind ourselves that each one of us, together in

that place, is a human being, with a heart and feelings.

I remember the trepidation I felt the first time my wife and partner Liz and I anticipated going behind the walls into a juvenile correctional facility. Some of these "kids" were in for murder. How would we approach them? Even scarier to contemplate, we wondered how they would approach us. I looked for the fire starter in my own Possibles Bag. I rubbed my hands together, touched my heart, and remembered that we are all human. And then, I remembered the story of "The Lion's Whisker."

Like so many deep and heart-full stories, there are versions of this tale from around the world. A favorite version comes from Ethiopia, best known in Margaret Read MacDonald's retelling in her book *Peace Tales*. In this version, a stepmother wishes to win the love of a new stepson. A wise elder sends the heroine on a quest for the whiskers or hair from a fierce beast in order to make a love potion. The woman approaches the beast slowly and ever more closely over a period of time, until at last the prize is won. But victory seems to turn to defeat when the wise one tosses the whisker into the fire and announces that a love potion is impossible to make. "You already have the knowledge," the elder says, and the new mother understands that if she approaches her stepson slowly and cautiously, she eventually will win his heart.

This is the first story we tell, and it resonates. Our listeners can relate to the son or stepmom. Many have faced rejections and betrayals. They have become adept at pushing adults away. Others relate to the lion, feared by many, but with a big heart and ready to help if they could only see a way. Directly to the point of the program we are about to begin, we acknowledge that our staff and students must be like the woman in the story, approaching each other slowly and respectfully if trust is to develop. To that end, we also begin our program by emphasizing that we do not need to know and will not ask what crimes brought our students there. No matter what, we are all human beings deserving of respect. Inwardly I remind myself to try and see beyond the person in the moment and sense the person who may yet become.

Having introduced a first compelling story to a group of teenagers who may rightfully be wondering what stories have to do with their lives, we go on to emphasize that stories are about possibilities, the future, and are powerful when the listener asks, as storyteller Pleasant DeSpain has pointed out, "and then what happens…?" We are careful not to tell stories with overly explicit morals. We do not ask students to think about stories in close relation to their particular problems. In fact, we don't spend much time talking about problems. When students are asked by independent evaluators what they most enjoy about the program, they often express appreciation that we do not use stories to "point fingers." Willingness to suspend judgment is a crucial ingredient in our Possibles Bag.

Several weeks after we first told "The Lion's Whisker" to a group of girls in one of our programs at the Youth Diagnostic and Development Center in Albuquerque, the girls came to class brimming over with excitement. "We used one of your stories! We told 'The Lion's Whisker' in our cottage!"

"Why that story?" we asked.

"One of the girls who isn't in this class is about to be released. She has a young son she hasn't seen for almost a year. She was in tears, afraid that her son is going to reject her. We thought of the story. It was perfect! She got it!"

A year later we met one of these girls "on the outs" in a local restaurant. She looked good, she was doing well, and she ran up to us to say hello. I remembered my own initial fears and thought, "Ah! The stories and the telling of the stories were part of the love potion that made this moment possible."

Performance Day arrives. The staff rover leaves with the list of students who are scheduled to perform. Perry is with him when he returns! So is Manuel. (Since Manuel was there, Jack didn't perform. But because Jack had made the commitment and practiced, we invite him to the final party for the performers.)

After 200 young men, along with their teachers and cottage staff, file in, Perry opens the program. "Once there was a mouse who spent all his life, as mice do … in the grass. All he ever saw was grass, grass, grass. Then one day he heard a faraway sound, a whooshing sound. His family and friends didn't hear it. They thought he was making it up. But he was curious and began to work his way through the grass in the direction of the sound, fearful of the hawks above." Mouse was off and so was Perry! His classmates in the audience were beaming. His teachers were beaming. Most of them had never heard him utter a word in class. Here he was, confidently telling a long and complex tale with feeling, expression, and passion. Mastery, belonging, independence, and generosity in action!

As we continue to do these programs, the stories pile up. When our students write original hero's journey stories, they share them with adult prisoners in England who tell them to their own children. Story fever hits the lodges. There is an endless demand for the books that we bring to class. None are assigned. Most are checked out. We get word that kids who never read are reading stories silently and out loud in the lodges. Months after the program ends, our students write us and ask for more books. They offer us more stories that were waiting to be told.

Fences and saplings

Walking near Jewel Lake in the Berkeley Hills, I once noticed that some small tender saplings had been recently planted. The young trees were surrounded by a flimsily built fence of small-diameter red osier dogwood canes, cut from the nearby swale. I recognized the work of the local Junior Rangers. "This fence won't last more than a couple of years," I thought to myself. And then I realized that the fence didn't need to last any longer, because within a couple of years the saplings would have grown enough to be able to withstand both the animal and human traffic that would pass by. The fence would literally fall away and would in fact enrich the soil where the trees were growing.

A story can serve as a fence that falls away. The tale can buffer a young person from the assault of having to look his own crises in the eye. The story will hold, nourish, and provide strength, acting in concert with added experience, perspective, and guidance, until the youth is ready to claim the piece of ground that is his own story.

How to work with juvenile offenders? Approach slowly. Make respect your compass. Be willing and able to suspend judgment. Carry a well-equipped Possibles Bag of stories. Meet needs and create challenges. Juvenile offenders are released into our midst, every last one of them. We must find ways to make their circle of courage whole. We must welcome them and guide them towards opportunities to succeed. Above all, we must look for ways to help them do what in their deepest hearts they yearn for: to make a contribution and to be recognized. To the extent that we can all succeed, beautiful new and true stories can come into being.

EXERCISES

- **Positive power:** When faced with a difficult challenge, we are strengthened by reminding ourselves of our powers and strengths. In Mali in Central Africa, a lion hunter girded himself for the ordeal of the hunt by wearing a shirt festooned with talismans that reminded him of his ancestors, his village, and the important events in his life.

  Brainstorm a list of words and phrases that evoke images of power. You may also want to brainstorm a definition of power. We have found the following definition useful: "You have power when you can transform yourself or a situation to meet a challenge." Because there are obviously negative and destructive powers that fit that definition, agree to concentrate on the positive. We keep an extensive list of words that have been generated in past classes so that if the brainstorm stalls, we can rekindle the discussion. We like to play the "musing dummy," asking questions like, "Is forgiveness a power? How about patience?" Refer to stories that have been told in class. What powers did the heroes call on? What powers did they lack that could have helped?

When the brainstorm is complete (challenge the class to generate a minimum of 30 powers), ask the students to reflect silently on the list for a minute or two. Ask students to identify the four words or phrases that they feel are their strongest powers. Then ask them to identify four powers that they feel they would most like to develop. "If you could ask Magic Frog for a new power…?"

• **Create power talismans:** Begin with 8½ x 11 paper cut into quarter sheets. Fold each quarter sheet twice and then unfold. Each quarter sheet now has four squares.

Ask students to write their four strongest powers on one side of the paper, one power in each square. On the other side of the paper they will write one power they would like to have in each square.

Refold the paper so that the one strongest power is on the top. This "bundle" will now be wrapped and tied. You can use anything from brown paper to beautiful art papers. If you use undecorated paper, students can color, paint, or draw their own designs. Tape down the edges of the wrapping with scotch tape, then tie off the bundle using colored yarn or raffia. Add feathers, beads, and glitter. The power talisman may now be worn, carried, or put in a special place for safekeeping.

Remind students to connect with their talismans and their powers when they face a challenging situation.

For additional resources, contact:

Alternatives to Violence Project.
P.O. Box 300431
Houston TX 77230
713-737-9999

Reclaiming Youth International
www.reclaiming.org

VIOLENCE PREVENTION AND INTERVENTION

The Dragon's Tear

DAN KEDING

Once there was a boy who lived in the foothills of a great mountain range.
His job was to take the sheep each day up into the high valleys to graze.
His task wasn't hard because his dog did almost all the work.

She herded the sheep, guarded them as they grazed, and brought them back to him at the end of the day. The boy usually found a shady spot where he could sit and play his tambouritza. He loved the old songs that his grandparents would sing and play each night. While the sheep fed, he would sit and play each song over and over again until he knew it by heart.

One day, he and his dog took the sheep deeper into the hills than ever before. There they found a hidden valley with long, lush grass. When the sheep saw the grass they ran into the valley with the dog at their heels. The boy explored the gray hills around him and soon found a rocky cliff. Against the face of the cliff there was a cave so dark that he could only see a few feet into it. At the mouth of the cave there was a big rock, and there he sat down to play his songs. He played for an hour. He played for two. And then he got hungry. He put down his instrument and reached for his lunch. That's when he heard a low and rumbling voice coming from behind him.

"Don't stop playing." The boy looked around, reached for his tambouritza, and was going to run when the voice said, "Please." So the boy played.

After the boy had finished, the voice in the cave told him a story. Then the boy played again, and the voice told him another story. And so it went, all day, story for song, song for story. At the end of the day the boy was filled with wonder. The voice in the cave asked, "Will you come again?" And the boy said, "Yes, tomorrow."

Every day the boy returned to the cave. And every day he heard more stories. Stories of knights in battle, stories of adventure, stories of romance, stories of great humor and great sadness, stories of promises kept and promises broken.

One day, the boy stayed later than usual. As the sun dropped low over the valley, the voice in the cave grew sad and began to tell its own story, one of loneliness and fear. As the boy listened, he understood that the storyteller was the last of its kind.

Soon the rays of the evening sun began to reach deeper and deeper into the dark cave. As the boy watched, he saw the light glint off razor-like talons and climb up powerful legs. Then it reached a huge body that was covered with scales and stretched deep into the darkness.

Finally, the light followed a long, serpent-like neck that arched to hold a great head. Wreathed in smoke and framed by curving horns, the head

swayed as the creature spoke. The boy was looking at a dragon.

As he stared at this amazing sight, the boy
saw one tear fall from the dragon's eye. Stepping
forward, the boy reached out and touched a
leathery wing. Suddenly, the great golden eyes of
the dragon flew open.

"Aren't you afraid of me?" he roared.

The boy laughed. "No."

"I could rip you apart with my claws."

The boy smiled.

"I could reduce you to a pile of ashes with a
single breath."

The boy looked deep into the dragon's eyes.
"I can't be afraid of you," he said. "I know your
story."

The dragon stared deep into the boy's eyes
and nodded. "Will you come tomorrow?"

"Yes."

Every day, for many days, the boy came back
to listen to the dragon's tales and share the songs
of his village. One day, as the sun began to set, the
boy picked up his tambouritza and turned to face
the dragon. "Why do you stay here alone? You
could live in the village. My people would love
your stories."

The dragon laughed. "Your people and my
people have been at war for a thousand years. If I
came to your village, the men would all reach for
their swords and spears and there would be a
great battle. Many would die, maybe even I."

As the dragon spoke, the boy realized that the
dragon's words were true. He made himself a
promise to find a way to help his friend.

That night he listened to his grandparents
sing and play. When the music stopped, his
grandmother said, "Isn't it sad that no one comes
to visit our village anymore? They all go to the
village by the river. And we have such good
singers, don't you think?"

Hearing his grandmother's words, the boy
had an idea. Without waiting for even a minute,
he ran to the mayor's house and pounded on the
door. The mayor answered the door with a gruff
"What are you doing here at this time of night?"

"Is it true that people have stopped visiting
our village?"

"Yes, everyone has forgotten us. Why do you
ask?"

"I know someone who could bring the people
back. A storyteller. A truly great storyteller."

The mayor smiled. "A storyteller. Yes, everyone likes a good story! I'll go and meet this teller
tomorrow and invite him to our village."

Quickly the boy answered, "No. That will
never do. You see, he is very shy. He lives in a cave.
You will scare him."

"A shy storyteller? I've never heard of such a
thing. How am I going to meet him?"

"Well, maybe if you were blindfolded you
wouldn't scare him."

"Blindfolded?!"

"Yes. I'll take you and the village elders to
meet him. My dog and I will lead you there."

The next morning the boy and his dog led the
mayor and the village elders to the dragon's cave.
Before they reached the top of the last hill, the
mayor and all the elders pulled their blindfolds up
and tied them fast. Holding hands, they followed
the boy. When they reached the mouth of the
cave, they sat in a circle on the ground. The dragon slowly stepped out into the light and began to
tell his stories. He told them stories of adventure
that stirred their blood, stories of romance that
warmed their hearts, funny stories that had them
rolling on the grass, The dragon told them sad
stories that made them cry through their blindfolds. Finally, he told them his own story of loneliness. As he spoke, one great tear rolled down his
face and landed on the mayor's hand.

Slowly the mayor lifted his blindfold, looked down at the tear, and then looked up. With one hand he reached out and touched the dragon. With the other hand he touched the woman next to him. She took off her blindfold and reached out. Around the circle it went, until each person was touching the dragon.

The dragon opened his golden eyes and looked at the mayor. The mayor looked back. He saw an ancient face, creased with untold years of wisdom. "We have come to ask you an important question," he said. "Will you come to our village and be our storyteller?"

In an instant, the dragon replied. "Yes. Yes, I will."

The mayor turned and looked at all the surrounding hills. Then he turned to face the drag-on again. "May we ask one favor?" he said with a smile.

"Anything," roared the dragon.

"May we have a ride?"

The mayor, the village elders, the boy, and the dog climbed up onto the dragon's back. He unfolded his huge wings and flew them home. People came from far and near to hear the dragon's stories of promises kept and promises broken.

Years later, when the dragon passed on, he didn't die alone in a cave. He died surrounded by his friends, his great head resting on the lap of a man who had once been a boy and had sung him songs. All the hate and all the fear had disappeared with one tear. 🐚

Connecting jewels

LAUREL WELLS

THE LYRICS TO A TURTLES' SONG from the 1960s run through my head as I pull up to the Unitarian Universalist Church one Sunday morning to teach our youth group. The song is "Happy Together," and it goes "Me and you, and you and me, no matter how we toss the dice, it has to be ...." Today I will be teaching a group of 10- to 14-year-olds the Unitarian Universalist Principle of the Interdependent Web of Life. Although this principle came out of the ecology movement and generally reflects our connections to the natural world, my lesson today will focus on the social aspect. Recent acts of violence committed by our children tell us that our connections to each other are debilitated. In order to heal them, we must communicate to our children what they need in order to understand and participate in this vital connection. But we are unsure of what to tell them when our world is changing so rapidly. For what are we preparing them? Regardless, one thing is clear: if we don't give our children the tools and experiences to overcome alienation and conflicts in a productive way, they will have an even more difficult time becoming responsible and socially conscious adults.

In a world of phone, fax, e-mail, and beepers, we can communicate with each other faster and easier than ever before, and yet it is partial communication at best. Without the actual face-to-face interaction that our ancestral environments have encoded in us over the ages, we are at a definite social disadvantage and are more at risk for miscommunication and mistrust than ever before in human history. Just as our communication technology prevents us from interacting fully with each other, our entertainment technology — television, films, and video games — desensitizes us to the reality of violence. Violence is often portrayed as something that is funny or that does not hurt. When a character is killed in a video game, chances are he has a few more lives to complete his journey. So how do we demonstrate the power of human connection to our children when they live in a world that increasingly isolates them from each other and removes them from the reality of violence?

One way is through story. It is the oldest form of education and the means by which culture and beliefs have been transmitted since the beginning of human society. Through the ages, stories have increased our connections with one another and our world, reminding us that we are not alone in facing difficult life issues and that we have a place in the natural world.

The hum of the congregation welcomes me into the church. There is a lot of excitement among the adults as they discuss the calling of our new minister. When I reach my classroom, two girls are at the chalkboard drawing ying and yang symbols. After a few minutes, when everyone has arrived, I call them into a circle on the floor. I light the chalice candle and we center ourselves with this chant:

Listen, listen, listen to my heart's song
Listen, listen, listen to my heart's song:
I will never forget Thee,
I will never forsake Thee;
I will never forget Thee,
I will never forsake Thee.

Initially, some are a little hesitant to join in, but before long their voices blend together with such sweetness that an adult pauses to listen at the door. After we sing through it several times, we stop and they are ready to listen to the story. I tell them it is a Buddhist tale, based on the ancient text of the Avatamsaka Sutra, and written by Jeff Wilson. Everyone gives me their attention as I begin ….

The Net of Indra

A FOLKTALE FROM INDIA RETOLD BY LAUREL WELLS*

When Indra, the king of the gods, heard that Buddha planned to use his powers to ascend to the Tushita Heavens, he began to prepare his palace for the World-Honored One.

As splendid as the palace was, Indra was not satisfied and so he gathered together a hundred billion trillion jewels of every type — diamonds, sapphires, rubies, pearls, amethysts, and more until the great palace was filled with an uncountable number of jewels, strung together in a giant net, like a rainbow-flashing spider web. Indra then spread the net across the ceiling and the walls of the great hall in the palace, creating a blaze of dazzling light.

When Buddha arrived, he entered the great hall of Indra's palace and saw the sparkling net of jewels draped all around him and marveled at the infinite number of brilliant stones twinkling in the palace. And then he said to Indra, "This great net of beautiful jewels is indeed wondrous to behold; the nature of reality is just so as well. Observe in every flashing jewel the reflection of all the other jewels, and within those reflections, the reflections of all those reflections, forever and ever, until every jewel is all at once in every other jewel as well. Just so is the nature of reality. Observe how we are reflected in all the jewels, and within those reflections are the reflections of us in all the other jewels as well. This is the ultimate truth of interdependence and great universal interpenetration. At every moment, all that is of the world is within you, and you are within all that is of the world. Although you may be said to exist independently in one sense, in a greater sense you are a part of the vast interpenetration of all things. You could not exist alone. Only by the glorious existence of all other things can you exist. Take care, then, to always cherish the things which support you, for they are as much a part of you as you are yourself."

Swept with joy at Buddha's words, Indra vowed to remember the glorious truth of interdependence. He took the great net of a hundred billion trillion jewels and spread it over the entire sky, so that all who looked to the heavens would be able to see and understand the glorious nature of all things. And every night it shines still. 🍂

There is a glimmer of understanding on most faces, but one boy looks puzzled. I reach in my bag and pull out a ball of multicolored yarn that has a shiny metallic thread running through it. "Remember how Buddha said to cherish the things that support you? Well, we're going to do just that as we form our own great net with this yarn." I hold the end of the yarn and toss the ball across the circle to a girl who is usually quite comfortable sharing herself with the group. "Would you tell us about someone or something that supports you?"

"My parents support me," she says," but so does my best friend, Stephanie." She looks to me for acceptance of her statement, and I smile and say, "Yes, that's good. Now throw the yarn to someone else." And we continue crisscrossing our web around the circle, sharing answers that range from the silly to the sublime, until everyone has had a turn and our great web has been spun. When it is time to begin the next activity, we leave the web one by one, noticing how much it is weakened. Just so is the nature of reality.

At the end of class we return to the floor for our closing. As we all hold hands, I say this prayer:

As we sit here quietly,
we are aware of our connections with each other
in this room;
we are aware of our connections with people all
around the world;
we are aware of our connections with all of
nature — in fact, the universe itself.
May we truly experience and appreciate our
interdependence with all of life.

These are the kinds of messages I think our children need to hear. Messages that honor, encourage, celebrate, and respect the bonds between us. I think we may have to help some hold up their piece of the web. If we can sit among our children and tell them stories from our hearts, if we can give them opportunities to listen and be heard, if we can show them how we are connected and how they are connected, we give them the treasures they need to learn to be fully human. And, just maybe, we even give them the chance to be so happy together.

Taking off Superman

ROBERT REISER

IN 1996, I RAN A STORYTELLING GROUP with some men in Sing Sing Prison. It all began when a friend, who was a member of the local Quaker Meeting, heard me talking. I told him I could relate to people who, because of a moment's indiscretion or stupidity or bad luck or a combination of the three, had become outcasts from society. My friend said that I sounded like a candidate for the Quakers' Prisoners Committee that met with prisoners at Sing Sing every week. The suggestion scared me greatly, but I decided to walk my talk and try it.

My first visit to the prison was chilling. Not only was I afraid of the prisoners (these people had, after all, done some scary things), but here I was being locked up with them. When the iron gate slid closed behind me, I knew I was inside, and honestly, I had no idea if I would get out.

During the worship meetings with the prisoners, I gradually got to know the men — talkative, courteous, quiet, frightened, genuine, manipulative, guilty, sad, angry. They were not cliches from a prison movie. They were real people — a thoroughly mixed bag of humanity. After a year, the prisoners asked me if I would run a writing group — a natural enough request, since they knew that I was a writer. I hesitated because I felt that this would reach only those drawn to writing; instead, I suggested storytelling, which could include everyone.

I had been telling stories for awhile and had begun to suspect that there was great healing power in stories. People will open their hearts to a tale, when well-meant advice often makes them close up. The listener has the right to accept the story as his own and take it to heart or reject it. It is completely in his hands.

The prison authorities agreed to our storytelling group, provided we followed prison rules — meaning no recorders for taping the stories and no candles. So in the half-darkened room, the men and I sat around a flashlight and pretended that we were sitting around a campfire.

In the beginning, I told all kinds of stories: old ones, new ones, funny ones, sad ones. Slowly, using exercises and some of the wonderful advice from Robin Moore's book *Awakening the Hidden Storyteller*, I got the men to began to open up and tell their own stories. My goal was to try to move the men from their often-repeated prison tale ("I didn't do it" or "I shouldn't be here" or "It wasn't my fault,") into new, creative stories. Gradually the men responded, telling about learning to ride a bike or daring to smoke their first cigarette.

As the men got deeper into their own memories, I could see the pain and anger from their youth beginning to rise. I had the choice of letting them follow their inclination to turn the stories into confessionals, or steer them into stories of the imagination. Since I was no therapist, I felt that I couldn't adequately respond to the terrible pain that I heard in their personal recollections. I decided to try to turn them towards imaginative stories.

Little by little, they entered the world of tales and fables. It turned out to be a tremendous relief for them. In the midst of this place of continual shouting voices, blasting horns, and clanging iron gates, the storytelling group, with its chance to escape into a world of princes and tricksters and animals, became a refuge for the men.

The moment I told the men to close their eyes and relax, they were gone, deep into themselves, deep into their imaginations. I could see their faces relax, and there was almost an audible "ahhh," as if they had stretched out in a hot bathtub.

As the men opened their eyes, one looked up and smiled. "Now I can take off my superman suit." The men laughed. The tough, hard-assed superman suits, the most important part of their prison garb, were put aside. For an hour or two they could just be kids, trading stories. Stories began to flow from their own imaginations.

As it turned out, many of them were big fans of fables and animal stories. Thanks to them I discovered the wonderful Bidpai Tales from India, precursors to Aesop's Fables.

I told only one story a session, leaving most of the telling to them. I felt that the stories I did tell needed to have a healing component. However, a healing story cannot just dispense advice. It needs to accept and appreciate both the best qualities and the pain of the person receiving the story. As an outsider who had no real concept of prisoner's lives, I knew I had to be both respectful and completely indirect, for if the story seems to preach, the listener will simply not hear it. In the following story, I sought to subtly acknowledge the condition of the men's lives and transform it into new possibilities.

The Raccoon

ROBERT REISER

He was big and round and fat and sassy.
He was the biggest, fattest, sassiest raccoon in the entire forest.
More than anything in the world, he loved to eat.

He could eat anything: turnips and petunias and rutabagas and coffee grounds and banana peels. He loved to eat …. There was nothing in the world he loved more than to eat and eat and eat until he could hardly move. Well, this winter had been particularly hard. The snow began falling early in the season, and it kept falling and falling, covering the plants and the roots and the grass and the trash bins, freezing over the streams, until there was nothing at all to eat. So he did what any raccoon would do in the circumstance. He crawled into his den in the hollow in the big old tree, burrowed into his pile of leaves, and went to sleep.

While he slept, he dreamed of food, of course. Orange peels and bananas and nuts and eggplants danced in his head as he snored away those cold, cold weeks. Then, one day, something new came into his dreams … a smell, a delicious sweet smell like grass growing, like old leaves warming in the sun. He opened his eyes. Something was different. There was all kinds of chirping and tweeting outside his hole, and that smell of fresh grass was as strong as ever. Spring! Spring had come to the forest!

Then he peeked out of his hole and sniffed. The snow was gone. The forest was full of food!

Was he going to eat? He would eat and eat and eat until he could bust. He leaped out of his hole and stopped. Right in front of him, at the end of a long branch high up on his very own tree, stood a bird's nest. Not an ordinary bird's nest, but a giant bird's nest made of mud and sticks and straw. It was amazing. What is more, right in the middle of this bird's nest sat an egg. An egg! Not an ordinary egg, but a humongous egg, oval, brown and white, and probably the biggest egg he had ever seen in his life. What a breakfast to celebrate the end of winter! The best thing about this egg was that there was no mother bird. It was all alone, ready for eating.

In a second, the raccoon was across the tree, jumping into the nest and grabbing the egg. It was heavy. He wrapped his arms around it and lifted. Then slowly he tottered out of the nest and hoisted the egg and himself onto the tree limb. Suddenly there was a sound.

"Screeeeeee!"

He froze. It was a horrible sound. He looked up and he saw the mother standing right on the branch above him.

"Screeeeeee!"

He shivered. This was no ordinary mother bird. No sir! This was an eagle mother, with a long sharp beak and beady eyes and great powerful wings and long, long razor-sharp claws. She screeched again.

"Screeeeee!"

Grasping the egg tightly in his paws, he began to scramble back to his hole in the tree. It was too late. She was coming straight at him. Suddenly — bang! She swiped at him with one of her great wings. Bang! She hit him with her other wing. Bang! Now she was standing on the tree limb right between him and his hole. He turned and started to run back towards the nest.

"Screeeee!" She had leaped into the air and was slashing at him with those sharp claws of hers. "Screeeeee!" She sounded furious.

Holding the egg tightly in his front paws, he slowly rolled himself to the bottom side of the branch and hung onto the tree with his back paws.

Suddenly she stopped her scratching and banging and landed on the branch right above his head. She didn't want him to drop the egg, but she didn't want him to get back to his hole. He was stuck, hanging upside down with the egg in his paws. He wasn't going anywhere. His back paws ached, his claws were beginning to slip. He knew he couldn't hang on. If he let go of the egg, the mother would slash him to pieces in a second. Minutes went by, hours. Any moment he knew he would slip from the tree. He couldn't let go of the egg. He couldn't hang on. So he did what any intelligent raccoon would do in the circumstance: with his front paws he shoved that egg into his mouth.

He couldn't swallow the egg. It was much too big, so instead he sucked it right into his cheek. Then he grabbed the tree with all four paws.

"Screeeee!" the mother eagle shrieked in fury. She stomped up and down on the branch, but there was nothing she could do.

But there was nothing he could do either. He lay upside down with all four paws wrapped around the tree limb, and he waited. Hours passed while the eagle stood on the branch, staring at him. Evening came. But he knew the moment he closed his eyes, the mother would grab him and the egg and pull them into the sky. The evening passed, night came. Everything was dark except for the clear eyes of the mother eagle staring at him.

Dawn came and still he hung on. He was so tired. The raccoon could see his friends scampering around below him on the forest floor, grabbing all the roots and nuts they could find, while he hung on. They were eating and playing while he was stuck upside down in a tree, starving to death with an egg stuck in his cheek. For a second, he thought about nibbling a little on the egg. But as soon as the idea crossed his mind, "Screeee!" The eagle leaped into the air and slashed her claws down toward him. She could tell what he was thinking! Why did he ever let himself get into this mess? It wasn't fair! He could feel the hot tears roll upside down off his face.

The day passed and evening came and still he hung on, and another night and another day and another night. The mother eagle never left her perch on the branch. She never took her eyes off him. Three days passed. Four days passed. Every muscle in his body ached. He hadn't eaten a bite. He hadn't slept a wink. He was exhausted. Five days passed. Six days passed. The raccoon knew that he couldn't last much longer ....

That's when it happened. It began as a funny, fuzzy, tingly feeling in his cheek, like there was something buzzing and shaking against the side of his mouth. Then it became a kind of pinching, like something was biting at the inside of his cheek. He felt a terrible sharp pain in his cheek, like something had bitten him. Suddenly the whole side of his face was jumping around. Then he felt something pushing his mouth open from the inside. It was unbelievable. It was weird. It was unlike anything that had ever happened to him before. The raccoon's mouth opened very slightly, and out popped the head of a baby eagle. The raccoon's jaw dropped in disbelief as the baby bird walked out of his mouth and up onto the branch above his head. For one unbelievable moment, he and the baby eagle stared at one another. Then the mother eagle snatched her eaglet from the branch and carried him off to safety.

The raccoon hung onto the branch, his mouth sore, his eyes dizzy, his head ringing in exhaustion. Finally he gathered his strength, pulled himself up onto the branch, and crawled back to his hole in the hollow of the oak tree. He burrowed deep into his pile of leaves and, shivering and shaking, fell asleep.

He was awakened by a startling change. The hollow in the tree had suddenly grown dark. A great shadow stood at the entrance. The raccoon opened his eyes. It was the mother eagle, only inches from his face. She was staring at him. Something was different. The eyes weren't flashing at him like before. Her whole face seemed softer. Then she made a sound he didn't know she could make, a soft "Screeeeeee…," nothing like the angry screech she had made before. Then she was gone.

The raccoon lived for many years after that. Of course he never ate eggs again. He became known as one of the wisest creatures in the entire forest. All of the creatures respected him because he was the only one in the land who was on speaking terms with the great eagles. The great birds called him "uncle," though none of the creatures knew why.

One magnificent eagle would often stop by and talk to the raccoon. All of the creatures kept their respectful distance from these meetings. But if they had been close enough, they would have heard that this extraordinary bird called him "father." ❧

The men's first reaction was delight. The story was fun!! They related to the fun-loving raccoon who had gotten himself into an impossible pickle — stuck out on a limb because of his own actions. Although no one jumped up and shouted "That's me," there was a smile of recognition. They especially loved the end of the story. Many of them had children on the outside. Fatherhood was one thing they could point at with unabashed pride, so the ending, with the special bond between the eagle and the raccoon, was doubly meaningful.

Slowly, talk shifted to the transformation in the story. The men were fascinated by the accidental good deed that transformed disaster into a wonderful victory. "Sometimes there is gold buried in the trash," said one of the men. They started telling stories (real and imagined) about transformations they had known.

Alas, the program lasted for less than a year. Prisons are easy budget-cut targets for ambitious politicians — no one loves a crook, especially one who may have once been violent. Money is not available for their rehabilitation, only for their punishment, so the program ended.

I still go to the worship group a few times a year, and the men still ask, "When are we going to get our story group back?" "Soon, I hope," I say. But they know it will be awhile.

A healing story can be told by anyone. The most extraordinary moment I ever saw in prison happened during a Sunday Meeting. The men were sitting in their usual circle as a tiny inch-worm worked his way between their workboots into the middle of the group. Every eye watched him. Any moment anyone could have lifted his foot and squashed the worm. These people had once done much worse. Yet no one moved. As the worm finished his crossing and left the circle, everyone breathed. Twenty people — one sigh. The inchworm was safe. He knew he could trust us. He knew us better than we knew ourselves. That healing tale was told by a worm.

The Golden Phoenix

A FRENCH-CANADIAN FOLKTALE RETOLD BY MARY LOUISE CHOWN

There was once a king who was very wise, and he became wise because a magic tree grew in his garden. Every night, this tree bore one silver apple, the apple of wisdom. Each morning, the king would eat the silver apple and he would rule wisely for the whole day.

One morning, there was no silver apple on that tree. It had been stolen.

"This is terrible!" said the king. "How can I govern my kingdom? Somebody must find out who stole the apple."

The king called his three sons and said to them, "Whichever one of you finds out who is stealing the silver apple will get my kingdom and my crown when I am dead."

The first son volunteered to keep watch that night to catch the thief. He took some food to eat, but instead of keeping him awake, it made him fell asleep with a full stomach. When he woke up in the morning, the silver apple was gone. "Well, there goes the kingdom for me," he said to himself.

Then the second son said, "I'm sure to do bet-ter," and he kept watch on the next evening. He brought a deck of cards with him and planned to play solitaire to keep himself awake, but he too fell asleep.

The third son was called "Ti Jean" — Little Jack. Jack volunteered to keep watch on the third night. Both his brothers laughed, "Well, how can you even try? You're the youngest and the small-est and we've both failed."

But Jack replied, "I can only do just as you have done and no worse." On that third night, he waited under the tree. When Jack felt himself going to sleep, he climbed up into the tree, plucked the silver apple, and hid it in the inner pocket of his shirt. "Now at least the thief can't steal it when I fall asleep."

Jack woke up suddenly in the middle of the night. Something was pulling at his shirt. He grabbed with both hands, but whoever it was got away, and all Jack had was a handful of golden feathers. Now at least he had a clue as to the identity of the thief. When Jack showed the feathers to his father, the king was amazed. "These are the feathers from the Golden Phoenix. So that's who has been taking my apples! I've heard that the Golden Phoenix lives on the other side of the glass mountain in the country of the sultan."

The king and his three sons set off at once and climbed to the top of the glass mountain. They could see the country on the other side, but they couldn't climb down the mountain because there was only a steep cliff. "Look!" said Jack. "A trap door!" His two older brothers didn't believe him, "A trap door on the top of the mountain?" But there it was, and when they lifted the door and looked down, it was completely dark, with smooth sides like a well. The king suggested that they could lower down a basket with a bell attached. Whoever went down could ring the bell when he needed to be pulled up.

"Who will go down?" asked the king.

"Not me, I'm afraid of heights," said the oldest brother.

"Well, I'm afraid of the dark," said the second brother.

"Then I guess it's my adventure," said Jack, and he climbed into the basket.

He was lowered down into the darkness until he felt a bump and the basket stopped. Jack stepped out of the basket and felt along the walls with his hands. Up ahead he saw a light, and so he headed in that direction.

Soon he came to a large cavern. He saw a door on the other side of this cavern and there, in the middle of the cavern, stood a unicorn. Before Jack had a chance to speak, the unicorn lowered its head and charged. Jack was too terrified to move. As the unicorn came closer, something made Jack jump sideways. The unicorn rushed right by him and its horn became stuck in the cavern wall. Jack opened the door and started to pass through, but the unicorn cried out, "Pull me out of this wall!"

"I will when I come back," promised Jack.

The door led to another room with another door on the far wall, and this time a huge lion was waiting for Jack. The lion crouched, ready to pounce, but Jack begged it to let him through.

"Please don't kill me. I'm looking for the Golden Phoenix."

"Alright," said the lion, "but I'm bored guarding this cavern. Talk to me. Tell me a riddle that I have to guess and I won't kill you."

So Jack asked the lion, "How far is it from the earth to the moon?"

"I don't know. Ask me something else," roared the lion.

"What is the swiftest thing in the world?"

The lion could not answer that one either. "I'll have to let you through, but you must promise to give me the answers on your way back. There's no other way through the glass mountain."

Jack passed through the door, and he found himself in another cavern with another door. This time the way was guarded by a snake with seven heads. Each head hissed at Jack and seemed to follow him wherever he moved, and this gave him an idea. He ran around the snake, and each head kept staring at Jack as he circled. Soon all seven heads were tied in a great knot, and Jack was free to open the door. He found himself on the other side of the glass mountain in the country of the sultan.

At that very moment, the sultan came riding by on his horse. He stopped when he saw Jack. "Who are you and why have you come into my country?"

Something told Jack that he should not say why he had come. "I'm Jack and I'm just a traveler along this road."

"All who come into my country cannot leave before they have supper with me."

So Jack had no choice but to accompany the sultan to his palace. Supper was served in the palace garden, and the sultan's daughter ate with them. While they ate, Jack heard a bird singing somewhere in the garden and the song was beautiful. As beautiful as the sultan's daughter.

"Tell me, Sultan, what bird is that who sings so sweetly?"

"Oh, that is nothing. Just a plain little bird of no importance. Continue eating."

Jack guessed right away that he must have heard the Golden Phoenix. Later that night, the sultan's daughter visited Jack in his room and warned him that her father never intended to let him leave. "In the morning he will challenge you to play a game with him and he always wins. No one ever leaves my father's palace." She also told Jack that the bird singing in the palace garden was indeed the Golden Phoenix, and whoever kept its cage controlled its coming and going. "My father locks the bird in the cage all day long and only lets it out each night so that it can fly over the glass mountain to steal the silver apple from the magic tree."

The next morning the sultan told Jack, "We're going to play a game of hide and seek. All my visitors must do this. I will hide three times. If you find me the first time, you can marry my daughter. If you find me the second time, you can take anything you like when you leave. If you can find me the third time, then I will let you leave tomorrow."

The sultan hid in his garden three times. The first time he changed himself into a goldfish, swimming in the garden pond. As Jack and the sultan's daughter walked through the garden, Jack noticed that one of the goldfishes had a mustache and so he knew that it was really the sultan in disguise.

"It won't be so easy the next time!" warned the sultan. And this was true. The second time, Jack had no idea where the sultan was hidden, though he looked everywhere in the garden, and so he resigned himself to his fate. Then he noticed a beautiful rose that reminded him of the sultan's daughter. He plucked the rose to give as a love present to the daughter, and it immediately turned back into the sultan.

"You were very lucky this time. What do you want to take with you?"

"Oh, I don't want much. I noticed a birdcage hanging in your garden. I'd like to take that," replied Jack. The sultan was furious, but he had to keep his promise. He hid himself a third time and Jack had no idea where he was. But it was getting on toward lunchtime, and Jack's stomach was growling with hunger. Just then he noticed a ripe pear hanging low on a nearby tree. But when he picked it and was about to take a bite, it suddenly changed into the sultan.

"I will let you leave in the morning, and you may go with my daughter and take the birdcage with you. But I'm not happy about this."

"Well, fair's fair after all," said Jack.

However, the sultan's daughter visited Jack again that night and warned him that her father did not intend to let Jack free. "It doesn't matter that you beat him at the game. He will never let you go. We must leave right now while he sleeps. Go and find two horses in the stable and wrap their hooves with your bedsheets to muffle their sound. I will take the cage from the garden and meet you at the stable."

When this was done, the two fled away from the palace towards the glass mountain. And it was none too soon, for the sultan woke up early the next morning and was soon chasing after them on his own fast horse.

Once they reached the glass mountain, Jack opened the door where the snake waited. Jack ran around the seven heads in the opposite direction and all seven heads became untangled. The snake promised him, "I won't let anyone past me into the mountain."

Jack and the sultan's daughter continued on into the room where the lion was still sitting, scratching his head and thinking.

"Oh good. You're back," the lion said. "Tell me the answers to the riddles. How far is it from the earth to the moon, and what is the swiftest thing in the world?"

Jack told him, " It is as far from the earth to the moon as it is from the moon to the earth. Thought is the swiftest thing in the world because it can travel in the twinkling of an eye."

"Now why couldn't I think of that?" moaned the lion, and he said to Jack and the sultan's daughter, " I won't let anyone past me into the mountain."

Finally, they came to the room where the unicorn was stuck, and Jack pulled his horn free from the wall.

"Oh, thank you," said the unicorn, " I won't let anyone past me into the mountain."

When Jack reached the basket, he rang the bell and the sultan's daughter climbed into the basket and was drawn up out of the depths of the glass mountain. The king and the two brothers had been waiting there all this time, and when they learned that Jack was still down there, they lowered the basket and up he came, holding the empty cage.

"Father, this is the cage for the Golden Phoenix. I won it from the sultan in the country on the other side of the glass mountain. Whoever keeps the cage controls the Golden Phoenix."

They all returned to their castle, and the king began once more to eat a silver apple each morning. But something had changed. The king and his sons could not bear to keep the Golden Phoenix locked up in its cage every day, so they let the bird come and go freely. When Jack's father died, Jack and the sultan's daughter became the next king and queen of the land. They ruled wisely because they had a silver apple to eat each day, and also the company of the Golden Phoenix and its beautiful song. ❧

Working with "The Golden Phoenix"

MARY LOUISE CHOWN

FOR TWO YEARS I TOLD STORIES to men who lived in two group homes and had been in trouble with the law. Most were sex offenders working off their sentences through community work, and several were at risk to offend again. Many of their offenses were committed against minors. The men ranged in age from 19 to their late 30s. Some were mentally disabled; all had low school achievement. Most were Native American.

The goals of the storytelling program as established by the staff were to foster a sense of self-worth among the participants, encourage problem solving, and help the men develop empathy for their victims. Residents from both homes gathered together regularly for sessions at one of the houses, and it was during this time that I was asked to come and tell stories. The combined group number varied from 11 to 18 men at any given time, and it included new residents as they arrived. I met with the men in the main living room of one of the houses, where we would sit around a coffee table in a circle of couches and chairs. Two staff members were always present. There would be a break, during which time most of the men went for a smoke and I had a few minutes to speak with the staff.

Each time I came, I brought with me some object that figured in one of my planned stories for that evening. I would place it on the coffee table and in the course of the evening, it would get passed around and discussed. Then I encouraged a retelling of one or all of the stories from a previous visit. I passed my rainstick round at each session for each man to hold as he responded to a question. I learned to be comfortable with silence, to wait for someone to speak or for the men to encourage each other to speak.

The stories I told were from five to ten minutes long. Sometimes I would tell only the first part of a tale at one visit: then we would pass the rainstick and discuss what happened. I would continue the telling next session. Later, I began telling parts of stories and asking the men to tell me what could happen next instead of finishing them myself.

As we became more familiar with each other, the conversation began to veer in all sorts of directions, to touch upon subjects brought up by the participants: their hopes, fears, dreams, and plans. The stories they heard, and the presence of a woman in their midst, combined to act as a catalyst upon the men, calling up associations and memories that they were not in the habit of voicing. These tangential discussions helped guide my choice of stories.

The story we had the most fun with was "The Golden Phoenix." I found it in an old book of French-Canadian tales collected by Marius

Barbeau, but it has changed through many tellings. By this time, the men had heard many stories in full and had also heard long stories told over two visits, and I thought they were ready to do some storytelling of their own. My intention was to ask them to tell their own versions of the story of the search for the Golden Phoenix. I would only tell them the ending I knew if they asked.

At the first session I brought a large feather with me and passed it around. As each man held it, the conversation centered on eagles, ravens, and crows that the men had seen or knew about. Then I told the first half of "The Golden Phoenix," up to the point where Jack heads for the light in the tunnel. I told the men that I was going to stop here because I wanted to know what they thought would happen next.

I asked these two questions: Who lives on the other side of the glass mountain? If you saw the light at the end of the tunnel, what would you find there?

We passed the rainstick around the circle, and each person shared his ideas for the rest of the story. Here are some samples:

- Two brothers live on the other side of the glass mountain. A golden eagle lives inside the mountain.

- There's a special apple tree on the other side of the glass mountain. There's a huge nest the size of a stadium inside the mountain. In the nest is a newly hatched phoenix, eating golden apples.

- There's a voice living on the other side of the glass mountain, a deep one. There's gold, jewelry, money inside the tunnel.

- A flying golden chicken lives on the other side of the glass mountain. Inside the tunnel are diamond rings, which are shining.

- It was a glass mountain that you could see through. There were people on the other side. You know what's on the other side 'cause you can see through. Inside the tunnel there is a reflection of light from the other side.

- On the other side of the glass mountain are three guys backpacking around a lake, fishing, and these three guys rescued the king and his sons. There is also a good spirit bird, a raven.

- There's an underground river, a mine, down the hole. Inside the tunnel are money and gold coins.

- On the other side of the mountain is a very bright light which lets them have whatever they wanted ... made them feel great about themselves, and happy. Inside the tunnel there are many other people who welcome you.

- The phantom of the opera lives on the other side of the glass mountain.

And the most popular one, judging by the intensity of laughs and applause:

- There's a big chicken in a Chicken Delight costume. [Laughter and the narrator holds up his hands for quiet and leans forward in his chair.] Stay with me, guys. There's this yellow light, and it's a factory with people working around a table. And they're all making copies of this apple in an assembly line, with the Chicken Delight chicken sitting on a throne, eating a bucket o' chicken. [Hoots of laughter again — the teller holds up his hands for quiet.] The youngest son, Jack, rings the bell, gets the brothers and the king to come down and see this apple

copying. Then everyone goes and has drumsticks.

The next time I came, I began the session by retelling the first part of "The Golden Phoenix," instead of asking the men to do this. Before coming, I had printed out all their words on separate strips of paper. As I read all their suggested endings back to them, they listened. Each man held the strip of paper containing his words as if it were a precious thing, some sort of tangible proof of his ability to create. I knew without a doubt that this experience added to the participants' self-regard. How marvelous that an age-old folktale about a legendary bird that no one has ever seen can touch the lives of grown men in this day and age. I am convinced that it is the very neutrality of the story that allows different listeners to make it part of their own story. Listeners don't expect that the story reflects their own lives and yet, somehow, it does.

Just like the lion in the story, the men loved the riddles and asked me to tell them more that they could try to guess. When I described the lion scratching his head and still thinking about the answers, the men nodded, and some said, "Yeah, I didn't know either." When the lion moaned, "Why didn't I think of that?" most of the men laughed out loud. When Jack ran around the snake to untangle the heads, one man said, "Well, that was easy!" Playfulness is an important aspect of imagination, and I was pleasantly surprised at the men's humor and sense of play. I felt that they were all seeing themselves as Jack, who used his wits and his sense of humor to get himself out of tricky and potentially dangerous situations. Here was a role model who demonstrated other ways to solve a problem besides resorting to violence. Their new insights were apparent when we went around the room and talked about the stories that I had shared. This impression was further corroborated by the staff of the group home, who told me that many of the men identified with the young male hero of the stories I told.

The men were receiving problem-solving training in hopes that this would encourage them to behave differently in the future. Both the staff and I experienced the benefits of storytelling for changing behavior. Listening to stories, discussing them, suggesting possible endings or "what happens next" increases imagination. There are no pictures to see, no words to read; all ideas must come from the imagination. Before someone can come up with different behavior patterns, alternative ways must be imagined. The very fact that the men relished the activity of suggesting outcomes and discussing them revealed that they were able to exercise their imagination and, moreover, they enjoyed it. These discussions were just the beginning, and I suspect they may have been the first creative experiences for many of the men. The participants would tell the staff, in between my visits, that they enjoyed finishing the stories because they could put in their own ideas and reasoning. Most of all, the staff told me, the men were glad the stories were about adults. It is quite common in my experience for adult and teenage listeners to be surprised and delighted to discover that storytelling is indeed for grown-ups.

I feel that this process of working with folktales invited the participants to look deeply into the richness of their inner lives. These riches are not material and at first may be as fleeting as a passing thought, as elusive as a daydream, or as brief as the men's stories about the Golden Phoenix. Their inventions drew upon their own personal repertoires of experiences and memories,

and yet were combined in an entirely new way. As a visiting storyteller, my role, as I saw it, was to take folktales and myths and adapt them for telling to a group of troubled men, and to invite my listeners to grapple with the story's meaning, drawing their own conclusions.

The staff informed me that the men usually did not tolerate visitors well, yet they eagerly anticipated the visits of "the lady with the stick." If too many weeks elapsed between visits, the men would ask the staff when I was coming again. A few men began asking to get books out of the library. My arrivals began to be greeted by a reception committee of two or three men waiting to hold the front door open for me, and usually one or two of them offered to walk me to my car at the end of the evening. When I agreed to be escorted to my car, a staff person came along as well, telling me afterwards that he wanted to be sure that the man didn't want my address, or a date with me. I appreciated the staff worker's concern, but as it turned out, the men simply wanted to show their care and respect for me.

During these visits, my own younger brother died suddenly, and some time passed before the group home asked me to come back. I was puzzled at the delay, thinking that they no longer saw my visits as valuable. I was so wrong, for when I did return I was presented with a wrapped gift and card. As I opened it, the men told me that everyone knew I was sad because of my brother's death, so they wanted to give me some time to myself. They gave me a carving of Coyote, a character in some of the early stories I told them. I keep it on a shelf near my books, and whenever I see it I am reminded of the faces of those men in the group home.

DOMESTIC VIOLENCE PREVENTION AND INTERVENTION

In search of happily ever after

ALLISON M. COX

OVER THE YEARS, I have worked as a mental health therapist, a health educator, a social worker, and a health promotion specialist. In all these positions, my job has required me to repeatedly focus on issues of domestic violence. No wonder. Domestic violence is the leading cause of injury to women ages 15 to 44 in the United States. Women of all cultures, races, occupations, income levels, and ages are battered by their husbands, boyfriends, lovers, and partners. It should be noted that, according to statistics from the National Coalition Against Domestic Violence, women are more than 10 times as likely to experience violence from an intimate partner than are males.

So many times I have heard the question "Why doesn't she just leave him?" Well, women who leave their batterers are at 75 percent greater risk of being killed by the batterer than those who stay. In the United States, 42 percent of murdered women are killed by their intimate male partners. In spite of this danger, 50 percent of all homeless women and children are on the streets to escape the threat of violence at home.

For several years I have told stories at the local battered women's shelter. The first time these women hear that they will be listening to a storyteller at their next group session, they usually ask whether they should bring the kids. We explain that the session is for adults. We want the women to be comfortable and create an environment where they can respond to the stories if they choose. There is no shortage of stories, going all the way back to ancient times. And yet the material is so current that I even had one woman run out of the room after one of my story sessions. When the women's shelter worker followed her and asked her what was wrong, the woman responded, "You told that storyteller what happened to me, didn't you? How else would she know my story so well?" We assured her that her story is, sadly, so much like that of other women.

After each story is finished, I offer a moment of silence for reflection. Then I ask simple questions, such as "What images stood out for you in that story?" and "What was your response to some of the characters in the story?" or "What was your favorite story among those you heard today and why?" Often this is all it takes to get the women talking. A shelter resident may begin a sentence discussing a woman character in the story, but in mid-sentence will switch to first person without missing a beat. For some, this is the first time they have spoken aloud of their battering experience. The dissociated viewpoint that the story allows them gives them the ability to discuss their experience from a safe distance, until they are ready to jump into the emotional thick of it. Many then bravely jump.

The greatest fear most of the women feel is that they will somehow find themselves in another relationship with the same problems as the last. So we discuss how one can tell if someone is potentially abusive. What are the warning signs? The stories hold up a mirror, reflecting back patterns that the women recognize: "As soon as that man in the story said that he didn't want her friends coming around, I knew she was in trouble!" "When her husband refused to do any work at all, well, she should have left him right there." And so, piece by piece, the women help each other build internal reference systems. Since a third of the women who are physically abused grew up in homes where this happened to their mothers, and one in five were abused themselves as children, it is no surprise that for some, learning what constitutes a safe and loving relationship is a new concept. It is hard telling stories to these women, knowing that many of them will return to their battering partner, for it often takes five to seven attempts to leave before they are permanently successful. Still, I keep returning to the shelter, thinking that it could be this time that will make the difference.

A woman once stopped me at the grocery store. "You're that storyteller lady, aren't you? Do you remember me?" she asked. I decided to agree that she looked familiar even though I completely blanked on ever having met her. "You told me to leave my husband and you were right!" I stood there, a bit flabbergasted. I have never, during any storytelling session at the shelter, told anyone what to do. But evidently this woman felt that the story spoke directly to her. "Are you happy?" I asked her. "Just look at these kids," she said, proudly pointing to two little giggling girls who were perched amidst the canned goods in her shopping cart. "And I'm going to school now. We're doing great!" It had been a long day in a longer week, but suddenly I felt like telling stories all night ....

Women's substance abuse recovery groups are another venue where I tell domestic violence-related stories, since many of these women are victims of abuse. Battered women are 15 times more likely to suffer from alcoholism and 9 times more likely to abuse drugs. Studies show that increased risk for substance abuse occurs almost entirely after the first reported abusive episode. These women will self-medicate with alcohol and drugs to numb the pain. As a storyteller, I have often visited a program focusing on pregnant and parenting women in recovery. Since we know that abuse escalates during pregnancy, we try to reach these women in any way possible before it is too late to prevent more violence. When new women in the program hear that I am going to tell stories, they respond, "Do you think we're a bunch of children?" But other women will jump to my defense, "Hey, you're really going to like this. Just wait till you hear her." And then the barrage of requests for favorite stories begins

One of the most powerful events I have taken part in has been the "Week Without Violence," sponsored by the YWCA during Women's History Month in October. For several years now the culmination of the week centers around the Silent Witness exhibit. The exhibit consists of life-size, wooden silhouettes painted red. Each silhouette bears a plaque with the name and story of a victim of domestic violence from our area. A women's group from a synagogue in Seattle has been sponsoring this project in our area. There are similar Silent Witness exhibits across the nation.

The first year I participated, we held a memorial service in a local church for those women who had lost their lives to domestic violence. At the memorial service, several community members spoke of ways to help stop the abuse and prevent the terrible loss of life. Next, a procession circled the church, and each time it encountered a silent witness silhouette at the end of a pew, a bell was rung and the woman's story was read aloud. It was then I noticed that some of the wooden cut-outs were draped with scarves, flowers, even stuffed animals. The families of the murder victims were sitting beside these wooden statues of their lost daughters, sisters, mothers, aunts, cousins ….

I wondered how these families would feel about the story ("The Stolen Skin") I was about to tell. Even though I had told it repeatedly with promising results, I had never knowingly shared this story with the surviving family members of women who had died from abuse. Still, I reminded myself that it was time to put my trust in the story.

After the service, members of the families came up to me. Some thanked me sincerely for the story. Others just squeezed my hand, touched my arm, or pressed gently on my shoulder, simple gestures that spoke so eloquently. Months later I still had people tell me that the story made a deep impression on them and they would never forget it. As for me, I will never forget the expressions on the faces of those people as they heard the story of their beloved read from the plaque on those cut-out statues. After each story, the entire church chanted "We will remember her." Once I got into my car, I cried all the way home, but I promised myself I will keep telling these stories until the violence ends.

The Stolen Skin

A CELTIC FOLKTALE RETOLD BY ALLISON M. COX*

Versions of this story are told around the Northern hemisphere in Iceland and Siberia, in the Celtic lands, and among the Native Americans of the Northwest. It is sometimes the emotional abuse of women that takes the greatest toll on their lives. Those women who escape from abusive relationships are often forced to leave their children behind. This tale echoes the painful choices that some of the woman at the shelter experienced as they attempted to reconstruct their shattered lives.

There once lived on the northern shores a lonely man.
He had always lived near the ocean bluffs, overlooking the descending
levels of the sea stacks.

The sea stacks are those great flat-topped islands of rock, carved out of the land by centuries of pounding waves. The man's days were spent fishing the ocean. He had little to do with the other people in the village nearby, choosing a solitary life for lack of knowing any other way. His only companions were the seagulls that wheeled overhead while he was fishing, or an occasional seal that would surface among the seaweed and search the man's face with its round, dark eyes, only to slip back into the depths again.

One midsummer evening, the fisherman was returning later than usual from the sea. He had worked a longer day, taking advantage of the late sunset and the early rise of a full moon to light his way back. When he approached the first and shortest of the sea stacks that marked his way to home shores, the fisherman caught sight of movement on its surface. As the boat drifted toward the rocks, he heard singing that was sweet, yet wild. After tying his boat to a scrub of a tree, the man slowly climbed up the side of the rock, urged on by the strange melody. To his surprise, he found a path and thought to himself, "Now that's strange. Who would make a path on the seaward side of the island?"

Upon reaching the top, the man found he was crouching in the shadow of a crag that jutted higher than the rest of the plateau. The man turned, balancing himself against the rock face, to see — shining naked figures dancing in the moonlight. As they whirled about, the beings laughed and called to each other between the verses of their song. They were women. Beautiful women with skin that shimmered like starlight. Their lilting voices reached deep inside the man, into places that he had closed off to others all his life.

There appeared to be dark shadows lying on the ground before him. As his eyes adjusted to the light, the shadows seemed to have substance. The fisherman reached out toward one ... it was soft fur. Seal fur. Without thinking, he quickly stuffed the sealskin into his shirt, and in doing so he lost his footing momentarily, sending rocks and pebbles cascading over the cliff. The dancers froze and then, at some unspoken signal, they all dashed towards the sealskins on the cliff's edge. The fisherman pulled back into the shadows, watching as the women draped the skins about themselves, transformed into the shape of seals, and then plunged off the cliff, into the sea. All but one, that is. For there was still one lone woman searching desperately along the cliff edge of the great rock for something that she could not find. She called out in an eerie voice to her companions below, and their cries echoed back from the waters, but these too vanished in time. Finally, all that could be heard above the crashing of the waves was the weeping of this solitary woman.

The fisherman crept out of the shadows and approached the seal woman. As he first drew near, she appeared terrified. He feared that she would turn and leap into the ocean after the others, so he stepped between her and the cliff's edge. He couldn't bear for her to go — she was the most beautiful creature he had ever seen. Then the mysterious woman drew a breath and stepped forward.

"Please, sir," she pleaded in a voice that sounded like the rippling of waves on the sands, "give back to me what is mine."

The man could think only of his own need. "Come home with me. Live with me. Be my wife."

The woman continued as though she had not heard him. "Without my skin, I can never go home to my family or my life beneath the waters." She began to weep again. "I will remain captive in the upper lands of the sun."

But the seal woman seemed so lovely to the man, even in her tears. The fisherman refused to consider letting her go. "The others have gone. You are part of my world now."

The man took off his coat and bundled it around her. The seal woman appealed to him, begged him, but the man simply answered, "Come now, we will go home." He picked her up, carried her down to his boat, and after lifting her in, untied the boat and turned it toward the shore. The woman continued looking out at the ocean as they headed to the shore. On the beach, the fisherman pulled the boat up out of the waves' reach, grasped the woman's hand, and led her up the steep path along the bluffs. All the way up the path she kept gazing out at the sea. She was still looking out at the distant waters when the man closed the door of his cottage, shutting her inside.

The two lived together many years. The woman gave birth to three children, with whom she spent most of her time. She avoided the people of the village, not wanting to answer their questioning stares when they saw the webbing between her fingers or listen to them whispering behind her back. As time passed, her long dark hair lost its luster, as did her once-shining eyes. The woman cared for her family, but would, at times, slip down to the sea. Sometimes, when the children woke from their naps, they would stand at the cliff's edge and look down at the bay. There they would find her, standing out on the rocks, calling in a mournful voice to the seals that slipped about in the water.

One night, the children were awakened in the sleeping loft by angry words. Their father's gruff voice whispered fiercely, "When will you stop speaking of this? It's been years now!"

"Life is ebbing away from me. I need my skin back," they heard their mother beg.

But the man had never admitted to having locked away the sealskin. Instead he answered, "And what would you do if you had this sealskin that you're always asking about? Would you just abandon your family? What kind of mother would that make you?"

The woman's gaze fell to stare at the floor of the cottage. "I don't know. I only know that I cannot go on living as someone other than who I am. I need my skin back. It is a part of me."

The man yelled, "You care only for yourself! What of me?"

The children heard a *crack*, and then the footsteps of their father as he stormed out, slamming the door, leaving their mother to weep alone where she had fallen on the bed.

Three children climbed down the ladder from the sleeping loft, slipped across the floor, climbed into the bed, and wrapped their arms around their mother. They stroked her hair and wiped her cheeks and covered her in kisses.

"Don't cry, mother," said the oldest. "Father will be back. We will make you smile till then."

And then the oldest urged the other two children, "Sing the song that mother taught us. You know — the one about the sea!" They began to sing and their mother could not help but smile.

"Do the dance too," coaxed the eldest. So the two little ones slipped off the bed and began to dance in circles, spinning in opposite directions, their nightclothes ballooning about them. Their mother laughed softly, which only encouraged her young to sing louder and dance with wild abandon. Suddenly the two children careened into each other and the wall all at once, bringing a high shelf crashing down on top of them. Their mother leaped to their aid.

"Are you alright?"

"We're fine," they answered, giggling, shaking off dust from the fallen shelf.

The oldest stepped around the others and lifted the board that had fallen to get a look at what had toppled down off the high shelf.

"What's in this old wooden box?" The boy knelt down on the floor, fingering the overturned object. "There's a lock on it!"

"I don't know," answered his mother. "I have never been able to reach up to that shelf to dust, not even from the chair." The woman bent down, reaching out to right what appeared to be a long, shallow, wooden chest. As she lifted it, bottom side up, the lid broke off and the contents spilled out onto the floor.

"Oh, look!" cried the youngest. "It's a fur." The three children fell upon the pelt, stroking the hide and guessing what it was from.

"It's from a bear," said one.

"No, it's from a seal," said the other.

The youngest buried her face in the fur and said, "It smells like mother."

Three small heads turned to look up at their mother, questioning. The woman stood, silent, barely breathing. But she did not hear the children. Instead, she heard the crashing of waves and the singing of whales. She reached out toward the sealskin and the children all lifted the fur up to their mother.

"Mother, what is it?"

"Ohhh," she sighed, clutching her sealskin to her chest. Then the woman held the pelt up to her face and breathed in the scent of the ocean air. She no longer saw the cottage before her, but instead saw images of sunlight filtering through waving seaweed, dolphins leaping in ocean spray.

The children interrupted her reverie again. "Mother, what is it?"

"It is time for me to go home, dear ones," she said.

"But you are home," insisted the eldest.

"No, I must leave you now."

The three children became very still. She knelt down and spoke gently to them. "If I stay, I cannot thrive — I will perish. I am a prisoner on the land. You know I have always told you that my real home is in the sea."

They nodded.

"I love you ... and I will always carry you with me in my heart." She kissed each one on the forehead and then the woman stood, turned, and headed toward the door.

The youngest cried, "Mother, don't go!"

She stopped in the open doorway. "If you need me, go to the flat rock at the edge of the sea. Call for me and listen for my voice." And then the woman fled into the night, clutching her sealskin to her chest.

It seemed only moments later when the fisherman returned home to find his three children standing in the doorway in their nightclothes.

"Mother has gone!" they cried.

He looked past them, saw the broken chest on the floor, and ordered, "Wait inside! Don't come out till I get back." And he ran off toward the bluff's edge. The man reached the cliff's edge just in time to see a seal dive off a rock, into the sea. He shouted her name over and over into the night — but his voice was lost in the crashing of the waves.

The fisherman never saw his seal wife again, and the villagers took note of this sudden disappearance of the fisherman's wife. They whispered about it to each other. And they also spoke of his children — those strange children.

"Did you know," they would say, "those strange children can be seen sitting on the rock at the shore's edge — and it appears that they are talking, laughing, and singing with a female seal!"

In time, all the villagers came to recognize this seal, and none would harm her for she became known as the guardian of the bay. And they always knew which one she was. They would point and say, "See, she's that one — that one there. The one with the lustrous dark fur and eyes that shine." 🐾

WAYS TO GET INVOLVED IN DOMESTIC VIOLENCE PREVENTION

- ***The Silent Witness Story*** is a book describing the Silent Witness Exhibit, with instructions for making the figures and ideas for fundraising, publicity, etc. Cost: $14.95. To order, contact Barb Zimmerman, 436 Penn Avenue South, Minneapolis, MN 55405; E-mail: HBZip@aol.com; Phone: (612) 377-8012; Fax: (612) 377-4769.

- **Organize a Benefit Concert:** During Women's History Month and Women's Awareness Week (a local event sponsored by the City of Tacoma's Women's Right's department) our local storytelling guild has sponsored storytelling concerts. Tellers donate their talent and share stories on the subject of women's issues. Whether the purpose of these concerts was to increase awareness or to raise money for the local women's shelter, the stories shared were of all types — myths, legends, folktales, personal stories, and literary stories. They were funny, sad, exciting, tender. The response we received from our listeners was that these stories needed to be heard and to please keep sharing the message. October is Domestic Violence Prevention Month throughout the United States and would be a perfect time to sponsor storytelling events to increase awareness.

- **Tell Stories at Your Local Shelter:** Both women and their children are hungry for stories that will nourish their spirit. I have told to families together, or just to the women alone, and each time I felt that the stories were deeply appreciated. Think of having your entire life torn apart — no home, no possessions except what you could carry out the door. Where will you go? What will you do? These are people who could use a healing story. A simple gift of story can mean so much.

- **Silence Speaks: Digital Storytelling in Support of Healing and Violence Prevention:** Violence shapes the lives, experiences, and dreams of countless adults and children each year, yet few opportunities exist for survivors to tell their stories in their own words. In an effort to help survivors and witnesses of violence tap into their creativity, move towards recovery, and bring their voices to the forefront of violence prevention and social justice work, Third World Majority (TWM) has created Silence Speaks. Three-day Silence Speaks workshops integrate aspects of creative writing, oral history, art and narrative therapy, and digital media manipulation to help people tell stories as short digital videos. The workshops bridge the digital divide by demystifying multimedia technology and offering participants a separate, intimate space for personal exploration and collective healing. With the permission of participants, organizers feature selected stories on the Silence Speaks website (http://www.silencespeaks.org/) and screen them in community settings, in order to raise public awareness about the complexity of violence and to mobilize people to get involved in anti-violence organizing and advocacy. For more information about Silence Speaks, please visit www.silences-peaks.org or contact Amy L. Hill at 510-653-2580 or amylenita@compumentor.org.

The Lady of the Lake Waters

A WELSH FOLKTALE RETOLD BY ALLISON M. COX*

There are multiple versions of this Welsh tale of a spirit woman appearing from a lake. The conditions of her agreement to marry and the occasions that cause her unexpected behavior and departure have provided material for discussions of abuse and the qualities that promote healthy relationships. I have used this tale both with adults and in Grade 4 classrooms.

There once was a young man who drove his sheep up into the hills, seeking greener pastures by the shore of a mountain lake. One day, after walking the flock to the lakeside, the shepherd was astonished to see a beautiful woman, dressed in white robes, seated on the calm surface of the water.

She was the most enchanting woman his eyes had ever seen. The woman, unaware of being watched, was combing her long hair, using the reflecting lake as her mirror. The man gasped and moved closer to the shore to see her. It may have been the sound or the movement that startled the woman. She looked up, and seeing the man standing, with his arms beckoning toward her, the woman quickly dove under the water and disappeared.

The shepherd called to her, "Wait! Don't leave. Stay here with me." But she did not reappear that day.

The shepherd began to visit the lake daily. He would leave gifts for the woman by the shore. He would find his offerings gone the next day, but still no sign of the woman. Eventually, the man could think of nothing else. He began to neglect his flock. He became obsessed. He started to visit the mountain lake at night as well as during the day. He would call out his love to the woman: "Lady of the Lake Waters, I love you. Please come to me." He was certain that he could see, at times, a faint glimmering in the water at the spot where he had once seen her.

Months passed and the shepherd persisted, consumed with his desire for what he could not have. By and by, some of his sheep wandered off and became lost, but he did not search for them. His thoughts were only for his unfulfilled longing. Finally, one evening when the moon was full, he sang out again over the lake, "Lady of the lake waters, I love you and I will never be happy until you are my wife. Please ...."

But then he stopped, for there, rising from the lake, was the woman he had sought. She glided over the surface of the water towards him, her shining white robes and long hair flowing with the soft breeze. The woman gently placed her hand on the shepherd's extended palm and stepped ashore.

"Shepherd, I consent to be your wife," she said and then held up her other hand to prevent him from speaking yet. "First, you must agree to this one condition. If ever you were to lay a rough hand on me three times, I would vanish from your life, never to be seen again."

"Dear lady," cried the man, "never would I ever think of harming you!"

He grasped her hand and began to lead the woman home when he heard sounds coming from behind them. He stopped to turn and see. There, climbing out of the lake after the woman, were a flock of sheep and a herd of cows. The man was overjoyed. Now he possessed the woman of his dreams and wealth as well!

The couple married and for several years seemed happy. The shepherd was now raised to the status of a farmer because of the flock of sheep and herd of cows that his wife had brought him. Because of this, they were often invited to attend the gatherings of the local villagers. One day the shepherd and his wife were asked to come to a christening, where, to the surprise of all present, the spirit woman began weeping.

Her husband gave her an angry glance and asked her, "Why are you making such a fool of yourself?"

His lady, having the ability to see into the souls of others, answered her husband between sobs. "The poor babe has entered a family where it is not wanted. His mother is worn from too many children and has scant enough food or time for yet another. The man of this house beats them all. Misery lies ahead for the child. Why should I rejoice?"

The husband shoved his wife to keep her quiet and to stop her from embarrassing him in front of the others.

The lady lifted her head, looked him steady in the eye, and said, "That's one."

Time passed and the farmer and his lady were invited to the funeral of the mother of the child whose christening they had attended the year before. At the memorial service, the lady now laughed and danced and sang.

Her husband angrily asked her, "Why are you making such a fool of yourself?"

The lady said readily, "The woman's sorrow is over. 'Tis sad that she died, but no longer will she struggle with being poor or mistreated. She is at peace now. Why then should I weep?"

The husband shoved his wife to keep her quiet and stop her from embarrassing him in front of the other villagers.

The lady lifted her head, looked him steady in the eye and said, "That's two."

Life went on and the farmer and his lady appeared to live contentedly together, as before. At length they were invited to attend a wedding where the bride was young and the groom was an older man of money. In the midst of the mirth and celebration of guests who had gathered from all the neighboring countryside, the lake lady burst into tears.

Her husband grabbed her by the wrist and pulled her to him, whispering fiercely, "Is there nowhere we can go that you do not embarrass me by making a fool of yourself? What is wrong with you now?"

"I weep because youth is married to age for the purpose of riches. It is a bad bargain and I see misery beginning here for both of them."

The lady wrenched her wrist out of her husband's grasp and added, "Just as I see it beginning here for you, my husband. For you have laid a rough hand on me for the third and last time. Farewell."

With that said, she left the wedding banquet. Her husband hurried after her shouting, "I'm sorry. Forgive me! Please, come back."

But the lake lady moved at such a pace that she was quickly out of sight and beyond hearing. The man finally reached their farm to find it empty. His wife as well as the flocks and herds were gone. He ran up into the hills to the lake where he had first found her. He reached the top of the hill that overlooked the lake just in time to see the woman's head disappear beneath the surface of the waters, followed by all the sheep and cattle. Moments later there was no trace of their passing. The water's surface was calm and the hillside empty. The only sound that could be heard in that mountain valley was the weeping of a man. A man who knew that he would never again see that which he had once prized above all else, but had forgotten to love. 🐦

The Princess and the Pigeon

AN ITALIAN FOLKTALE RETOLD BY DIANE F. WYZGA

Over the years I have told so many stories at the Human Options Shelter, which offers emergency and long-term housing and other services to women and children escaping domestic abuse. I often go with some ideas of what I would like to tell, but what story I share with the women often depends on what is going on for them, what they express when they throw their burden into the imaginary fire, what story is asking to be told. So intuition, readiness to tell a story, and the ability to be flexible are critical. The following is one of the stories I've shared.

One morning a princess sat by an open window of her apartment, combing her beautiful, charcoal-black hair, when suddenly a pigeon swooped down out of the sky and picked up the scrunchie she intended to use to tie back her hair, held it in his beak, and flew away. "Humpff!" said the princess.

The next morning the princess was sitting by an open window of her apartment, combing her beautiful, charcoal-black hair, when suddenly a pigeon swooped down out of the sky and picked up the Armani scarf she intended to use to tie back her hair, held it in his beak, and flew away. "Humpff!" said the princess.

The following morning the princess was sitting by an open window of her apartment. She had just finished combing her beautiful, charcoal-black hair when suddenly a pigeon swooped down out of the sky and picked up her tortoiseshell comb, held it in his beak, and flew away.

"That does it!" said the princess. And she stood up and marched out of the apartment building and down the street in search of the pigeon.

The pigeon was waiting, and it would fly ahead and stop and wait, and fly and stop and wait, and fly and wait and fly and wait and fly and wait. And in that way the princess was led to a deep dark forest where she had never been before. In the middle of the forest was a clearing, and in the middle of the clearing stood a really miserable-looking hut. As the princess stood there wondering what to do, out of the really miserable-looking hut came a tall, dark, and handsome man. In fact, he was the tallest, darkest, and handsomest man the princess had ever seen.

She said, "Yo! I'm a princess from back that way somewhere and I was wondering if by chance you've seen a pigeon fly by here with a tortoiseshell comb in his beak? Every morning for the past three days this stupid pigeon has been stealing stuff from me. Today he took my comb. So I followed it here and now it's gone. Have you seen a pigeon like that around here?"

The tall, dark, and handsome man said, "I know all about that pigeon. You see, I'm the pigeon. And I'm under a spell. I have no idea how I came to be under this spell or even why I turn into a pigeon, but I know that you are the only one who can break it. So I led you out here."

"Me? Only me? There isn't some other princess out there somewhere who can do this?" And the tall, dark, and handsome man shook his head. So, being good inside, to say nothing of the fact that she was quite taken by the tall, dark, and handsome man, the princess dropped her attitude and asked, "What do I have to do?"

And the tall, dark, and handsome man said, "All you have to do is sit on the chair by the window inside that really miserable-looking hut and wait for me to turn into a pigeon. When I turn into a pigeon, I will fly away over the mountain there. You must watch the spot where I disappear for a year, a month, and a day, and then I'll never have to be a pigeon again."

"Are you sure I'm the only one?"

"Yup," he said. "You're it."

So, without another word, the princess walked inside the really miserable-looking hut, sat on the chair by the open window, and waited till the tall, dark, and handsome man turned into a pigeon. And when he did, he flew over the mountain, and the princess began to watch the spot where he disappeared.

And the sun shone in the window, and her skin burned and cracked and peeled, and burned and cracked and peeled, and cracked and peeled, and cracked and peeled, and cracked and peeled until it began to look like the bark of a tree. And the birds of the forest flew in the window and made nests in her hair. And the rain came in on her, and the sleet and the snow, and her clothes turned moldy and green. But still she sat and watched and waited.

Then the tall, dark, and handsome man came walking back. When he saw how hideous she had become, he said, "Look at you! Blech! You did all this for a man?" Then, "Puttt," he spit on her and walked away.

The princess had been sitting for so long that she could not stand. So she slid out of the chair and out of the miserable-looking hut and into the clearing, where she began to cry big heaving sobs and cried herself to sleep. She slept for a very long time.

When she awoke, she was looking at three old women, sisters, who said, "We've watched this whole mess. We know what happened to you and we're going to help you get it right." And with that, the first woman touched her hair and it became more lustrous than a L'Oreal hair color commercial. And the second sister touched her skin and it was smoother and more supple than a baby's bottom. And the third sister touched her clothes and before she could say "Martha Stewart," the princess found herself in a gorgeous five-story condo with a panoramic ocean view and the three old sisters for company.

Now, it happened that the princess's five-story condo with the panoramic ocean view was right next to the not-so-shabby home of the tall, dark, and handsome man. And when he awoke he could not remember any five-story condo blocking his panoramic ocean view. And while he was standing at his balcony and deciding whether to call his lawyers, he saw the most beautiful woman he had ever seen. She had charcoal-black hair and she was sitting at a window of the condo. He knew he had to have her. So he sent his valet next door to arrange a meeting.

The valet returned and told the tall, dark, and handsome man that she would meet him, but only under the following conditions. "You must build a wooden bridge from your balcony to hers with carved handrails. And when it is built, cover it two inches deep in rose petals. Then you must wait on your balcony. You must not set foot on

the bridge and you must not speak. She will walk from her balcony to yours and then you two will meet."

So the tall, dark, and handsome man hired the best contractors in town and had them build the bridge. And he had all the FTD florists in town scour the countryside for rose petals. In time, the bridge was ready.

When it was ready, the tall, dark, and handsome man stood on his balcony, taking care not to step on the bridge and not to speak. The princess stood on her balcony with the three sisters, who said to her, "OK, chickie, this is how it works. You start walking across the bridge. When you're about one-third of the way across, pretend to step on a rose thorn and faint, then leave the rest to us."

"Works for me," she said and she started walking across the bridge. When she was about one-third of the way across, she cried, "Oh, it's a thorn in my foot. You're trying to kill me to get my five-story condo with the panoramic ocean view." She collapsed in a heap. The three sisters stepped over the balcony, picked her up, and dragged her back, all the while glaring at the tall, dark, and handsome man.

The tall, dark, and handsome man was beside himself. He wasn't allowed to speak or set foot on the bridge, so he stood and watched and waited and watched and waited while the doctors ran to-and-fro from the condo, and the rumors flew. "She's going to die from that rose thorn." And still the tall, dark, and handsome man watched and waited, and the rumors flew. "She won't die, but her leg, you should see, it's 20 times its normal size." And still the tall, dark, and handsome man stood and watched and waited until in time he learned that the princess was fully recovered.

He decided to try again. So he sent his valet to the condo to inquire whether he and the princess could meet. The valet returned and said, "She has agreed to meet you, but only under the following conditions. You must tear down that really miserable wooden bridge and build one of steel in its place. And when it is done, you must cover it four inches deep in jasmine petals. Again you must stand on your balcony and not speak. Above all, you must take care not to step on the bridge. The princess will walk from her balcony to yours, and the two of you will meet."

The tall, dark, and handsome man ordered the contractors to tear down the wooden bridge with the beautifully carved handrails and erect one of stainless steel. And he ordered all the FTD florists in town to scour the countryside for jasmine petals. In time, it was ready. And the tall, dark, and handsome man stood on his balcony and waited.

The princess stood on her balcony with the three sisters. They said, "OK, chickie, you know how it works. This time, walk about halfway across before you pretend to stub your toe on a rusty rivet."

"Works for me," she said, and she climbed over the balcony and began to walk across the bridge. About halfway across, she cried, "Oh, I've stubbed my toe on a rusty rivet. You're trying to kill me to get my five-story condo with the panoramic ocean view." She collapsed in a heap. The three sisters stepped over the balcony, picked her up, and dragged her back, all the while glaring at the tall, dark, and handsome man.

The tall, dark, and handsome man was beside himself. He wasn't allowed to speak or set foot on the bridge, so he stood and watched and waited and watched and waited while the doctors ran to-and-fro from the condo, and the rumors flew. "She's going to die from that rusty rivet." And still the tall, dark, and handsome man watched and waited, and the rumors flew. "She won't die, but her leg, you should see, it's 20 times its normal size." And still the tall, dark and handsome man stood and watched and waited until in time he learned that the princess was fully recovered.

He decided to try one more time. So he sent his valet to the condo to inquire whether he and the princess could meet. The valet returned and said, "She says she will not lay eyes on you until you are stretched out in your coffin."

The tall, dark, and handsome man sent for some coffin makers and had a coffin made to his exact size and shape, except without the lid, of course. Then he climbed in and stretched out in his coffin.

He had his friends and relations lift the coffin and carry it through the neighborhood saying, "Come see the tall, dark, and handsome man stretched out in his coffin. Come see the tall, dark, and handsome man stretched out in his coffin."

The princess stood on her balcony and waited. And when the procession came by, she said, "Look at you! You did all this for a woman?" Then, "Puttt," she spit on him.

Somehow these words seemed vaguely familiar to the tall, dark, and handsome man. He sat up in his coffin and took his first really close look at the princess. He saw that, indeed, she was the very one who had so willingly sat for a year and a month and a day to break a spell for him.

So he climbed out of his coffin, went to her, and said, "First, I'm terribly ashamed for what I said to you that day in the forest. Will you forgive me for the way I treated you? And second, could we start over?"

Well, being good inside, the princess forgave the tall, dark, and handsome man. But as for starting over, that's another story, indeed. ❦

When I have told this story at the shelter, the women have responded, "Doesn't it just figure — you go and do all this stuff for some guy, and what do you get?" They like the idea of women helping women in this tale. They also like that the princess can get the prince to jump through hoops to prove himself in return. They are suspicious of what he wants: after all, they recall that he sees this fine-looking woman and decides he has to have her — like property.

What I found most interesting when I told this story was that these women insisted on changing the ending. They accepted that if they held a grudge and did not forgive, it would eat away at them — provided, of course, that they were ready to forgive. So the princess forgiving the prince was alright with them. But as to starting over, no, they weren't ready for that. That is another story. They all agreed on that.

Each of my storytelling sessions at the shelter opens with a ritual and closes with one. The closing ritual is always the same. I invite all the women to stand in a close circle and extend their right hands. Each places her right thumb into the palm of the person to her left, and each set of fingers is curled over each thumb until a circle of hands is formed. This circle is our story well, and all the stories shared are within it — just reach in and grab one of these stories. I tell them that this particular well is unique because we have created it in this moment and time, which will not exist again except in our imaginations. So it is important to keep imagination, and thereby connection to each other, alive and well. And then we bid each other goodnight and pleasant dreams, and blow out our candle.

The Little Boy Who Couldn't Sit Still

W. KIRK AVERY

The U.S. Advisory Board on Child Abuse and Neglect suggests that domestic violence may be the single major precursor to child abuse and neglect. Child abuse is 15 times more likely to occur in families where domestic violence is present. Exposure to domestic violence can have lasting negative effects on children. The following story gives us a glimpse into the world of such a child, struggling to understand and survive.

— *Allison M. Cox*

"The Little Boy Who Couldn't Sit Still" has very personal meaning for me. I had attended my first Sharing the Fire Storytelling Conference and sat in on a workshop led by a presenter whose energy and spirit I especially admired, and who was scheduled to tell dinosaur stories at a children's museum near where I live. I wanted to watch how she told stories; the vision of myself as a storyteller was still very new to me at the time.

While I was there, I witnessed the scene that I have written about: a little boy forcibly removed from the crowd of children gathered together, carted off like a board in his mother's arms. There was such a terror in his eyes, such anguish; eyes that for just a fleeting tortured second directly pierced mine, his silent scream for help. The first draft was written in longhand, straight through, that very same night.

Five years later now, and counting, the resulting story has evolved through numerous revisions and various retellings. As various people responded to the story, I learned more about myself. What had started as my own attempt to record a little boy's particular experience and thus, somehow, to "preserve" it (in truth, probably as much for myself as for him), has opened up for me what I have only begun to understand as the wonder and the hopeful promise of storytelling as a healing art. For to share such a story is ultimately not so much to "preserve" it at all, but, rather, to release it and to share that very releasing, for it is in the shared releasing that mending first seems possible. In that spirit, application would seem appropriate in any number of theme-related groups, but perhaps most of all, gently, one-on-one, one survivor's hand reaching out for another.

"The hitting sounds late at night," suddenly so clear to the little boy when he gives his mother one of his magic colors, what those sounds might actually mean, no child anywhere ought ever to have to experience, nor should their mothers.

Once there was a little boy who had trouble sitting still.
He knew this bothered his mother and he really didn't mean to make
her nervous, but it was just that sometimes he couldn't help himself.

He could see such pretty colors in his heart. When he tried to tell about them, how they were magic, no one would listen. The harder he tried, the more tongue-tangled his words describing them became, and what came out were only strange sounds, not what he saw, not what he felt.

So he jumped up and down sometimes. The magic colors were so special to him, and because they were, most of all he wanted her to know. Maybe then she wouldn't be so afraid of his father. Maybe then they could keep *her* safe, too.

Now one day he heard a radio voice saying something about dinosaurs, how a storyteller was coming to the town library to tell stories about them. Dinosaurs he knew about because two of them were in his favorite coloring book. He made each one a special color. That way, neither would feel alone and each could always see the other one coming for company. That's what his magic colors were for, to give away.

He just couldn't sit still when he tried to tell about them.

His mother agreed, finally, that he could go, but only if this time he would behave himself: not jump around, not make any strange noises, not do anything that would call attention to himself. He knew how important all of that was, that he not embarrass her, especially because lately she had seemed even more nervous than usual. But he wanted so much to go, and he promised with all his heart that he would sit quietly, *but please, please ...*

She said, "Oh, all right then," and he pretended not to see the look that crossed her face when she did, the same way he also pretended not to hear the argument with his father in the kitchen a few minutes later about whose *turn* it was to take him, nor the breaking of the dinner plate against the sink.

Two days later, she walked in with him very straight and stiff, her hand gripping the back of his neck. He was so happy to be there. Right away he made himself invisible so no one could see how that made him feel, her hand so tight as though he couldn't quite be trusted to walk in by himself.

The way it was planned was for the children to sit on the floor up front, closest to the storyteller. There were three rows of folding chairs toward the rear of the room where the big people were to sit. The children were all elbows and knees scrambling for places, most of them about his age or younger. A face or two he recognized, but he knew she would be upset with him if he waved or called out hello. She ushered him quickly off to one side, so far outside it was almost the same as not really being with the group at all.

He sat frozen, could feel as though his hair were on fire, her eyes burning the back of his neck.

His secret wish was for someone to notice him and say, "Hey, little boy, come over and sit with me, please." But he really didn't expect that to happen, so he made believe it happened. He sat cross-legged the same as the others and wriggled as close as he dared. He knew how hard it would be to sit without moving for the whole story, but his magic colors suddenly danced to life, promising to help. He did wonder why the other children didn't have to sit so still, but they were at least together and perhaps that was why.

The storyteller was such fun. She became the friendly dinosaur, and he forgot right away how alone he felt, how in that whole crowd of children there was no one sitting with him. The friendly dinosaur seemed to be smiling directly at him. *Yes!* he was so sure of it. His magic colors were suddenly thousands of balloons, brighter than the sun, taller than the sky. He was so excited, and then there was this happy place in the story and he hopped up and down, up and down with all his might to give one of his colors away, *yes! yes! yes!... when quickly her hand so tight* was there. He was grounded again so roughly it hurt.

"Sit there! What … did … I … tell … you? *Don't* jump up and down like that!" Both hands now, fingers pinch-digging into each arm. "Don't you DARE embarrass me in front of all these people!" Lifting him, grounding him; up, down harder. "You *know* how excited you get sometimes! *Do … you … understand?*"

He didn't want to cry, but her hands had hurt him, her voice a whispered stinging. It hurt him because … well, because her fingers were cutting as nails and it hurt him in another way, too — maybe there even more. He obeyed, did what she wanted, sat very quiet like an unsmiling stone, and hoped the friendly dinosaur hadn't seen, jumping up and down now only inside his heart beyond the hurting place. He hid there often, his secret garden, where no one else could see or ever know. But this time, even his flower fort was no longer safe, and he felt very sad, very alone.

As he cowered there, his magic colors floated gently closer, touching his cheek. Such was their soft music, he heard something, noticed someone not there before. Way … way … way to the other side, as far from the center of everyone as he was on his side, there was a little girl sitting by herself, too. She had a knitted cap on her head, a pulled-down-tight stocking cap. He wondered about that because it was spring, and *why* would she have that hat on?

The way she was sitting, he could just tell she felt separated, outside, the same way he did. She had this pretty dress on and he wished he was over there with her. He wished with all his magic colors because maybe then she could be his friend. Maybe he could be *her* friend, which would be even better.

He thought about that, and the friendly dinosaur seemed to smile, nodding yes. The story caught his attention once more, his colors spinning, *her hands on him again* almost before he started to hop. His colors slapped away, he shut off his ears, retreating as before to that make-believe place inside where he could hide and no longer hear how much he upset everyone. He had meant to be quiet. It was just he wanted so much to ask the friendly dinosaur about the little girl, to give her one of his pretty colors.

When he thought it was safe to come out of hiding, by that time he had missed the ending and the story was over. The storyteller was motioning for everyone to crowd closer to play a very special dinosaur game. He wasn't sure if she meant him, too, because he wasn't supposed to move, but when he looked across once more for the little girl, he noticed that she had crowded closer with the rest so maybe it would be all right for him as well.

She was still wearing her knitted cap, darker red it was, with what seemed like tiny snowflakes or maybe white blossoms. He just had this feeling about her cap. There must be some reason, maybe like his magic colors ... when suddenly his guarding color sounded the danger alarm. Behind her back, where she could neither see nor protect herself, there was a movement: this other boy pretending to crowd forward with everyone else, but instead shifting ever so slightly sideward,

ever so slightly closer, closer to where she sat. The magic colors rushed to her defense; he could imagine it before it happened, what this shifting shadow intended.

The dinosaur game had started, the children completely caught up in it. From deep within his secret garden, almost as though in slow motion because he knew he couldn't possibly get there in time to prevent it, the little boy was up and running, circling behind the children still crowding forward, before the eyes of the big people who sat there frozen, pretending not to notice.

A sudden lurch, flashing hand: *her cap was off.*

Her hands tried to cover, shield from sight her bald head, slumping then inside herself, hunched down, hunched down.

Even as he rushed to her, he could feel that hurting so inside: how much she wanted to disappear right then, her shame. The storyteller was wonderful because right away she started a story about how different people are pretty in different ways, and even though some of the children laughed and pointed at first, none of them did very long.

The little girl's mother hugged her.

The little boy heard none of it: not the commotion, not his mother's voice demanding he stop, *stop fighting this instant!* He charged that dragon, tackling him to earth, retrieving the stolen crown ... and for just that one wonderful moment, pushed away the cruel warrior to stand proudly now like a little prince before the gentle princess. He held out her cap with all his secret garden heart, almost as though he knew how important it was that she put it back on her own head herself.

"Here," he said, his words so soft and true and clear, not mixed up at all. Her mother moved slightly back so the little princess might receive his ever-so-very-special gift. "It's okay," he said. "Don't be afraid." Her eyes were as warm and kind as he could ever remember eyes being. As though brushing back strands of hair, with dignity and grace, she then cradled the cap to recover her head.

Every magic color he had ever made-believe opened his heart…when out of nowhere, time fast motion again, he felt himself snatched, yanked away. It was as though he had been slivered through the middle, no more than a warped, weathered board to be removed from sight, carted away for fighting, for causing such a scene.

He tried to cry out how it was, but his words failed him once more, so desperate was he to scream them — about the little princess, about what had been in his heart to make right, how he knew what that was like, to feel such shame, to be so alone. And so it was like the board he appeared, he stopped struggling; no sounds emerged. Inside, he reached for his magic colors, but there was only such a very cold wind blowing them all away. There seemed nothing left, the little prince, wounded, slowly dying ….

But sometimes magic really does still come true, each fallen sparrow's song heard. Just before the little boy was about to be carried out the exit door forever, suddenly, big as life, there she was, the little princess, not about to allow her prince to be disgraced like that.

"Stop," she commanded, and everything did, the tableau behind her frozen in place: her mother; behind her, the gathering of children, heads turned now; fronting them, the friendly dinosaur, who seemed to know exactly what was happening. The little princess, however, had spoken up for herself, moved away from them on her own, all four-feet-tall of her.

She blocked the exit door. "Put him down," she said, not a question, not a request, not a doubt, and so was the little prince put down. "Let him go," and thus was he freed, his magic colors returning.

She held out her hand, her eyes very quiet and warm again, revealing the tiny rubber dinosaur. "He's my friend," she said softly. "He goes with me to treatments and keeps me safe." Her smile was as soft as her voice. "But he gets sad sometimes. Do you know anybody who could play with him, maybe cheer him up a little?"

The little prince's heart beat 10,000 miles a second. "I could do that," he said, his words so clear. "I could do that," the tiny dinosaur fitting just right in the very center of his hand.

She turned again to face his mother. "We're going back with the others," she said. "You can sit anywhere you like," and although he could not have explained exactly why, the sight of his mother slumped in the very last chair of the row, head down, tugged at his heart. "I'll be back," he said, "don't cry," and he left one of his magic colors with her because it came to him right then maybe why she was so nervous: the late-at-night hitting sounds, his mother's wounded weeping ….

"Come," she said, and they turned now to where the other children still waited: the little boy who had trouble sometimes sitting quietly and the little girl with the dark red stocking cap. The storyteller welcomed them back with a wonderful story about two dinosaurs she said she had never told before, how each was very lonely but had given a special gift to the other and because they had given away what meant the most, no longer were alone, were now new friends.

The little boy jumped up and tossed all his magic colors high … high … high in the air where they sparkled in the make-believe sun, twinkling with music and heart and life, such rainbows as he had never imagined before.

He turned to show her.

It was very warm in the room and the little girl took off her pretty cap with the tiny snowdrops, the better to see. 🙙

SUBSTANCE ABUSE PREVENTION AND INTERVENTION

Communicating with heart

Margaret Jones

WITH FUNDING FROM Maine's Office of Substance Abuse beginning in 1995, Day One, an adolescent substance abuse agency, has developed an innovative model that uses storytelling as a way to help both youth and adults increase insight into personal behavior and to communicate with one another. Meaningful communication among peers and adults, problem-solving skills, and a connection to the community as a whole creates resilience, which is a major protective factor against substance abuse. Professionals work with high-risk in-school youth in substance abuse support groups and alternative classes, and with out-of-school youth, including recovering adolescents in a long-term treatment program, teenage mothers, and foster children.

Working sessions consist of anywhere from 6 to 20 meetings, lasting about one to two hours in length, with the storytelling component woven throughout. Day One's storytelling model uses both personal and fictional stories with particular themes to awaken memories that act as catalysts for listeners to share stories of their own. Through carefully crafted activities, participants share stories leading to a deeper understanding of themselves and others. Additionally, through stories, the facilitator teaches participants skills to better solve problems, as well as to create a healthier connection to peers and to the world around them.

Day One has also created a training component for professionals who work with teens and high-risk populations. Professionals learn how to use stories as an aid in their therapy practice or in the classroom. The training prepares them to write and tell personal stories, helps them memorize fictional stories, and equips them with activities to use in small or large groups. It also teaches them to be better storytellers! In addition, a support network has developed among professionals committed to helping others adapt to the world through the use of story.

Through a series of evaluations to measure behavior change among these clients, we have received a consistent response: participants feel more connected to others as a result of stories, and clients have increased understanding of self and increased problem-solving skills. This increase in skills affirms that stories assist in the prevention of substance abuse and other destructive behaviors.

Many happy returns

Each week for a year, the program routine was the same. At 4 p.m. I would pack my bowl, a bag of rock salt, some small white candles, and a story and drive five miles to an apartment complex housing teen parents and their children. With kids screaming on their laps and half-eaten pizza left on the table, they'd eagerly meet me at the door. One called the rest of the apartment complex to let them know "the storytelling lady" had arrived and the hour-long session was about to begin.

Four or five of them came regularly, dropping their children off with the babysitter in the living room and gathering around a table in the counselor's office. I would pour the rock salt in the bowl and place it in the middle of the table, then hand each teen mom a candle. The room quieted as each participant solemnly prepared for storytelling.

I began with, "So, let's have a check-in. On a scale of one to five, one being the pits and five being great, how are you today?" The first participant reached for a match, lit her candle, and placed it in the rock salt. "Well, I'm about a two today. My boyfriend left last night and he hasn't come home yet." The next participant followed suit. A candle was lit, placed in the bowl, and a number given. When all had spoken, including the counselor and myself, we began our stories.

Each week, we chose a theme: loneliness, relationships, parenting, love. Once established, someone would begin the story. "Once upon a time …" For about three minutes she would weave a plot in whatever fashion she wanted. Oftentimes it began with a little girl who lived a hard life in some way. When times got too tough, she embarked on a journey to find her freedom or fulfill her dreams. When three minutes were up, a second participant would pick up the story. The plot always had several obstacles, reached a natural climax, and almost always had a spectacular ending.

My responsibility at that point was to process the story so the "storytellers" could reflect on what meaning was found in their tale. Their tales of tragedy and triumph were the stuff of legends. Each week they would set out on an adventure and face the battles of life. With each other's support, they received guidance. I asked questions such as "What characteristics did the little girl have to possess in order to leave such a hard life?" A conversation would then ensue around charac-

teristics such as courage, strength, and hope for a better life to come. My next question would be "So which characteristics do you see in yourself?" This created a perfect opportunity for them to see how they, too, had some of these traits. Often I ended our session with a boast. Each teen mom picked a characteristic that she identified with and made a statement using the phrase "I am." Statements like "I am as strong as a tree" or "I am hopeful that I can take care of myself" were passed around the circle. There would be a distinct change in the tone of the room by the end of each session. A few more bites of pizza and a swift good-bye brought me back to my life until the next week, when I did the whole thing over again.

What was it about this storytelling project that was so successful? Upon reflection, it was the consistency of the project — the reliability of my return week after week — that made this project work. Many storytellers say that when they tell stories to small children, the children often want to hear the same story over and over again. In the world of teenagers who have no regularity in their lives, a repeat appearance from the same person each week is a monumental step towards trust. They came to my storytelling sessions because they knew what to expect. There were no surprises, only a candle waiting for them and an hour where they could bond with people their own age. They could look forward to being imaginative and creating a world where the little guy (or girl) triumphed over obstacles. In a supportive, non-judgmental atmosphere, they knew that they would almost always feel better by the end of the session.

This feeling of well-being in a safe environment could only contribute to better parenting skills. The counselor told me that she observed the teen mothers telling stories to their children between storytelling sessions. I knew that by role-modeling consistent patterns and activities that activated the imagination, in some small way I helped them become better parents.

By year's end, these teens could tell stories like ancient bards. By learning to trust that I would appear each week and metaphorically tuck them into bed, they allowed themselves to enter into the powerful and magical world of storytelling. I can only imagine that they are doing it still, perhaps around their own kitchen table or beside their child's bed, with a candle cradled in their hands.

The White Wolf

Margaret Jones*

Winter. It was just past midnight when the two wolf pups were born. Quietly, they lay sleeping alongside their mother, who licked them clean, tucked them near her belly, and settled in until the sun rose early the next morning.

Father Wolf awoke them when he burst into the cave. He had been out hunting when his babies were born. "Where are they?" he exclaimed. "I want to see my new family."

"We're over here," said Mother Wolf. "We have two beautiful pups."

They both peered down at their newborns and smiled. The pups lay where they had slept the night before, but turned their heads when they heard their parents' voices. One wolf pup was the same color as her mother, a muted gray with flecks of black around her nose. But the other wolf pup was very different. She was as white as freshly fallen snow. She lay slightly apart from the rest and reflected the light as the sun shone through the cave opening.

"Oh my!" said Mother Wolf. "Our second pup is so unusual. I wonder what she will be when she grows up."

Father Wolf agreed, and even though he loved his two pups equally, he was quite proud of his white wolf pup.

Time passed and the pups contented themselves with playing games inside the cave where it was warm and safe. Every afternoon Mother Wolf gathered them together. She insisted they take howling lessons, as it was very important for a wolf to howl out in the wild. When they all got together, they howled in unison. But each time they howled, White Wolf's voice rose above all the rest, for her song was vibrant and strong.

"What are you doing?" cried Sister Wolf. "Are you trying to make me look ridiculous! I can't sing that loudly so you should just keep your voice down. Why can't you just be like the rest of us."

White Wolf was terribly embarrassed. She didn't mean to be different. She just had a song in her heart and she wanted so much to let it out.

She wanted to share it with anyone who would listen. But she loved her sister and heeded her scoldings. So as the family continued to howl together, White Wolf kept her voice down and tried hard to fit in with the others.

Warm weather finally arrived and the wolves were ready to come out of the cave. Sister Wolf came out into the sunlight and marveled at the world around her. She could see into the deep forest and see the animals who lived there. She knew that her home would welcome her.

As White Wolf started to follow her sister, a terrible feeling overcame her. She could not shake the feeling that she would be laughed at. What if she should howl too loudly and her neighbors shun her for making such a racket. She took one look out the opening, yelped in fear, and turned back into the comfortable darkness of the cave. No amount of coaching could lure White Wolf into the sunlight. She stayed in the cave day after day until the night sky enveloped the forest. It was only then that she would allow herself to come out. As day slipped into night, White Wolf would pass her family as they entered and she exited the cave. They would settle themselves in and watch her as she entered the darkness. Mother Wolf shook her head as she could not understand her daughter anymore. Sister Wolf and White Wolf rarely spoke to each other, and Father Wolf watched from a distance. He grew worried for her but did not know what to say. So he said nothing.

While her family slept, White Wolf slipped out into the dark forest. White Wolf loved the darkness. She could howl as loudly as she wanted because most creatures were sleeping and never bothered to scold her. The ones who were awake were too busy looking for food, so they never bothered her either.

One night White Wolf was foraging for her evening meal. She wandered down a path that took her deeper and deeper into the forest. Eventually it led her into an open field. White Wolf stopped. A cool breeze blew on the top of her head and a whisper blew gently into her ear. "Look up, White Wolf. We wish to speak to you." White Wolf looked up and saw a marvelous sight. She saw stars sprinkled across the sky like diamonds. They shone ever so softly and illuminated her white fur. These stars became her friends and her audience when White Wolf howled her song. They sparkled in appreciation and encouraged her to continue no matter how embarrassed she became. So every night, White Wolf walked into the darkness to dance and play with her new friends.

One night as White Wolf passed her family on her way out of the cave, her sister stopped her. This was a rare occurrence and White Wolf was taken aback. Sister Wolf looked into White Wolf's eyes and said, "White Wolf, I have not been fair to you. I have been jealous of your beautiful white fur and your strong vibrant voice. I have scolded you and advised you to be like us, but now I know I was wrong. You didn't ask to be different. You just are who you are and I have blamed you for that. I say this to you now because I will be leaving the cave soon to join a new clan with my new husband. I realize that I have missed you and want very much to be close to you again. Will you come and visit me when I settle in with my new family?"

White Wolf was stunned. She always thought that her sister disliked her and never thought there was any hope of being close. She was deeply touched and replied, "Of course I will visit you, Sister Wolf. I, too, have missed you."

It was a bright sunny day when Sister Wolf's new family came for her. The Wolf family had planned a large celebration and had asked the animal kingdom to attend. As they gathered around the cave's opening, White Wolf paced inside. She very much wanted to participate in the festivities, but she was afraid. She would step towards the light but could only get as close as the opening.

Sister Wolf realized that White Wolf was absent from the celebration and broke away from her new clan just long enough to speak to her sister. She stood before the entrance to the cave and said, "White Wolf, it's my time to leave our family, but I don't want to go without seeing you one last time. I know you are afraid, but if I can leave the forest I have called home, you can come out of the cave. Please come out, sister."

White Wolf took a deep breath and did something she thought she could never do. She stepped out of the cave. The warm sun illuminated her white fur, but this time she did not feel afraid. She looked around and saw the entire animal kingdom before her. There were creatures there that she had never seen before! They were all shapes and sizes, colors and dimensions. She was awed by the sight.

A deer stepped forward and bowed before White Wolf. "Welcome to our humble forest in daylight. We have heard wonderful things about you from your family and some of us have heard your howl when we were unable to sleep at night. It's a beautiful voice, White Wolf. Would you howl for us now as we send your sister on her way?"

White Wolf was honored. She looked up into the sky where her star friends twinkled their invisible support and opened her mouth. She let out a howl full of joy that could be heard well into the next several days and several nights. &

DISCUSSION GUIDE AND ACTIVITIES FOR "THE WHITE WOLF"

Many of us grow up in an environment where there are conditions that prevent us from realizing who we really are. This story was created to address some of the reasons why we don't become who we are meant to become, and to provide avenues for thinking of ways to surmount barriers placed along the path. Adolescents as well as adults respond favorably to the images and message in "The White Wolf." I often pause for a moment after I tell the story to let teens digest the images and collect themselves before responding to the questions and activities.

- **Questions to ask after telling "The White Wolf":** If you could be anywhere, anything, or anyone in this story, where, what, or who would you be? What are you feeling as a result of hearing this story? What do you think this story is about?

- **Positive and negative messages activity:** Ask the participants to write words or draw pictures of negative messages that they have heard from the people in their lives — messages that stopped them from growing emotionally or prevented them from being who they really wanted to be. Next, ask them to add to the drawing or words listed on their paper selected words, names of people in their lives (past or present), and colors that represent the positive messages that helped them become who they really are. After all participants have completed their drawings, ask them to share whatever is comfortable for them to talk about. Focus on how much better it feels to hear the positive and how positive messages help us come out of ourselves and grow.

- **Questions in an envelope activity:** Prepare a list of questions or topics that relate to the story. Write each question on a separate sheet of paper. Fold them up and put them in an envelope. There should be at least one question for each participant to pull out of the envelope. Design the questions to prompt personal sharing among the participants. These could include:
  - Tell us a story about an animal to which you have a connection — either one that you know personally or an animal that you feel connected to in the wild.

- Tell us about a time when you felt positive about yourself.
- Tell us about a negative message you received that is not true.
- Tell us a story about someone who has positively influenced you.
- Tell us about something you are good at.
- The stars supported White Wolf in the story. Do you feel supported by anything other than people?
- White Wolf loved the darkness. What do you love and why?
- Have you ever done something you thought you could never do? If so, tell us about it. If not, what would you like to do but think you can't?

Embracing the Shadow: Dancing with Dashkayah

TERRY TAFOYA*

Long ago, when the sun still shone without embarrassment, and mountains were the size of salmon eggs, The People feared Dashkayah. Dashkayah was bigger than Bigfoot and covered with long, dark, greasy hair, and she smelled bad because she didn't bathe very often.

Dashkayah was very ugly and looked as if she had fallen down an Ugly Tree and hit every branch with her face. Her eyes were round and yellow like an owl's, and the way you would always be able to recognize her was the way she held her lips. She would carry them round as a circle, pursed round as her yellow eyes. Old people would tell children, "You better listen to your elders, or Dashkayah will come into your bedroom at night and suck your brain out of your ear!" But the real reason she had her mouth that way was — Dashkayah would whistle.

Dashkayah would only come out at night, looking for young boys and young girls. If she found you, she'd hold out her hand and it would be filled with food — maybe dry fish, or deer jerky, or berries. If you reached to take her food, she would pull out her other hand from behind her back, and it would be full of sticky sap from the trees. If you took the food, she'd slap you across your eyes with the sticky sap so your eyes would be glued shut and you couldn't see to run away. Then she'd grab you up and throw you inside her basket. And her basket was so large, it could hold ten children. And that was her favorite meal — ten children — because she was a cannibal and ate human flesh.

And now — you're ready to hear the story. Sometimes it takes as long for people to get ready to hear a story as it does for the telling itself. Sometimes therapists try to rush into working with clients before the clients are prepared for a certain direction, as if they want to harvest corn before it's even planted.

It was early in the morning, and a young boy woke up. Now the first thing the old people teach you to do when you wake up is to go take a bath. And so the boy went down to the river to bathe, and it was so early the sun was just starting to come up. It felt warm and comfortable on his face, and he sang a song to thank the sun. When he was finished, he went out fishing to get food for his family. But he realized he had gone out so far, he wouldn't be able to get home before the sun set, so he decided to camp out where he was.

It was late at night and the moon was full. White People tell us there's a man in the moon, but our old people in the Pacific Northwest tell us it's really a frog. Just so, the frog in the moon was looking down at the sleeping boy when clouds came up and covered the moon. In the darkness, the boy awoke — he could hear heavy footsteps, coming closer and closer. Then he heard that strange whistling sound.

In working across cultures, you discover that even through we all may have the same physical experience of reality, our cultures teach us to interpret that reality differently. In a number of European cultures, people are taught there is a "man" in the moon. In a number of Asian cultures it's a "rabbit" in the moon. In some cultures it's a "woman," and for Native Americans of the Pacific Northwest it's a "frog."

When you work with clients, you will find that sometimes a crisis helps people "wake up" in terms of dealing with the challenges they face in life, whether or not those challenges come whistling ....

The clouds blew away from the moon and he could see Dashkayah standing there in the darkness. She called out, "Don't be afraid. Those stories they tell about me are just to scare children. I'm really a very nice person. In fact, I have some plump, juicy berries for you," and she held out her big hairy hand that was heaped high with the berries.

Isn't it interesting how addiction often starts this way too? A denial of danger and then something tempting is offered ....

As the boy reached to take the berries, he noticed that instead of fingernails, she had long sharp claws, like an owl. She took her other hand, which had the sticky sap in it, out from behind her back and slapped him across his eyes, so he couldn't see to run away. She grabbed the boy and threw him inside the basket she carried on her back.

She ran through the woods, whistling, until she came to a clearing where she had built a great fire. She dumped the boy out of the basket into a circle of other children that she had stolen. She was going to barbecue them in the way we barbecue salmon outdoors.

She was so pleased that she was going to have a fine meal of the children, she started singing and dancing around the fire. The boy was worried because he knew he was going to be eaten, and he wished the whole day could start over again. He remembered how the day had started, and how good the sun felt on the side of his face.

The warmth of the sun reminded the boy of the warmth of the fire, and so he leaned even closer into the fire.

If you were about to be burned up in a fire, would you lean even closer into it? As a therapist, I find what you fear the most gives you the most insight if you have the courage to look deeply into it — whether it's about addiction, sexuality, or grief. It's those aspects of ourselves that our cultures teach us to separate from and see as our shadow selves.

As he leaned into the fire, the heat of it began to melt the sticky sap on his eyes, just as candle wax melts when it gets near the flame. Pretty soon he could see out of one eye, and he watched Dashkayah dancing around the fire. This gave him an idea, and he whispered this idea to the girl sitting next to him, who whispered it to the boy sitting next to her, until it went around the circle of children.

As the boy watched, Dashkayah finished her dancing. She was now so tired she could hardly stand up, and that's when the boy shouted, "Now!" And the children pushed her into the fire, where she started to burn. But she didn't burn the way ordinary things burn. She burned like sparklers — like fireworks on the Fourth of July. And as the children watched these sparks fly into the air, they turned into mosquitoes. And that's why mosquitoes bite. Because they still live off the blood of young children, even today. ❧

In this traditional Native American story from my relatives — the Georgie Miller family of the Skokomish Reservation in Washington State — the monster woman wears the Twana name of Dashkayah. In my mother's language of Sahaptin, at the Warm Springs Reservation in Oregon, she is called another name. If you travel to northern California, or to Alaska, The People will know her story, but use their own language to name her.

One of the things I find fascinating about this story is that it teaches if the boy had kept his insight to himself, he would still have perished. But he shares his insight with his circle of support, and it allows him to mobilize his community to bring about meaningful transformation and change.

The Dashkayah story differs from the familiar European fairytale "Hansel and Gretel" —

about an old witch who likes to eat children, but who is eventually pushed into her own oven where she's burned up — in a fundamental way that reveals the differences between the two cultures. In European thought, there is always a witch to burn. There is always a dragon to slay. Evil can be identified, and then there is an obligation to destroy it.

But Dashkayah isn't destroyed. She is transformed, which seems to be an essential element in Native American tradition, where striving for harmony is stressed. Just so, many clients come with a very "binary" way of thinking: clean/sober; happy/depressed; male/female; on/off, where one is 100 percent successful or 100 percent a failure. Native American tradition understands that harmony is really a function of difference.

Another common Native theme is The Dance, where, by the definition of dance, one doesn't remain static, but one moves according to The Dance, so one position is not continually held. In working with addiction issues, for example, for some people the challenges don't disappear because of therapy, but, as in the case of Dashkayah, those challenges may become something manageable, something that one can survive. For that reason, this is a legend that I also use with suicidal clients. If one is contemplating suicide, it's as if one's life is like Dashkayah — something huge and monstrous that's eating you alive.

Interestingly, in the Pacific Northwest, where The People are still actively involved in Spiritquests or Visionquests, to receive the vision of the Dashkayah is considered a great blessing.

She is a cannibal who devours children, but she also is associated with great wealth and power. I had an old friend — Joseph Campbell — who died a few years ago. He talked about traveling to India and China where he found "temple guardian figures" that in many ways resembled the totem pole depictions of Dashkayah. His take on the temple guardian figures, which were very frightening, was that they existed to keep out the uninitiated. If one is not ready to face the truth that dwells within the temple, one should stay out.

In the Pacific Northwest, where masks are often used in ceremonies, there is a special type called a Transformation Mask. When a hidden string is pulled, the mask will split open and reveal a hidden face within. There is a Dashkayah Transformation Mask, and when you pull the string, the monster face opens and reveals a human face. Just so, when we meet people different than we are, we first see them through a mask of otherness. When we get to know them better, that mask of otherness splits open and reveals the essential humanity that unites us all.

This paradoxical combination of what frightens and what heals that so defines Dashkayah is crucial in understanding her, since healing can take place only when we fully embrace all of ourselves, even the parts that society has taught us to fear. In the Indo-European roots of the English language itself, the word "heal" is linguistically related to the word "whole," which itself is related the word "holy." In the structure of the language itself, healing is the process of being restored to wholeness, and is, by definition, a sacred act.

Using stories in addiction treatment

MARY DESSEIN

AS HUMANS, WE are attracted to telling our life story. Stories contain a component of our experience, our hopes, or maybe an emotional truth. Telling one's story to a group of fellow alcoholics and/or addicts is a fundamental part of the 12-Step program during recovery from addiction: we share our experience, strength, and hope in order to remain clean and sober as well as to support others. Using story in the more structured setting of a treatment facility dovetails with what the client may already be experiencing outside treatment in such meetings or other abstinence-based support efforts.

As an addiction counselor, I have found storytelling goes naturally with a balanced approach to dealing with a person's addiction. Balanced refers to the many facets of a person's life, since being abstinent from the drug is not enough by itself. Lifestyle changes, beliefs, and one's self-concept are all affected by addiction and must change if a person is to remain abstinent. Abstinence is the pivot in a complete and satisfying life, not just a life that would be great if only the person could use again.

Often, introducing story as a therapeutic tool is initially a challenge. Many adult clients associate stories with "kid's stuff." Most of the clients I work with have come to treatment as the result of someone else's plan, perhaps a probation officer, a judge, or a social worker who determined the client was having trouble with alcohol or other drugs. I use various exercises to get clients acquainted and relaxed about the idea of using stories as tools to help towards their participating in treatment and, ultimately, their ongoing recovery process.

Opening doors with personal story

Having a longer group time, say two hours, gives us time to set up and do two or three exercises. One exercise I use incorporates personal stories. I ask group members to tell the funniest or wildest or maybe the most embarrassing thing they ever did when they were "loaded." This always brings out a wealth of experience: talking with a fish, seeing gunmen under the neighbor's hydrangea bushes, forgetting where they left their car, driving over someone's mailbox several times, not knowing where they left their clothes, coming home with underwear on backwards and no socks, repeated driving around the block thinking the cop would not notice and go away, and even asking the arresting officer to hold their drink while they find their license!

Another personal story exercise is asking clients how they came to have the name they use. Names can be an important part of the using life. Street names also need to be left behind, not used now in the "clean life." Asking about their many names (do they like their given name? Were they named after a family member? Do they go by their middle name?) can be a non-threatening, easy way to start the client telling a story. What is the story their family tells about their name (it was my great-grandfather's; it was the name of a town my mother drove through just before I was born; my mom loved Mickey Rooney; etc.)? Then perhaps we hear about what the person's nickname is and why. The clients' comfort levels go up as they are talking about something they know and are interested in. They are relieved that they are not being asked to "spill their guts" and make self-disclosures that are too personal for a new group.

The search for authenticity

I have used many different kinds of stories, both traditional and contemporary, in my groups depending on time and group dynamics. One favorite is "The Black Prince." Storyteller Laura Simms has recorded this ancient Egyptian story. In summary, a poor young man falls in love with the princess and believes she would never love him as he is. He trades his one worldly possession, a flute that he plays beautifully, to a magician who changes the young man's soul into what the young man believes the princess will love. In the end, he finds the princess loved the simple, flute-playing man and not the charismatic and powerful leader into which he has been transformed. And there is no going back.

There are many uses for this story in addiction counseling, for each client must continually search for authenticity. People so often believe that, as themselves, they are unlovable and inferior. They seek to change this feeling of inadequacy by using drugs. Not that drugs actually change the person, but individuals may feel changed or believe that some aspect of their character is enhanced. There is a feeling of power and invincibility that comes with the use of certain drugs, notably crank (methamphetamine) and cocaine. The feelings of confidence that can accompany using, as well as feeling very sexual, are desirable states for many people. And then the decrease of inhibitions that accompanies drug use in turn makes behaving sexually very easy. All of these, ironically, may move individuals further away from their authentic selves. Just as the young man traded away his most important possession, his flute, to be what he thought he should be, drug users trade away important parts of themselves in order to feel differently or to become more like the person they think they want to be.

One of the poignant parts of this story is how the young man had no idea how profoundly he affected the princess. His hope was that she loved him, but he had no idea how much she loved him, his true self, which he had valued so little.

Clients commented:

- So sad. There's no going back.

- Once I burned my bridges, I couldn't get back what I had lost.

- Why didn't he stay and try to convince her? Why did he leave?

- Once a cucumber is a pickle, you can't go back to being a cucumber.

- He lost everything in one fell swoop. My using never looked like a problem to me. Until I lost everything, too.

- He willingly traded his soul. God, I did that and didn't even know it, all to get my drug.

- I can't undo what I've done, to myself or my family.

- We always want to be something we're not. With alcohol, I thought I could be someone else.

Learning to trust

Another story I like to tell in my recovery groups is "The Man Who Had Black and White Cows." Laurens Van Der Post collected this African Bushmen story in Africa, along with many others. Briefly, a man is pleased with his fine herd of cattle until his cows stop giving milk. He discovers that beautiful women from the sky — Star People — are taking the milk. The man captures one of the women, falls in love with her beauty, and asks her to marry him. The Star Woman agrees to marry him on the condition that he never look inside her basket. The man promises and keeps his promise until some months later, when his curiosity leads him to peek. He sees nothing. His wife returns home that evening, and the man confesses. She tells him that if only he had waited, a wonderful future awaited them, using the gifts in the basket, but she had to teach him how to see the gifts. Since he has broken his promise to her, the Star Woman leaves, returning to her home in the sky.

I am often startled by the different ways people understand the same story. I was barely finished speaking one time and a man chimed in, "And I bet she got the house, too!" I was so surprised. I never would have thought of that, since she left with only that with which she came. Yet the man's comment showed clearly where his emotions and experience were.

We talk about why she left. What else might she have done? What does this have to do with addiction? Can trust be rebuilt? When is it time to leave a relationship? How does one deal with boundary violations?

Clients responded:

- Trust takes time to rebuild. I destroyed the trust my family had in me. After 15 months of me being clean, they still check my breath and look at my arms when they think I don't notice.

- She had to leave. If he broke his promise once, he will again.

- She should never have left. It wasn't a big deal. What about commitment?

- She should have forgiven him. Everyone deserves another chance. Forgiving ourselves is a huge part of recovery.

- My addict boyfriend made me all kinds of promises. Never kept one, except that I wouldn't care that he didn't.

- Once trust is broken, you may want to forgive and forget, but you can't.

- Is this the message we want to give, that magic people will come from the sky to make you happy?

- He made one mistake and suffers the rest of his life? That's not fair.

I tell the group that there are no right theories or wrong ones about this story and press further. What did the basket symbolize? Who was the woman? Who was the man? What other "characters" were important in the story? Was the ending inevitable? Are the results of addiction inevitable?

An interesting discussion came up once about the idea of "magic people" being necessary to make us happy. Many stories are not meant to be taken literally. That the woman was one of the Star People could denote simply that she was a very special person who came into the man's life. People like that can wander into our lives. Magic can mean "not easily explained." There is no magic to recovery, by which some combination of action, sponsor, and meetings will allow someone to achieve and maintain abstinence. For most everyone it takes hard work, commitment, pain, humility, willingness, forgiveness, shame, and finally acceptance and surrender.

Our problems teach us

Another story I like to use is the Asian Indian tale "The Cracked Pot." A water-bearer carries two large pots up the hill from the river to his master's house each day. One has a crack and leaks half its water out on the way. Finally, after years of arriving half-empty and feeling guilty, the cracked pot apologizes to the water-bearer. The man smiles and tells the pot to take note of all the lovely flowers growing on the side of the path over which the cracked pot was carried. They grew so lovely because of the water the cracked pot had leaked. There are no flowers on the perfect pot's side.

This story works well in the recovery world and the community of 12-Step programs because it provides a counterbalance to the strong focus on an individual's deficits. This focus is appropriate, as it is aimed at awareness and then positive change. However, sometimes people get stuck on their deficits, seeing only their own flaws. "The Cracked Pot" reminds people that even their deficits have a function. As a therapist, I believe the problems in our lives and our character defects are also some of our best teachers. Groups almost always indicate an awareness of the message when they hear what the water-bearer says to the pot. That awareness, however, is often very shallow. Really believing it is difficult for many people.

Of course, the play on words — cracked pot is close to the expression "crackpot" — is fun for clients. They have commented:

- If that was whiskey and me carrying it, the entire pot would've been empty.
- We are our harshest critic.
- I never measure up to someone else.

- Sometimes we do good we don't even know about.
- My bad traits are easier to see.

I have a group exercise that I use with "The Cracked Pot." Each group member draws a line down the middle of a sheet of paper. On one side, they write "How I see myself." On the other, they write "How others see me." I usually get a lot of resistance as clients claim they don't know how others see them. But after some examples and a little thought, most begin to see some positive aspects about themselves as well as some contradictions. Also, they acknowledge that others tend to see them in a more favorable light than they see themselves. Just like the cracked pot.

Sharing the load

There is a Chinese folktale in Margaret Read MacDonald's *Peace Tales* titled "Holding Up the Sky," which I call "The Hummingbird" when I tell it. A hummingbird is lying on her back, feet in the air. She tells elephant that she heard the sky was going to fall and she is ready. Elephant laughs and asks what could such a tiny creature do to hold up the sky. Hummingbird says she doesn't plan on doing it herself, but she is ready to do her part.

This story is aligned with a crucial tenet of abstinence-based support groups: "I can't do it alone." There are also many facets of a balanced recovery program here, including willingness, humility, unity, hope, and perhaps even surrender. These are excellent elements for clients to explore in story and then, in turn, to find in their lives.

Story is a natural tool for use in addiction treatment. There are endless issues to be explored. There are endless stories. Story is a safe way to examine some very difficult areas, ones that can be frightening or shameful to have to admit too soon in the recovery process. One of the wonders is that in the group setting, people explore issues together and very often find what they have in common, not just their differences from one another. This then allows candor, personal scrutiny, increased awareness, perhaps some empathy, and, just maybe, some trust. Each person has to find his or her own answers. Story opens the door.

 The Coat

BRUCE TAYLOR*

I met Bruce Taylor, the author of this story, as a co-worker when we were both working at Harborview Medical Center Inpatient Psychiatric Services in Seattle, Washington. Bruce told me that while he was working in mental health services for the past several years, he had also written and published a book of short stories (*The Final Trick of Funnyman and Other Stories*). When I read his book, "The Coat" leapt out at me. It was immediately apparent to me that this tale was perfect to use with populations in recovery from chemical dependency because of the non-threatening way it addressed the issues of family dysfunction, family "scripts," and the ability of families to "enable a user." After Bruce gave me permission to tell his story, I wondered about how to abbreviate the story and still do it justice. While the story is a bit longer than most that I tell in a therapeutic setting, I decided that one could only be faithful to the true essence of this story by telling it in its entirety. It has proven to be a story that stays with the listener over time, and it is fascinating to hear the diverse interpretations of the story and how each listener finds meaning for his/her own unique situation.

— *Kevin Cotter*

Now, you see, it's like this. Little Nicholas Jackson was born into his father's heavy black coat. And soon those were the first memories of Nicholas, struggling and wearing that ill-fitting dark coat and trying like hell to love it even though he hated it.

But his father, Nicholas Senior, saw that not only was his coat good enough for him and his name, but if it was good enough for him, then everything he had would automatically be good for his son, and of course the son, young Nicholas — how could he know otherwise? So, of course, Nicholas wore his father's heavy black coat — it was all he knew for it was all his father ever knew, for it was all his father knew. And that's all there was to it.

And so, here was Nicholas, hereafter called Nicholas Junior, wearing his father's dark coat.

And it really was a ridiculous coat. What strange first memories young Nicholas had: a strange mixture of a world of sunlight and bees and blue sky and yellow sun and the coat — that immense, huge, suffocating, black, heavy coat.

Honest to God, how absurd. The only place where he could feel the wind was on his face. No other place, save his hands and his feet when he tried to go barefoot (except he kept stepping on the coat). Nicholas Senior saw Nicholas Junior at times uncomfortable but simply said, "My father had to wear it. I had to wear it. I don't know what your problem is, but I'm sure you'll get used to it, just like I did."

By which Nicholas Junior knew that his father meant there wasn't anything he was going to do about it because if there was, he would realize he might have to do something about his own coat that he had to wear and, for whatever reason, he wasn't about to do that.

Oh, how absurd, but at the time, Little Nicholas didn't know what to do about it at all. He didn't have the faintest idea that he could do anything, and whoever realizes that until they are many years along and then decide that the coat really isn't their style and then make a decision to take it off and drop or shred it, and leave it neatly at the parent's feet or sometimes necessarily throw it in their faces. Ah, would it not be wonderful to decide one's wardrobe so early in life? But not so for Nicholas Junior. Not so for him at all.

Now, you might wonder where was Nicholas' mother in all of this? Did she not realize that Nicholas was wearing too heavy a coat for the occasion? Any occasion, actually. Did not she wonder when Nicholas was just a baby what that dark aura was about him? Didn't she wonder when he, in the baby carriage, kept getting lost in the heavy black coat that something was wrong? Didn't she ever say, "Nicholas, my baby and darling Nicholas, that coat will make you ill. That coat is much too heavy for your constitution." Now, how was it that the mother did not see? How could she be unaware that when Nicholas went swimming, he stayed and struggled beneath the surface of the water for really too long periods of time? (After all, such a heavy coat simply became waterlogged so that swimming was no fun, and was certainly just a struggle.) And where other children glided like pale fish through the sun-sparkled water, Nicholas just floundered and gasped like a fish out of water. Or how was it that on those lovely hot days, Nicholas, with face beaded and shining in sweat, almost suffocating in that black coat — how was it that she did not see Nicholas' discomfort?

That is indeed a good question. Perhaps she didn't really want him, and by him being miserable, that way she could justifiably love him. Doesn't misery always bring out the caring in people? But maybe that wasn't it at all. But she did not see. For whatever reason, she did not see and Nicholas, wearing that black, heavy coat, got his mother's love. Time moved on and you know how that goes.

Even though Nicholas knew the coat was somehow the very worst thing he could wear, well, not knowing any better, perhaps he wore it anyway. He grew into it. Sort of. Now just because you grow into something doesn't mean it fits any better. No, no, oh, not at all. It just means you distort your body enough to fit the form — what else can you do? But what can you do when you're a day old? Two months old? A year or so old? What choices have you about certain clothes that you have to wear for the rest of your life and no matter how ill-fitting, the only advice you can possibly get is that "You'll learn to love it as you grow into it for there are no other alternatives in this family for you." So what are you to do at age two? Shove off the coat and risk rejection? And even Nicholas Junior, minutes after birth, knew the folly, the impossibility, the ludicrousness of that. The black and heavy coat stayed in place, ah, sad, sad, anchored by survival need and quest for love, the coat stayed in place.

It stayed in place in spite of the admonishments of his best pals; Kenny, for one, who wore clothes of bright colors and whose parents always respected his tastes and asked him what he wanted to wear, so Kenny was quite the individual with a trust in his tastes and his own sensibilities. He always looked at Nicholas and said, "Gee, don't you ever get tired of wearing that coat? Look how black it is and how frayed the sleeves. The buttons are coming off and it's way too large. Don't you have other coats you can wear? Or other clothes? I can see this in winter when it's dark and gloomy and then everyone can't help but wear coats like this — but all the time?"

To which Nicholas replied, hurt and defensive, "But what's wrong with it?"

Kenny asked, "Is that really your coat?"

"It's the only coat that I know."

"But is it your coat?"

"Yes."

"And you choose to wear it?"

Desperately, Nicholas said, "Yes."

Kenny looked puzzled, unsure what to say for he saw the desperation, didn't know how to talk about it or much less what it meant, and finally said, "Oh." But he really meant, "I don't know what's going on with you, but that black coat that you always wear is a mean-looking coat and I have a hunch you're wearing it for the wrong reason and it's not even your coat. What do your clothes really look like beneath that old coat? What are you really wearing? Polyester? Cotton? Wool? Plaid? Blues? Greens? Red? My friend, what are your clothes and true colors beneath that black coat?"

Ah, poor Nicholas, what was he to say? For everyone's worst fears are such that if they have been taught that they must wear a dark coat, it must be because that which is beneath the coat is so worthless or so secondhand or so colorless that if they showed their wardrobe to the world, their clothes would be found to be utterly rejectionable; therefore, your worst fears about that which is beneath the coat are thereby confirmed. So of course the coat remained in place. Nicholas wore it at school dances, and while everyone was showing off their glorious but (of course) adolescent wardrobes, Nicholas just assumed that once the coat was in place, it would always be in place and that was the only wardrobe he had, there were no other clothes to wear.

But oh, how hard it was to dance in an ill-fitting black coat that enshrouded Nicholas like a great black sack of space. And oh, how that coat made it so hard to dance; Nicholas might try to turn, but the momentum of the coat simply made him ungainly. He'd try a new step, but the coat got in the way and he'd end up falling. He'd reach out to touch hands, but the coat sleeve flopped over his fingers and the only touch anyone ever got was a fistful of fabric and a handful of darkness. And when everyone else danced, their new wardrobes became more lively in color, more solid in hue, poor Nicholas; it was as though his coat became heavier, the fabric denser and darker and what, what, what was poor Nicholas ever to do? And to make it even worse, whenever he went home, his father always said, as he sat unconsciously distorted and destroyed by his own coat, "My, my, what a fine-looking coat that is. You should be grateful that I gave you that coat. Why, if it weren't for me, you'd not have that wonderful coat at all. Wear it well and make me proud of you."

His mother, still, for whatever reason, unable to see that black coat even now, did notice his discomfort and always gave him much loving concern.

Who can refuse? Ah, that parental love is the strongest there is, and who can refuse. To such overwhelming love and concern, of course he said yes and yes. And every time he said yes, it was as though the coat became darker and fit closer, or he was like tender meat crammed into a shell. He made the coat fit as best he could, but oh, the pain, the sense of pain was always there. Nicholas could only guess that was the way it was — but his friend Kenny appeared very happy. And Melissa, she always wore bright colors and had gay and happy parties. And his other friend Jackie, my how he loved reds and yellows, and on the dreariest of days he wore the brightest of colors as if defying the clouds, the very dark side of the moon, the unending dark and deep well of space, to try, just to try to snuff out that blaze of bright fire known as Jackie.

At what point does one make a decision to remove one's coat? At what age? At what time? How is that decision made? Perhaps it was when Nicholas was 16. Perhaps it was because of Meredith that things began to change. Meredith MacKenzie was as sweet a young lady as you could find anywhere, what with long hair and delicious smile. She liked Nicholas and Nicholas could not figure out why.

All this came about because she was in his art class with him and tremendously enjoyed the sketches he made, although to him they seemed of small consequence, even though everyone else liked them, too. It was the only thing he could do without the coat getting too much in his way, but the long sleeves did make it hard to draw, and frequently the vast folds of the coat made it difficult for him to sit and be comfortable, or to draw without smudging the lines or colors. But in spite of the coat, that at least was one place where Nicholas could accept a little color into his life, though how colorful it really was, was as yet rather beyond him.

But one day, while sitting in the lunch room, sitting in his vast coat and trying to be as comfortable as possible in that dark and thick hand-me-down, Meredith came over and said, "Hi, I really liked the sketch you did."

And Nicholas, almost choking on his cold corned beef sandwich, said, "Uh, oh, gee, uh, thanks — it wasn't really anything all that good —"

Meredith smiled. "Everyone liked it."

Nicholas smiled a grim little smile and it was as though somehow the coat felt closer and bigger than ever before.

"Uh, well, gee," he said, "um, thank you —"

"May I sit with you? Can I join you for lunch?" Her look was gentle and patient.

"Oh, uh, yeah, sure," said Nicholas.

And she sat.

And he did not have the faintest idea what to do and he seemed to lose himself in that coat even more.

"Don't you ever get tired of wearing that coat?"

"Huh?"

"That coat. That heavy black and dark coat. Why do you wear such an awful coat?"

Nicholas looked at her with a mixture of shame and guilt as if there was something terribly wrong with the coat, and not only was the coat wrong, but what was beneath it was also wrong. And he did not know what to say so he sat there, but with very dry mouth, eating a corned beef sandwich and feeling very unhappy indeed. But she was patient. And she kept smiling. She dug in her brown bag and brought out a tuna fish sandwich, a big red apple, and a small bag of potato chips. She ripped open the top and offered them to Nicholas.

"Care for some?"

Guiltily, Nicholas accepted.

"It's okay," she said.

"Thank you," he said.

"You know," she said, munching a chip, "my father used to wear a coat just like yours."

Nicholas stopped eating and stared at Meredith.

She crunched another potato chip. "It took a lot of work for us to help him take it off. He just couldn't believe that the natural clothes he wore beneath the coat were actually okay." *Crunch*, another potato chip, and she offered him some more. From the depths of his coat, he looked at her, comprehending but no, not comprehending at all.

"Of course," she said, "the hardest thing for him to realize was not only that he was wearing a coat in the first place, but that he could take it off." She sighed. "He just did not understand. But after you've known someone who wears such a coat, you see it on others."

Nicholas shrank even further into his coat. "I know you probably don't understand," she said. "My father didn't either, not for a long, long time. But finally he let us become close to him because he finally saw that he was okay…" And before she knew it, she had her hands up to her face and began to cry.

Just then, without even thinking, Nicholas, in spite of the heavy and dark coat that he wore, he right then reached through all that fabric and touched Meredith right on the arm, and as he moved, his coat pulled away from him, oh, just a little way for him to look down to see a shirt he was wearing beneath suddenly become a blaze of reds and yellows and greens and blues. And Meredith, suddenly looking at Nicholas, looking through her own tears, said simply, "Thank you, Nicholas," and then softly, "Thank you very much."

Nicholas, still blinded by the colors of what he really wore beneath that dark coat, began to grasp the nature of the decision that he had to make. 🐌

⚊ Snake's Jive ⚊

AN AMERICAN FOLKTALE RETOLD BY ALLISON M. COX*

Versions of this tale motif — of someone warming a frozen snake, only to have it bite them — are found worldwide. A Native American variant of the story is currently used in drug and alcohol counseling with Native American children in the U.S. Since I grew up in the city of Chicago, I wondered what it would be like for a street kid to find a rattlesnake waiting for him in the alley. I designed this retelling of the old tale to lend itself to rap, hip-hop, or even the old scat or beat poetry that I remember from when I was young. After the story, I usually ask my audiences "Who or what are the snakes in your life?"

I tell this story to third graders (and older) in Tacoma, Washington, as part of my work in substance abuse prevention for the health department. When I ask inner-city elementary school students who or what are the snakes in their lives, many respond with "gangs, guns, and drugs", in that order. These kids have seen shootings as they climb on the school bus and run on the playground. Most are still too young to belong to the gangs, and many are angry at the toll it has taken on their lives.

I usually add the question "What are some of the things that your parents and teachers tell you to stay away from?" and the children eagerly list all the possible dangers while we brainstorm ideas about ways to deal with each danger. Teenagers answer, "Friends." The first two times I heard that response, it sent a chill up my spine. I heard that learning who you can trust is a big issue, and I share with these youth that even as I get older, I am often still trying to figure this one out. So we discuss developing internal reference systems, our own set of criteria of learning when to allow someone into your circle, and how to pay attention to the internal whistles, flashes, and feelings that go off when it is not safe. Adult audiences have often told me that the snake is an ex-lover or ex-spouse.

Given enough time, these conversations often turn to the fact that the snake is merely holding the mirror and we are ultimately responsible for our choices. It is interesting to me that it is always the youngest who are the first to point out "The snake didn't make him pick it up — he did it to himself."

A boy went out walking,
it didn't matter where.
Just get out o' the house
was his only care.

Dad had come home drunk
and was sleepin' it off.
Mom was mad. She cried,
"I won't put up with this stuff."

Sis just got home,
she was out all night.
She and mom started yelling,
had a screamin' fight.

The boy was worried, scared,
didn't know what to do.
Seemed like the whole house
was gonna break in two.

So the boy went out walking,
with his head hung down.
When, what did he spy,
stretched out on the ground...
but a rattlesnake, stiff from cold,
looking dead.
So he crouched down,
near the viper's head.

Now, what happened next
really blew his mind,
'cause that snake started talking
like humankind.

102

"Oh pleassssse, pick me up"
was his pitiful cry.
"Pleassse hold me and warm me,
or I'll sssssurely die."

Well, the boy was young,
but he was nobody's fool.
He listened in the streets.
He learned at the school.

"If I pick you up,
you'll bite me!" he said.
"I sssee," said the snake,
"ssomeone'ss filling your head
with misssinformation
about usss reptilesss.
Let me sset you sstraight,"
said the snake with a smile.
"All that ssstuff about bitin'
and poisssin'sss a lie.
Sso pleasse hold me and warm me
or I'm cssertain to die."

But the boy wasn't buying
this snake's hissin' jive.
"If I warm you, you'll live,
but I won't survive."
"Oh no," said the snake.
"Sssnake'sss honor I ssswear!
Pleassssse hold me, don't leave me,
or don't you care?"

Well the boy didn't want
the old rattler to die.
Still, it's hard to tell
what's true, what's a lie.
His parents, his teachers,
the man at the zoo
all said, "Gettin' near rattlers
is bad for you!"

The snake could tell
the boy didn't believe him
so he said, "Just to show ya
that I'm not decssseivin'
I'll tell you a sssecret
that sssnakes usually hide.
I've got powersss that'll make you
feel good inssside.

My magic can make you
feel great all day.
You'll be cool, any problemsss
will ssslip away.
Ssso pick me up, my man.
Hold me clossse, you'll sssee.
My high will make you
fly legally."

The boy thought about home
and all that had happened
and decided he'd go for
what this snake was rappin'.
"If pickin' you up will
chase away my blues
then warmin' a snake
is a job I choose."

He bent and picked the serpent
up from the dirt
and stuck him inside
his coat n' sweatshirt.
The snake grew warmer,
started movin' and then
the boy asked, "Well,
when does the fun begin?"

"I thought you'd never asssk!"
the snake hissed.
And round that boy's chest
it started to twist,

slithered down his sleeve
and wrapped around his hand
and sank his two fangs
into the palm of that young man.

"OW!" screamed the boy.
"You bit me! You lied!

You said I'd feel better.
Now I'm gonna die"
The snake dropped to the ground
and as it slithered away
said, "I'll alwaysss be a sssnake,
no matter what I sssay!" 🐌

LOOKING
FOR A HOME

Homelessness tales for holidays

David H. Albert

We are Quakers. As a religious matter, "Friends" (which is what we call ourselves) don't celebrate holidays. Or to be more accurate, Friends consider all days to be holidays because they have equal potential for revealing the Divine to us and within us.

In our household, we don't consider this to be a restriction, but an opportunity. As a cultural matter, we've chosen to celebrate all kinds of holidays: Hindu, Christian, Jewish, ethnic, birthdays of famous composers, artists, writers, and scientists. Some — such as the Feast of the Three Little Pigs — we just make up ourselves. Food is often an important element in our celebrations. Santa Lucia Day is celebrated Neapolitan style, with pizza and five different kinds of olives; Mozart's birthday with Viennese cream puffs; Diwali (the Indian Festival of Lights) with spicy lentil curry; π Day (March 14) … well, you get the idea. My two daughters provide music for each of these occasions. Visitors are welcome to join us.

Our family is fortunate to be able to celebrate — we have a home. Every first Monday of the month, when my daughters and I serve meals at the local soup kitchen, we inevitably meet families, along with the larger number of single adults, who are not so lucky. One learns from their stories that these families become homeless for a variety of reasons: women with children escaping abusive husbands or lovers; families, often leaving rural areas or small towns, who have fallen on economic hard times; young couples, barely adults themselves, who, now with children of their own, have been abandoned by their own families, friends, schools, and social institutions. Each family has its own unique story, but what they all share in common is that they are families in transition.

I wrote "Another Chanukah Story" during a transition of my own. After a lengthy illness, I moved a thousand miles away to a new city in the Pacific Northwest with my wife and two young children. Both my wife and I were unemployed and came seeking a new start. We were not homeless, nor in any real danger of being so, but in a time of transition.

In "Another Chanukah Story," I sought to find a way to commemorate the Jewish holiday in all its cultural manifestations — through food, music, lights in the darkness; to celebrate family togetherness and resourcefulness; to suggest that miracles can come about as a result of our own generosity, which is not reserved to the rich; and to remind ourselves that with transitions come new possibilities. We light the traditional Chanukah candles with blessings each day for eight days, eat the traditional foods, and retell our story daily with ever-growing embellishment. The kids began creating new stick puppets each year — simple paper cutouts mounted on dowels (we've usually used chopsticks) — and presented the story as narrated on a makeshift cardboard stage. We soon found ourselves on cable TV and have been invited to present the tale at community alternative and international holiday celebrations. At one telling in our home to a group of neighbors and friends, when we came to the part of the story where there is a knock on the door, there was indeed a knock: it was the UPS driver bearing holiday gifts!

So here it is:

Another Chanukah Story

David H. Albert*

Once upon a time and space — for a time without a space is like a nose without a face — at the far northern edge of the town, which was at the far northern end of the county, which was at the far northern end of the country, at the far northern edge of the continent, which was at the far northern end of the northernmost world, there lived a very poor family consisting of a mother, a father, eight children (four boys and four girls), and an old cow.

In the cold northern winters they didn't have much to eat, or enough fuel for the fire to keep warm, and they couldn't afford electricity. Still, they were happy enough and kept themselves happy by singing together every evening.

One cold and windy day in deep, darkest December, the youngest daughter met an old, shriveled woman at the northern end of the town square. The old woman was wearing a tattered brown cloak that covered her whole body and which she drew up over her head. The old woman complained that she had no place to stay and nothing to eat. "Come home with me," said the girl. "We don't have much, but I'm sure we'll share what we have."

And so they went home together. The family welcomed the old woman, even though there wasn't much in the pantry to eat. (In fact, they were so poor they didn't even have a pantry.) They had a bunch of potatoes that had lots of black spots in them, so they cut out the black spots and made potato pancakes. They had a bag of wormy apples, so they cut out the worms and made applesauce. The old cow gave nothing but sour milk, so with their potato pancakes and applesauce they had sour cream.

It gets dark early in deep December in these northern climes, and the house had no electricity, so the father went to the candle box, but he found only one small candle left. The father lit the last candle, and the family gathered around the table to sing songs for the old woman, and also for themselves. The music was beautiful and somehow the light of the candle seemed brighter as the family sang. Soon, one by one, first the children and then the mother and father drifted off to sleep in the old family bed, where they huddled together with the old cow to keep warm. The old woman slept in the old armchair by the table.

The next day when they got up, they were all surprised to see that the candle was still lit. In the evening, they gathered together again to eat their dinner of potato pancakes and applesauce and sour cream, and to sing songs around the table. And as the singing seemed to get more and more beautiful, the old woman seemed less shriveled. People began to gather outside to hear the singing, their noses pressed against the one small window.

And so it went. Every evening the family ate their poor dinner of potato pancakes and applesauce and sour cream, and sang around the table, their faces and the one small candle still shining brightly. And the crowds around the window grew larger and larger.

On the eighth day there was a knock on the door. It was Mayor Mayer (the mayor of the town) who, having heard the singing and liked it so much, offered the family a job singing at city hall. At that, the old woman stood up and took off her tattered cloak. Underneath she was wearing a robe made of gold. She reached into her pocket and took out a small crown of rich red rubies and placed it on the little girl's head, and out of her cloak she brought a bale of fresh green grass for the old cow.

"I was hungry and tired and you took me in," she said, "and it gave you such joy to do it. I have a castle where any tired travelers, rich or poor, can stop and have a meal and spend the night. And since you have been able to make the poorest fare seem like a feast, I want you to come to my castle and take charge of the food and the singing and the hospitality. And bring the cow!"

And they did. And to this day we celebrate the family that made a feast out of the poorest fare of potato pancakes and applesauce, and the cow who could only give sour milk, and the one small candle that stayed lit for eight days by the light of their singing. 🐾

⚒ Joseph's Annunciation ⚒

DAVID H. ALBERT*

By far the most famous homeless people in Western culture are Mary and Joseph. (In Islamic cultures, the most famous are the Old Testament's Hagar and Ishmael, from whom Islamic peoples trace their descent.) Much of the focus in the Christian tradition during the Christmas season has been upon Mary, who gave birth to Jesus in the manger, having left her home in Nazareth for reasons that are wholly unclear in the two New Testament accounts.

But what about Joseph? Here is the tale of a young man, almost too young, choosing to stay with his loved one after, he is sure, she has become pregnant by another. He has no idea what the future holds in store for them both, only that they must leave their homes and everything they hold dear. He will have to look for work among strangers, without friends or family to support him or Mary or the child. Most of all, he has to come to terms, again almost too young, with being a father, the transition from childhood to adult responsibilities. He can't know what tomorrow may bring. All he has working in his favor is his commitment, born of his love.

It is unfortunate the New Testament is virtually silent about Joseph, for his could be the most contemporary of stories, a tale of a young man on the edge, who feels constrained by family, oppressed by the legal system, witness to the violence of the society around him, and seeking, if unwittingly, a way to give meaning and purpose to his life. And the revelation would come, not yet, but soon enough.

The impetus for writing "Joseph's Annunciation" came from witnessing, around Christmas time, the trials and tribulations of a young friend of mine. As a teenager, he had fathered a child. Though estranged from the child's mother, who now lived some great distance away, he maintained a strong interest in his son's life. The mother had fallen into a series of abusive relationships and was prone to substance abuse. My friend, now well settled, was seeking

with great difficulty to try to provide some stability in the child's life. He had now grown, if belatedly, into fatherhood.

I have told this story to adult audiences and used it to spark dialogue among adolescents. Unlike most tales told orally, this story is an interior dialogue, the kind, if I can remember that far back, a teenage boy might indeed have had with himself.

In the case of a virgin who is pledged to a man — if a man comes upon her in town and lies with her, you shall take the two of them out to the gate and stone them to death; the girl because she did not cry out for help in the town, and the man because he violated his neighbor's wife. Thus you will sweep away evil from your midst.

— Deuteronomy 22:23-24

Then Joseph her betrothed, being a just man, and not willing to make her a public example, was minded to take her away in secret.

— Matthew 1:19

*He loved her, deeply he loved her, but he didn't believe it. Not a word of it.
And he was quite certain she didn't either.*

She was already beginning to show a little. This tale about visitations by angels and impregnation by God was strictly her way of covering. The God part was the parlance of the day, just a manner of speaking. No one knew why children were visited upon us, or why, sometimes, they weren't. It wasn't for lack of trying. Children were God's blessing. In this case, would it be His curse? No one believed in angels.

But what else could she say? He knew the child wasn't his, although if that had been the case, at least there wouldn't be any shame in it. He wondered if it was her uncle, who beat her beyond reason and without mercy. Or maybe she had a lover? He doubted that. The story about the angel was told so poorly, with so little art or subtlety, with such lack of conviction. She wasn't telling the truth, her eyes red with weeping told him as much, but most definitely it was not love she was hiding. And the way she spoke, with such fear in her voice and trembling in her limbs. Her whole body pled, do not reject me, and do not ask.

He wouldn't ask. It would be better if he didn't know. They were already betrothed, but the wedding had been planned for next spring. He would be justified in breaking the engagement. If his father found out, the marriage would surely be called off, and her uncle would throw her into the streets to escape his family's shame, or even his own. His father could demand her younger sister, who was as yet merely a child, even if but two years younger, in her stead.

This would be the best that could occur. His brothers could require her death. The law required it, as she was pledged to him and didn't cry out. The penalty was the same as for adultery. They would not likely await the law's verdict. Her uncle would eagerly render her up. In his mind's ear, he could hear the stones cast by his brothers as they cracked against the side of her skull, and he could see her frail body left limp and bloody beside the gates, to be carried off at night by strangers to an unmarked grave.

And what if she gave up this tale of heavenly visitation and surrendered the name of her attacker? It had all the makings of a blood feud. He would be asked, no, required to lead it. People had long given up any hope of obtaining justice from their own courts, which had surrendered even the appearance of impartiality. Faced with Solomon's challenge of determining an infant's mother, they would have sold the baby to the highest bidder. And sometimes parents who could not afford to redeem their first-born male children, pledged by law to the Temple, did just that. The Roman courts? Even if one could manage to understand them, very few people ever returned from Roman jurisprudence still in pos-

session of their lives, let alone with their worldly goods intact.

No, blood feud it would be. Throats cut, the acid of fear and rage admixed eating at their bellies. That's how it had always been, and perhaps always would be. His brothers and father would settle for no less. And if he wasn't killed in the process, the Romans had a cross waiting. For him.

But he loved her. He still loved her. His whole being ached with love. Strangely, he loved her even more now. He loved her more for the strange story she told, and the strain she manifested in the telling.

He saw clearly they would have to leave. In the middle of the night, like thieves, steal away. Forever. There would be no wedding and no goodbyes. They would leave no trace behind. He would take his carpenter's tools. She would change her name. To Mary. He would lie about his lineage so as not to be found out. Something safe. Common. Something that would never be questioned. That was easy. All his countrymen who had left Judea, be they merchants, criminals, or thieves, especially thieves, claimed they were descended of David, or so he had been told. Abroad there were probably more descendants of David than of Abraham. How many generations would that be? His mind ached. He would have to figure that out later.

He loved her, but what of this child? Leaving now would put the child out of Herod's reach, as if that mattered. Kings were always threatening the death of children as a way of extracting tribute and taxes. He himself had been born under a similar proclamation, as had many of his brothers. The decrees were read, and fathers would ransom their children through the tax collector. When the proclamations were cancelled, fathers were expected to offer tribute in thanksgiving and gratitude. This was an old story. The greater danger for the child would be to be born in the alley outside the city walls beside the fields of the dead, where she would raise the child, to be raised among the dead and among strangers, without a future and without a past, not even one which could be invented.

He loved her, but could he accept this child? He wasn't sure. He didn't even know what it would be like to be a father. Certainly he had not planned on it so soon. The flight would be rough on them, and he had little money. The child would likely be born on the road, perhaps at an inn, maybe under a tree, or, he had a vision, in a manger? He liked that. In his experience, animals, more so than humans, were accepting of each other, at least of their own kind, the black sheep with the white, the pure brown cow with the brindled. He could imagine the animal smells, and she lying there, her brow bathed in sweat, the baby suckling at her distended breasts, and he standing there, useless and curiously, and utterly, alone.

He loved her, but what child would this be? Unto them the child would be born, but not of his flesh and blood. Of that he was certain, though what to make of this fact had him confused. He as of yet had no experience of sex and would not touch her while she was with child. Would he ever? For him, forever for him, this would be a virgin birth. Would there ever be other than this child born of sorrow?

He loved her, but the child, would he grow to hate the child? Child of a vile, hateful act, could this be a child loved? Would he revenge himself upon the child, even as he could not bring himself to do, or have done, upon her? Would the child be a stranger to him, reject him, scorn him, grow to despise him, father to grief, an outcast father in a foreign land?

He began to sweat. This could not be the way. This way was the madness of the world, that which would make him lose his home, his family, his world, all that he held dear, all, but her. He thirsted. The way, the only way, was forgiveness. His head began to swim. Forgiveness. Unmerited. Undeserved. Unasked for. A new law, a new beginning. His body shook. Uncontrollably. A rule of forgiveness that would cause princes to bend, would govern kings and vagabonds, soldiers and slaves, architects and carpenters, equally, and would brook no exceptions. If only he could convince them. A forgiveness that would shake the foundations of the world. Joseph's law, born of his love for her. This is what he would teach his child.

Love. He would love his child. Love his child as he loved her, unconditional love, with all his heart, with all his soul, and with all his might, love more than he loved himself. He would protect his child as he would protect her, keeping watch over them at night, like a shepherd in the field, keep them out of harm's way. He would love and teach his child, suffer for his child, continue to suffer, die for his child, if it was required, and he was called upon. He was ready, or would be, or so he thought.

At last. Thankfully. He was asleep. In the night. He dreamed. He dreamed he had been visited, and heard an angel's voice. He saw. He dreamed he saw. A great light. He loved her, and he saw a great light, and now he was sure. It would be a daughter. 🐚

An eye-opening resource on homelessness in contemporary America is *Street Lives: An Oral History of Homeless Americans* by Steve Vanderstaay. Vanderstaay traveled throughout the United States interviewing people who are homeless — recounting in their own words their condition, their history, their hopes, and their dreams.

Paul: A Christmas Story for People of All Faiths

RETOLD BY JOHN PORCINO*

Often, when I tell people I am a "storyteller," they say to me "I've got a story to tell you." That's how I first heard this story. I was moved by its simple power and was gifted the story to tell. The man who told me the story said it happened in his church in rural Pennsylvania. I've heard tell of several other variants since. Still, I believe this story happened somewhere and I know it is "true" in the deepest sense of the word.

Paul was an eight-year-old boy, labeled "mentally retarded." He could not run or jump like other children his age. When he talked, he struggled to be understood.

It was hard for him to grasp concepts that seemed so simple to other children. But you know, in some special ways Paul understood things that no one else could. And that night, that precious Christmas Eve, Paul gave a gift. A pure simple gift that, years later, lives on in many hearts.

It was decided early one fall day, at Paul's little church in rural Pennsylvania, that the children would reenact the story of Jesus' birth for the Christmas Eve service. The directors of the play wanted to include Paul somehow, but they knew it would not be easy. Finally, after some conversation, they decided that perhaps Paul could learn the simple role of the Inn Keeper. He would have to open the door when the characters of Joseph and Mary knocked, and say to them "No room at the inn," and close the door as they left. Well, it took as much work for Paul to learn just his one line as it did for the actors who played Joseph and Mary to learn all their lines. But, finally, at the dress rehearsal, Paul was perfect. When Joseph and Mary knocked on his door, he opened it, looked at them, and said, "No, no room for the likes of you here!" The room erupted with cheers. Hooray for Paul. He had done it. He could be part of the play.

At long last it was Christmas Eve. The church was beautifully decorated with candles, poinsettia, and wreaths. On stage, the sets were prepared. The actors and actresses excitedly bustled about in the dressing rooms, preparing for the play. Families, except for their young stars, nestled together in the pews. Finally, it was time for the play to begin. Everything was going beautifully. Joseph and Mary approached Paul's door and knocked. Paul was nearly perfect. He opened the door at just the right time. He looked at Joseph and Mary and said, "No, no room for the likes of you here!" There was only one thing Paul forgot. He forgot to close the door. He stood there watching as Joseph and Mary walked away looking so tired and sad. Suddenly, it was no longer a play to him. Then, with the whole congregation watching his eyes unmistakably fill with tears, he called out to Joseph and Mary, "Come back, come back — you can stay in my bed."

The Wolf's Eyelashes

A Japanese folktale retold by Susan Charters*

This traditional Japanese folktale is in many ways a modern fable. The homeless person, who may have become homeless through no fault of her own, is perceived as lacking in worthiness by virtue of her homelessness and may become convinced of her own worthlessness as well. The best that she can hope for is invisibility to hide her shame. But the tale is also a warning to us that, living as we do in the comfort of our daily existences and our overstuffed homes, we may be viewed through "the wolf's eyelashes," and we may not like how we are seen. In short, this story is a reminder that the homeless have eyes too.

— *David H. Albert*

In old Japan there was a prosperous merchant who was also fortunate in his wife and daughter. He loved them both, but his fortune turned one day and his good wife died.

He and his daughter lived for a time in great sadness, then began, slowly, to put their life back together. The daughter took on the tasks of the household and did them willingly and lovingly for the sake of her father. She was kind to her father's servants and workmen, who worked all the harder in order to repay her kindness.

Eventually, the merchant married again. His second wife resented the girl, Akiko, and found fault with her constantly. She was always pointing out flaws in the housekeeping to her husband, and railing at Akiko for her bad behavior. Through it all, Akiko kept her generous disposition.

The new wife especially disliked Akiko's willingness to feed any beggar who came to the door or to offer comfort to any poor traveler. "She will ruin your business," the wife told the merchant. "Who will come and buy from you with all these beggars hanging around the door? And why does she give away so freely all that you have earned?"

When Akiko was brought before her father to answer these complaints, she said nothing in her own defense. She was a traditional Japanese girl and only hung her head so that her tears would not show. But by the next morning she would be singing again at her work, and her father began to believe that she was deceitful, as his wife said.

Finally, the wife found a way to get rid of Akiko. "Look!" she cried at the New Year's celebration. "Akiko has used old rice to prepare the New Year's meal! Now the god of happiness will desert this house for a whole year unless you get rid of her. Send her away!"

And so, the father ordered her to leave the house.

Akiko went from door to door, asking for work in the other houses of the town. But everyone was busy with the festival and turned her away. "There is nothing for you here," they said. After she had gone, they said to each other, "Why would a girl from such a family be out on the streets?"

Finally, cold and hungry, Akiko went to an inn and knocked on the door. "Please," she said to the innkeeper, "will you give me some rice and a little fish in return for my padded jacket?"

"How do I know if it's worth anything unless I sell it first?" said the innkeeper. "Give it to me."

She gave him her fine coat and he slammed the door in her face. She stood in the snow, with her arms wrapped around herself in her thin kimono. At first she was not cold. She imagined finding work in a great house where she could care for beautiful things. Perhaps she would be able to arrange flowers in a delicate vase and prepare dainty things to eat. But the cold wind began to eat away at her, and her imagination failed. She waited and waited on the cold step, and finally knocked again.

"What are you still doing here? Get away!" yelled the innkeeper. "Such a young girl to be on the streets! A slut! I don't want you hanging around here. But it's the festival, so here, take this." And he threw out an old crust of bread and a piece of rough sacking. As he closed the door, he laughed, and the sound of rude laughter from his guests inside echoed his.

Hurt and ashamed, Akiko fled away from the town. She ran deeper and deeper into the forest, thinking, "Maybe some hungry animal will devour me and end my shameful life. I will be of use, at least, to the animal."

When she finally fell, exhausted, into the snow, there was a wolf nearby. He was watching her through half-closed eyes.

He came up to her. She rose to her knees and begged him, "Please, Mr. Wolf. Please, eat me and end my shameful life."

"Ah, no," said the wolf, considering her, "for you are a real human being, and I don't eat real human beings."

Akiko sat back and said, "I don't understand."

"When I look at you," said the wolf, circling all around her, "I can see that you are truly human."

"I ask your forgiveness," said Akiko, "but still I do not understand."

"Your problem is that you don't look at people carefully enough," the wolf said. "Here, I will give you two of my eyelashes. Look through them before you trust anyone, and you will see." He carefully handed her two of his eyelashes.

Akiko took them and thanked the wolf. Then she struggled on, as best she could, to the next village. When she got there, she saw a nicely dressed woman who seemed kind. She would have spoken to her, but she remembered the wolf's eyelashes and held them up. She saw the head of a chicken poking out of the woman's kimono, pecking and pecking angrily as she went by. So Akiko did not speak to her.

She went on to the market, which was full of people. But when Akiko held up the eyelashes, she saw a rich man moving through the market who was really a pig, pushing and shoving; a woman who was a donkey standing in front of a stall; a narrow-eyed cat selling its wares. She saw all manner of animals — cows, geese, a snake — but no humans. Finally, she thought the eyelashes must have lost their power because one man that she looked at was a man whether she held up the eyelashes or not. She looked at him long and hard.

Then she realized that she was looking at a real human being. She followed him, at a distance, out of the market, through the village, and down the road to his poor dwelling by the edge of the forest. He was a charcoal burner. After he had gone inside, she went slowly up to the door and knocked.

When he opened the door, she told him her story of the second wife and how her father had ordered her out of the house, how she had nowhere to go, and how the wolf had helped her. But long before she had finished, he brought her inside to the fire to warm herself and gave her a bowl of rice with a little fish.

When Akiko was feeling better, she went out to wash in the spring that bubbled up near the charcoal burner's house. Amazed, she discovered that it contained a fine rice wine instead of water.

She took the wine to the charcoal burner, who was surprised at her interest in it.

"This is ordinary water. I use it every day. Why does it please you so?" he asked.

"This is a fine rice wine," said Akiko. "It would delight travelers on the road."

He did not believe her at first, but she eventually convinced him. In time, Akiko helped him to build his small dwelling into an inn for travelers. In time, they fell in love and married.

The inn became famous, both for the wonderful wine and for the generosity of the hostess. Many people came and the business prospered. But Akiko always had a bowl of rice, with a little fish, for any beggar or wandering monk who came to the door, or for any poor traveler who could not pay.

One day, when she gave some rice and fish to a poor and tired old man, he burst into tears. "I once had a generous daughter such as you," he wept, "but I drove her from my door. I have suffered a hard life ever since, which is just, because of my hard heart."

Akiko recognized her father. She brought him in and cared for him. She told him about the wolf's eyelashes and how they had saved her, and he lived with her and her husband for the rest of his days.

And to the travelers at the inn, and when there were grandchildren for him to care for, the old man told the story, again and again, of what could be seen through the eyelashes of the wolf.

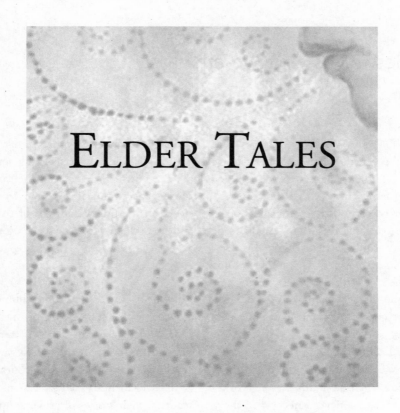

ELDER TALES

Our stories tell us who we are

Steve Otto

Our Stories Tell Us Who We Are. This was the theme of the Seattle National Storytelling Conference, and it holds a place in my heart. I do not have a long family history of telling stories. My grandfather was in on the 1889 Oklahoma Land Run. He took his team and wagon into Indian territory and settled down by the Canadian River near Norman. My mother would never tell me the stories of her years growing up in a sod dugout on the plains of Oklahoma. Those were not good times, and "you don't tell about bad times," she'd say.

I never heard about the Depression and how my folks raised a baby daughter with dad out of a job, and the joy when he finally started working in the stockyards. I never knew what they had to go through. I never understood why I always had to work from the time I was nine years old and save every penny I earned. I never knew why it was just expected of me to go to college.

I didn't know these things until my mother died. I had all her papers unopened in boxes in my basement for three years after her death. One day I decided to clean them up and found that Mom had diaries. She had written down the things that had happened to her and her family. From those diaries, I found the powerful, loving woman, wife, and mother that she really was. If only I had heard her stories! I decided that this

should not happen to others. That was the start of my "obsession" with teaching seniors how to tell their own stories and at the same time take those generations of personal stories that are stored in the musty cobwebs of the inner mind and share them with new generations.

His wife had made him come. John just sat there. All during the first session of my "Telling Your Own Stories" class for senior citizens, he just sat there, arms crossed and barely acknowledging anything. The class was to encourage seniors to go into elementary school classrooms and tell students their stories of growing up in a time so different from today. I wanted to have the kids realize that this powerful generation had accomplished so much without a lot of the perks that are considered necessities today.

At break time, I went to the back of the room with a Coke and gave it to John. I sat down and began talking about my own upbringing and finally asked, "Hey, tell me a story about something that happened in your life."

"Don't have any stories!" was his reply. "I've lived here all my life and nothing exciting ever happened."

I finally asked, "Were you ever in the service?"

"Yeah, I was in the Navy."

"Boy, if you were in the Navy, I know you have some stories …."

That was when it happened. The eyes were the first clue; they suddenly brightened and you could almost see wheels turning. He looked at me with a funny expression and said, "You know, come to think of it … I was on a heavy cruiser the day Pearl Harbor was attacked."

Not an exciting thing had ever happened to him! He had never told the story because no one had ever asked. The story began to flow, along with a few tears. I quickly realized that the story was way too long to be told in a single sitting, so we took it and broke it down into three separate stories, with an ending for the first two that left the audience in suspense till the next installment. John was already assigned to a Grade 5 class to assist the teacher in photocopying and refilling books, so I suggested that he take his story to his class to tell. He took his medals and Purple Heart the next day.

At the next session of our storytelling class, John was the first one in the room (it was easy for him because he was about three feet off the ground).

"You wouldn't believe it … They listened to my story!"

"Of course they did. It was a wonderful story."

"No, you don't understand … They're really great kids. They REALLY LISTENED!"

And all of a sudden, this thing called a generation gap was bridged by communication, by story.

What effect a simple little thing like listening to each other can have! John opened up and became a leader in the program. His wife commented how wonderful it was to have him "excited, really excited, about doing something! He used to just sit in the chair and watch that damn TV!"

Old people don't get crabby. Crabby people get old. Have you ever looked at the senior adults who are stimulated by using their minds? Most of them are healthier than their peers. They are more positive in their relationships with others. They are not as depressed. Dr. Rex Ellis says. "I truly believe that the power of storytelling is the one best hope we have to improve the communities we live in and the people we love. I have seen people with different backgrounds talk to each other for the first time. I have seen fathers, mothers, sons, and daughters who seldom speak to each other start laughing, reminiscing, and reconnecting because of storytelling. I have seen bridges built with storytelling, as listeners and tellers unite in ways that are more potent than a town meeting and more healing than a therapy session. It is pretty hard to hate someone whose story you know."

Look at Willard Scott's "100 Year Olds," oriented and alert centenarians featured during Scott's weather forecast on a popular morning television show in the U.S., and you see individuals who live by the motto "Getting Older is Inevitable … Growing up is Optional!" Our minds control the physical side of our everyday environment, and just as we exercise to keep our muscles strong, we need to exercise our minds in a positive way to keep them alert. Teaching storytelling techniques is a positive step toward creating a healthy environment for our seniors.

When looking for the methodology to teach seniors how to tell their own stories, I went back to my youth and began to figure out ways to enable individuals to visualize the events of their own past. I wanted to have them feel the story so that they were telling the experience not from their head, but from their heart. The final key was a workshop with storyteller Donald Davis, who had me up in front of an audience, leading me back to my grandmother's kitchen. I was suddenly smelling the Sunday dinner, It was roast with potatoes and carrots. I could feel the heat from the old coal stove. I could feel the warmth of Grandmother and the gardenia smell of her toilet water as she held me close. I could even smell the outhouse out back. IT WORKED! I developed the "Remember When" list of questions that can take the mind back to a time that may have been forgotten. These questions are not about life-changing events, but the small, seemingly everyday happenings that helped us learn life's lessons.

REMEMBER WHEN?

This list can be revised and expanded to meet the cultural and age differences of the specific audiences. Making the list appropriate to the group will be pivotal to the success of your program

The best stories are those that happened to each of us! Remember when you used to walk three miles to school … Uphill both ways … With snowdrifts over your head … Barefoot …?

Well, sometimes our memories are better that way. Let's go back in our memories and pick up some of those stories of events that made us what we are today.

1. LIVING CONDITIONS
- Did you use outdoor privies?
- Did your house have central heating?
- On what kind of stove did your mother cook?
- Did you always have electricity? What happened when you got it?
- What other things do you remember about your home?

2. FOOD
- What was your favorite food? Why?
- What was your least favorite food? Why?

Did you have to eat it anyway?
- Do you remember any special meal? Birthday, holiday, special day?
- Where did you eat meals? Did all the family eat together?
- Did you keep your food in a refrigerator, icebox, cellar?

3. HEALTH CARE
- Were you sick a lot? What happened?
- Do you remember having your tonsils out?
- Did you have a favorite doctor? Did he make house calls?
- Did you or a sibling ever almost die? What happened?
- What drugs did you take?
- Did your parents make home remedies for you?
- Can you remember a time you got sick at a very inconvenient moment?

4. TRANSPORTATION
- Do you remember your first car? How much did it cost?
- How much was gas? How long did the tires last?

- Did you ever take a long trip?
- Did your car have a heater? Air conditioner?
- Do you remember learning to drive? The first time you took the car out by yourself?
- Did you ever have an accident that you didn't tell your folks about?
- If you didn't have a car, how did you get around?
- Did you ever go on a date without a car? What did you do?
- Can you remember a trip that you would NOT want to take again?

5. YOUR FAMILY

- What kind of people were your parents?
- How many children were in your family?
- Did you play jokes on each other?
- Did you have responsibilities at home?
- What were some of the happy times you had?
- What was the saddest time?
- Did you do things together?
- Did you fight with your siblings?
- Do you remember something you did that you never told your parents? Did they find out?
- Can you remember a time you got in trouble for something you had already been told not to do?

6. ENTERTAINMENT

- What did you do for entertainment?
- Did kids in your neighborhood play Kick the Can or Hide and Seek?
- Do you remember the days of radio? Did you have a crystal set? What programs do you remember?
- Did you play cards? Dominoes? What else?
- Was going to the movies a big event?
- Do you remember "Dish Night" at the movies?

- Did you ever get caught sneaking into a movie or event?

7. WHERE WERE YOU AND WHAT WERE YOU DOING?

- The day the stock market crashed?
- On December 7, 1941?
- On V-J day?
- When the Korean War began?
- The day Kennedy was shot?
- (The day Lincoln was shot?)
- The day the first man landed on the moon?

8. HOW DID YOU CELEBRATE?

- Your birthday? Did you have a cake?
- Christmas?
- What presents did you get? Did you ever have a Christmas or birthday where you didn't get anything (or thought you wouldn't)?
- Did you decorate the tree or did Santa bring it?
- Did you celebrate any other religious or seasonal holidays?

9. TOYS AND THINGS

- Do you remember your favorite toy?
- When did you get your first bicycle?
- Were your toys handmade?
- Do you remember losing something special?
- What was your favorite gift?

10. CLOTHES

- What did you wear? Buster Brown shoes?
- Could you wear jeans?
- When did you realize that clothes were "important"?
- Did you have a favorite outfit?
- How much did clothes cost?
- Did you stand in the shoe store and x-ray your feet?

11. COURTSHIP AND MARRIAGE

- When was your first date?
- Did anything funny happen?
- Do you remember your first kiss?
- Did you marry him/her?
- Can you remember the names of high-school dates? What happened to them?
- What did you do on dates?
- Where did you go?
- Do you remember the marriage proposal? Who proposed?
- What happened at your wedding?
- Where did you go on your honeymoon? Did anything funny or bad happen?
- What were the hardest times during your marriage?
- What things do (did) you like best about your spouse? least?
- Where did you live when you got married? What did you eat?

12. CAREERS

- What was your first job? How much did it pay? What did you do?
- What was your first full-time job? Would you do it again?
- Tell about your boss. What kind of person was he/she? Do you think that your boss was as good/bad now as you did then?
- Did you change jobs? Why?
- Did you have to work hard physically? Were you ever hurt on the job? What happened?

13. REMEMBER?

- Do you remember the time when you got locked out of somewhere you needed to be?
- Do you remember when your first impression of someone turned out to be completely wrong?
- Do you remember when you learned something from your children?
- Do you remember a time when you were lied to or tricked?
- Do you remember a time when you almost won, but not quite?

14. MILITARY TIME

- Did you enlist or were you drafted? Why? What service?
- Do you remember experiences of basic training or boot camp?
- Was this your first time away from home?
- Do you remember your First Seargent, DI, etc.?
- What was your barracks like?
- Were you shipped out to go overseas? Where did you go? How did you go?
- Were you in battle? Tell about the experience of being shot at. Were you afraid? Did you lose friends? How did you cope with the experience?
- Were you married at the time? What did your wife/husband do?
- If you were left at home, what did you do? Letters, jobs, children?
- In retrospect, was this good for you? What did you learn?

To Everything There is a Season

Wendy Welch[*]

Inge is the hostess at our Quaker meeting. In her 80s, slim, with soft white hair that used to be long but is now cut blunt in an easy-to-comb style, Inge has senile dementia.

Her husband cares for her at home as she continues to forget who she is and what she's doing there.

At the Quaker meeting my husband and I attend, there are usually ten or so people: a young couple expecting their first baby, a retiree, a widow, a professor, a farmer, Jack and I, and Douglas and Inge. It is — no sarcasm intended — a quiet group. Every two weeks (which is how often we meet) we sit in a circle and keep silence for an hour, contemplating the One who made us and our own lives in relationship to that One. Then Inge makes us tea and serves us cake. That's how it has been and ever should be, world without end, amen.

But Inge began to have her troubles a year ago and had to stop making the cakes. So she put store-bought cookies on a tray and made the tea. We ate the cookies and drank the tea and everything was fine. This winter, Inge's hands began to tremble, the strength began to evaporate from her body. The hot water burned her. Other women of the group stepped forward, and Inge sat back — until the tea was made. Then her trembling hands shot out and took the tray, and she stepped with dignity around the circle. Her arms haven't the strength to hold the tray while the recipient

puts in milk and sugar, then lifts the cup and saucer from its place. The tea sloshes precariously in the sturdy church cups; things slide about, the sugar spoon gets wet.

We pay no attention, as each member has learned to unobtrusively brace the tray from beneath with a knee while spooning in sugar and making polite conversation. The tea makers put on fewer cups than they used to, and we wait with more patience for Inge's slow steps to circle us all with her gracious hospitality. Because Inge was the one who made the cakes, swept the floor, and prepared the tea for 40 years. If all she has left to hold on to is the tea tray, we won't be the ones to take it away from her.

Her husband takes her to the doctor, a difficult journey with a confused woman who doesn't know she is confused. He endures the looks of sympathy, the looks of derision, the looks of curiosity. He gets tired, he says, but what else is there to do? The world no longer has a place for Inge, who gave it so many cups of tea, except with him. And so it goes. The world closes inexorably around the place Inge used to occupy in it. The professor makes the tea now, and the farmer brings the cake. But Inge holds on to the tea tray, and we hold on to Inge.

Stories live at Neighborhood House

Leticia Pizzino

SHARING STORIES AT Neighborhood House is an extraordinary experience. The average age of clients is 79, and 80 percent are affected by Alzheimer's-type diseases. June (all names have been changed) can't put together logical sentences, but she shows her delight much as a child would — with smiles and giggles. With a big grin, she squinches up her eyes, wrinkles her nose, and waves. Steve closes his eyes most of the time and is a man of very few words. Ellen wants to share the same story again and again. When I tell stories at Neighborhood House, I'm ready for anything to happen. Participation of most any kind is encouraged and acknowledged because this is a special audience.

My work with these elders began with a phone call in August 1998 from the administrator at a Neighborhood House Adult Day Program facility. We met and discussed the needs of the seniors as well as the goals of Neighborhood House. I began storytelling programs almost immediately, funded by a grant from the Utah Arts Council/Arts in Education. Working closely with the activities director, I learned about Neighborhood House clients, how to communicate with them, and what stories or related activities best suit this population. My one-hour interactive storytelling programs occur from once a week to once a month. This project was so successful that word spread and the administrator of the other Neighborhood House in the area invited me to come and work with an even larger group of clients. I began storytelling there in March 1999, with funding from a private grant earmarked for arts in the facility.

Stories open doors

The Neighborhood House Adult Day Program provides therapeutic recreational activities designed to maintain physical, mental, and social skills — as well as the highest level of independence. The program goals are to prevent premature placement in a long-term care facility, provide respite for family and/or caregivers, offer a social rehabilitation model, and, it is hoped in this process, educate the community on what adult day care can offer. The staff strives to aid the seniors by reinforcing a sense of identity. These elders are encouraged to express their feelings; access memories; decrease negative, self-deprecating talk; increase their self-esteem. We want to recover/recreate images symbolizing significant life stages, issues, and self-concept.

The art of storytelling has provided tools to help meet these therapeutic and artistic goals. Along with telling stories during my programs, I often include music, encourage client storytelling, lead discussions, and conduct story-related activities. We discuss familiar topics and ask questions to help the participants recall and reminisce. Stories that are brief, familiar, and contain wisdom and humor work most effectively with my friends at the Neighborhood House. Some of the stories I tell are familiar, and the participants like to follow along and predict what comes next. Sometimes I ask them to help me retell these very familiar tales. When telling unfamiliar stories, I have learned to make sure these tales are short with uncomplicated plots. Long fairytales are best told elsewhere.

Sometimes the elders comment on what they think of the story they just heard or what they think it means. Those who do not comment or who share a seemingly irrelevant comment are still acknowledged. Stories sometimes remind them of their own experiences, and then they share stories from their own lives. At times this sharing creates discussion, and at other times it provides a springboard for other activities. We usually sing together and often incorporate dance, drama, music, and visual arts into these story experiences.

Story stimulates senses

Storytelling appeals to sense memory. I work to include sensory language in my storytelling to enhance recall. The participants have especially enjoyed stories with food in them or reminiscing about experiences involving food. When I told a story about bread, we had a lively discussion about making, smelling, and tasting homemade bread. Flowers and other objects are useful for eliciting stories. One spring day I brought a bouquet of daffodils from my garden and we talked about their color. Because we want the seniors to respond, we are positive about all contributions, even those given by an elder who has lost the ability to identify and/or express colors correctly. On this occasion, each person was given the opportunity to hold and smell the daffodils, and this experience was followed by stories about flowers. In return, we heard a wonderful story

that Rosa remembered and recounted about how Easter lilies came to be.

Even with factual memory gone, there is still emotional memory, which is used to connect with stories. Although some clients have struggles with memory loss, they still have strong emotional memory and respond to the stories with genuine feelings. This process provides a positive experience that helps the participants create good feelings about themselves. Humor is generally a good tool to reach this audience. With positive storytelling experiences they feel good about the situation; they feel good about themselves.

Enhancing listening skills

Storytelling helps people maintain and practice listening skills. It keeps minds moving and exercised. What is most amazing to me is how the audience at Neighborhood House can listen with rapt attention to the stories. They can become completely absorbed, and an hour passes quickly and unnoticed. The clients are quiet and attentive even though many of them have difficulties with short-term memory. We can stimulate their long-term memory to encourage comprehension and participation. These elders appreciate storytelling — perhaps because their generation was raised with stories. They speak of growing up with a slower paced lifestyle that would give more time for personal storytelling, such as sitting around the dinner table sharing stories with family. The seniors also speak of listening to stories on the radio.

Although they're content to just listen to me, I have discovered that some type of participation is a key to more enjoyable and successful programs. The seniors like to chime in on stories, helping me when I pause for them, or they help tell it in turn. One day my audience was taking turns retelling "The Three Little Pigs." When we got to the part where the wolf is on the roof, suddenly Loretta had Santa coming down the chimney. Obviously! Who else would come down the chimney? What a surprise for the third little pig and a delight for us.

The listeners lead

I share a variety of stories from fable to folktale to riddle to legend to true and more. Through experience I have learned to choose stories carefully and present them in a way the seniors would not view as childish. Always respecting and honoring my audience, not behaving in a condescending manner towards them, has been a concern for me no matter the age. Discussions have at times been lively as clients share their wisdom on what a story or fable means, or they remember a related or even an unrelated proverb.

When we share participation stories, the clients increasingly respond and show enjoyment. A favorite activity among these groups has been retelling a familiar story with a new and different twist. Sometimes the elders will help outline what will happen, and I tell their version back to them. I have come to realize that the storytelling is most effective when it is two-way.

The groups have also helped create stories using their ideas and imaginations. For one program I told some *pourquoi* stories (stories that explain the origin of natural phenomenon), including a couple of Rudyard Kipling's *Just So Stories*. Then, together, the audience contributed and created its own group story about how the rainbow came to be. It was titled "The Rainbow Letter." We created it in outline form. They chose for characters "us and our mothers and fathers." The setting was the sky. The beginning was "Once upon a time ..." 1) Our parents were in the sky writing a letter to say "I love you. I miss you."

2) The parents were crying so it rained. 3) They spilled the ink they were using to write the letter. 4) The ink dripped in the sky, making the rainbow. The ending was "This is why we have rainbows in the sky."

When I retold the story back to them, I filled in and added details and acknowledged each contributor with a smile or nod.. The sense of satisfaction was evident through their body language and their positive comments. They stated that they never would have believed they could help to create such a wonderful story. Through the process of creating and telling the story, opportunity was given and taken to express feelings and thoughts that were evidently on their minds.

It is the elders themselves who have taught me how important humor is to them. In one instance, Jacob, who likes attention and doesn't mind speaking out, had the full attention of the others. They were leaning forward, hanging on his words when he said, "I found the cure to forgetfulness."

"Really!" came the response.

"Yes ... but I can't remember what it is."

A ripple of healthy laughter filled the room as together they faced with humor something they struggle with in their lives.

One story leads to another

The elders have found satisfaction in sharing their own stories. Sometimes my reward for telling a true family or personal story is a story in return from them. Some are still able to exercise their long-term memories by recalling the days when they were younger. One highlight was when Dave's and Stuart's memories of pranks they played were jogged when I shared shocking stories of my youthful granddad's fascination with electricity. They both loved being in the spotlight as we laughed with them while they recalled boyhood pranks.

We could just imagine the scene as we heard Dave tell us how he rewired an old Model T crank to the driver's seat instead of to the motor. When they cranked the starter, this large woman in the driver's seat bent the steering wheel as she tried to escape the charge. Stuart had us laughing when he explained how he lassoed the outhouse and then had his horse pull it over. When Millie heard that, she confessed her memories of getting trapped in an outhouse when it was knocked over on its side, with the door facing down!

A staff member noticed how much storytelling affected Don. Don was 80 and generally did not speak except when it came time for storytelling. There was a clear change as the story program began — Don would become alert and talkative. He shared stories about his life on the ranch, as well as experiences from his youth, which included riding to school on a mule. If the staff had not shared with me that Don was usually silent, I would have never suspected it.

I also engage the groups in activities related to storytelling. For one project I collaborated with the visual art therapist. I told the group a story of my favorite place as a child — my grandmother's garden. Then the art specialist assisted as each person drew a picture of his or her own favorite place. The art specialist took a picture of each elder, and together they pasted the photo into the drawings. All the group members had an opportunity to share their artwork and tell a story or describe their favorite place.

For one November program, each person told the group what he or she was thankful for. I wrote down their responses in large letters on sheets of paper for them to hold. Then I sang a song.

We are thankful.
We are thankful.
What are we thankful for?
(Name) is thankful.
(Name) is thankful.
(Name) is thankful for (his or her response).

I went around the room singing their song. Those who wanted to were encouraged to participate in any way, from singing to tapping their toe. Even Steve opened his eyes. He beamed when we sang his verse.

Proven favorites

A popular participation story is the folktale "Too Much Noise," also known as "How to Make a Small House Large." In this story, a farmer finds his house is too noisy and too small. Following advice from the local wise man, the farmer brings more and more animals into his house. The animals make too much noise and crowd the house all the more. The clients enjoy making the sounds of the different farm animals. The ending is always satisfying and revealing to them as the farmer takes the animals out and is left with a house that is physically the same, but which seems quieter and larger to him. I have shared this story in many different programs, and the best "aha" and fit was when I brought a half-filled or half-empty jar and shared stories of perspective and we discussed attitude. The elders pointed out that from the beginning to the end of the story, the only thing that changed was how the farmer felt.

The "Name Story" also provoked wide participation. I had been telling regularly throughout my pregnancy. The elders were kind, interested in my progress, and offered advice. After my baby boy Rowan was born, they asked about him, so the staff encouraged me to bring Rowan with me when I told stories. When I brought the baby to these storytelling programs, we observed a positive effect. The mood was warm and the reaction wonderful. The attention of the group was focused, cheerful, and remarks were positive as individuals related to the infant.

The first time I brought Rowan and introduced him, everyone, including visitors, staff, and even those elders who don't always participate, joined in. I began by telling Rowan's "Name Story" — how and why he was given his name and what it means. Then I told my own "Name Story." Next, I encouraged others to share their "Name Stories." We began with volunteers. Then, in turn, elders, staff, and visitors began telling their stories as we went around the room. Incredibly, everyone shared. During the program there was quiet respect while others spoke. Listeners leaned forward, and they responded appropriately, nodding or laughing at times.

I enjoyed working with and getting to know the clients and staff at the Neighborhood House. I have grown to appreciate and love these fine individuals with whom I am privileged to work. The National Storytelling Network has recognized my work and encouraged its continuation by awarding me their annual research grant in July 1999. At the National Storytelling Conference in July 2000, I shared the results of this grant in a presentation, "Discovering Effects and Benefits of Storytelling for Special Needs Adults." Today, I am still working at both Neighborhood House facilities and the stories continue ....

⇜ Stone Soup ⇝

A FOLKTALE RETOLD FOR PARTICIPATION AT NEIGHBORHOOD HOUSE BY LETICIA PIZZINO*

I shared "Stone Soup" during several visits to build familiarity. Then I retold the story, and we all helped to prepare the ingredients for soup. Those who were able to chop onions or peel carrots did so. Those who could contribute by tearing the cabbage did that. We even discovered that Richard was a former chef. He peeled and chopped his potatoes quickly and was off helping others with their tasks.

When we were done, each person had a covered bowl with a soup ingredient. I retold the story and this time everyone took part. All remained seated except those portraying the three soldiers in the story. These three soldiers went to each person asking if they had food; each person said no, they didn't have any. Many improvised, stating their part in their own words. Although there was a bit of suspense as Lila hesitated — first looking at the soldier, then peeking into the bowl, and finally back to the soldier with uncertainty — in the end she played along as she claimed she didn't have any food either. The villagers in the story are convinced by the soldiers to contribute food, and in return they receive some delicious soup to eat. At this point in the tale, the clients added their bowls of food to a big pot with water and seasoning. The music therapist joined the process by using familiar tunes with new lyrics that she created to fit the story — much to the clients' delight.

Materials: Clean stone, pot, large spoon, water, salt and pepper, vegetables to cut or peel and break up for soup (potatoes, turnip, green beans, cabbage, carrots, onions, etc.), peelers, cutting knives, cutting boards, small bowls, and napkins for everyone.

Participants: Narrator, three soldiers, villagers.

Directions: Have the elders prepare the vegetables for soup by tearing, peeling, breaking, or chopping according to individual abilities. Put prepared vegetables in small bowls and cover with napkin. Make sure each villager has an item for making the soup hidden under a napkin (i.e., salt and pepper, a bowl of vegetables). The villagers sit in a large circle with the soldiers moving to each one. A lot of improvising is done, and often the elders say their lines their own way. The narrator can adapt lines so that the story continues its flow.

NARRATOR: *Once upon a time, there were three soldiers. Now these soldiers had been on the road a very long time, and they were tired. Their feet were sore, and they were hungry.*

They saw a village and they stopped there. They thought perhaps they could find someone who would give them a place to rest and some food to eat. But the villagers saw the three soldiers coming and hid all their food. The soldiers knocked at the first door. [Knocking sound.] The villager answered the door and said, "What do you want?" [Cueing the villagers and soldiers is optional.]

FIRST VILLAGER: What do you want?

SOLDIERS: We are three hungry and tired soldiers. Can you give us food to eat?

NARRATOR: The villager shook his/her head and said, "No. We don't have any food."

FIRST VILLAGER: No. We don't have any food.

NARRATOR: So the soldiers went to the next house and knocked at the door. [Knocking sound.] The villager answered the door and said, "What do you want?"

SECOND VILLAGER: What do you want?

SOLDIERS: We are three hungry and tired soldiers. Can you give us food to eat?

NARRATOR: The villager shook his/her head and said, "No. We don't have any food."

SECOND VILLAGER: No. We don't have any food.

NARRATOR: So the soldiers went to the next house and knocked at the door. [Knocking sound.] The villager answered the door and said, "What do you want?"

THIRD VILLAGER: What do you want?

SOLDIERS: We are three hungry and tired soldiers. Can you give us food to eat?

NARRATOR: The villager shook his/her head and said, "No. We don't have any food."

THIRD VILLAGER: No. We don't have any food.

(Continue and repeat with each villager until the soldiers have talked to every villager.)

NARRATOR: The soldiers thought that they would just have to make some stone soup since it seemed that there was no food in this village. They built a fire and put a large pot of water on it to boil. The soldiers found a stone and put it in the large pot of water to boil. The villagers saw the soldiers cooking a stone and were curious. They asked, "What are you doing?" The soldiers answered, "We are making stone soup. We have a stone and are cooking it up. It will be delicious."

The villagers wondered at that. Soup cooked from a stone. All the villagers gathered to watch this. Soup out of a stone. That would be amazing. The soldiers stirred the soup and said, "Mmmm. This looks good ... but it would taste better if we had some salt and pepper to put in it." A villager remembered that he/she had some salt and pepper.

VILLAGER: I have some salt and pepper.

NARRATOR: The villager found the salt and pepper and gave them to the soldiers to add to the soup. [Villager gives the salt and pepper to the soldiers.] They put the salt and pepper in the soup. The soldiers stirred the soup and said, "Mmmm. This looks good ... but it would taste better if we had some vegetables to put in it." A villager remembered a few onions ....

VILLAGER: I have some onions.

NARRATOR: The villager found the onions and gave them to the soldiers to add to the stone soup. [Villager gives the onions to the soldiers.] They put the onions in the soup. The soldiers stirred the soup and said, "Mmmm. This looks good ... but it would taste even better if we had some other vegetables to put in it." A villager remembered a few carrots ....

VILLAGER: I have some carrots.

NARRATOR: The villager found the carrots and gave them to the soldiers to add to the stone soup. [Villager gives the carrots to the soldiers.] They put the carrots in the soup. The soldiers stirred the soup and said, "Mmmm. This looks good ... but it would taste even better if we had some other vegetables to put in it." A villager remembered a few potatoes ....

VILLAGER: I have some potatoes.

NARRATOR: The villager found the potatoes and gave them to the soldiers to add to the stone soup. [Villager gives the potatoes to the soldiers.] They put the potatoes in the soup.

(Continue gathering vegetables from each villager in the same way until all the vegetables are in the pot.)

NARRATOR: The soldiers stirred the soup as it cooked. The villagers watched. The soup smelled delicious. When the stone soup was done, the soldiers invited everyone in the village to help them eat it. Some villagers brought out bread and butter to eat with the soup. Others brought drinks to share. They all sat down together to a wonderful meal. And what do you know? There was plenty of stone soup for everyone.

Baskets full of memories: Rediscovering personal archives of story

TERESA CLARK

I was inclined to assume that memories fade with the passage of time, until finally they disappear altogether. But I found this is not true. Some remain intact in the archives of the mind — dusty from disuse, perhaps, but still there — ready to be relived in detail if the mind's owner tries to summon them forth.

— Laura Ingalls Wilder

IT HAS BEEN SAID THAT Laura Ingalls Wilder was 60 years old before she wrote her first "Little House" book at the urging of her adult daughter. She said she wrote the series because it helped her keep those she loved and the things she loved alive. It was her belief that our memories become clearer the more we use them, that each time we close our eyes and go back in time to a memory, we enable ourselves to go back further.

Ruby was my grandma. Years ago she had given me the quilt and asked me to store it when she moved to a retirement village. It had been lovingly stored for years before I received it, and I simply followed tradition and kept it stored for the 20 years I had owned it, never completely taking it out of its packaging. It was obvious that it had never been used or laundered. The fabrics and the pattern of the quilt dated its creation to the early 1900s. It had never occurred to me to ask why it hadn't been used.

When I "rediscovered" the quilt in my storage room, I asked everyone I knew about it, but no one could tell me anything. I decided to go to Ruby, now 90, and ask her personally. Her children assured me she would never remember. They could not have been more wrong.

Ruby was already blind. When I placed the quilt in her lap she ran her fingers along the stitches and patches. She held the quilt to her nose. Then I asked her to tell me what she was thinking about. She shared an extraordinary story that most of the family had never heard.

Back in 1916, her mother had suffered from breast cancer. She'd had radical surgery and was sent home to recover. Living with them at the time was Ruby's aged grandmother, who had driven her own oxcart into the Salt Lake Valley of Utah back in 1847. She was blind and 82 in an era when the average life expectancy was 47. Ruby had dropped out of Grade 9 to take care of these two women. The three of them had made the quilt together during that time. Upon close inspection of the quilt, and armed with the knowledge of Ruby's story, an observant person can pick out three different stitching styles. Ruby's mother had eventually recovered. Her grandma had moved on to be cared for by another, and Ruby had returned to school and finally graduated at the age of 20. But that time with those precious women had become so special to

131

Ruby that she had never felt she could use the quilt.

When I asked her why she had never told us the reason the quilt had been saved for all those years, she said she had gotten so used to storing the quilt that she'd also gotten used to storing the memory. The quilt, a single tangible item, had triggered a flood of memories that had not been shared before. It became the catalyst that caused many more stories to resurface and be shared.

My experience with Ruby is what led me to create the memory basket exercise. After experiencing the powerful impact the quilt had on Grandma and her memories, I started looking at everything with newly aware, memory-seeking eyes. I wondered how many other memories she had stored away, and I wondered if I was doing the same thing. I discovered how easily memories could be triggered by the simplest of items when one takes the time to spend a few moments with an object. Whenever some little knick-knack or junk-drawer oddity triggered a memory for me, I tossed it into a basket. In no time at all I had baskets full of memories. I was amazed by what this simple exercise had done for me. I was remembering and sharing experiences I hadn't thought of in years. So was my grandmother. I tried the exercise out in a workshop. The result was so affirming it became a fixed tradition.

THE MEMORY BASKET EXERCISE

The memory basket exercise is an effective way to tap into the power of storytelling and open the doors of communication. This exercise works because many of the senses are called into use. As participants look, touch, and smell the various items in the basket, memories are triggered and stories are shared, often stories that have not been shared for years.

STEP ONE: GROUP DISCUSSION

The discussion leader comes prepared with baskets full of odd and assorted items. It seems just about anything will trigger a memory for somebody. Antiques and thrift store collectibles are excellent things to put in the baskets. So is any old object you may have lying around: tools, beauty accessories, recipes, keys, old postcards, letters, hankies, spices, medicine bottles, hats, gloves, toys, books, etc. If it has been around for some time, throw it in the basket — it will trigger a memory for somebody. There is no generation gap in this exercise. It works with youth as well as senior citizens. It is especially fun to do it in a multi-generational setting and hear the different memories triggered by the same items. Using this exercise, I've heard some pretty amazing stories that haven't been told in decades. I've also heard some recent memories that hadn't been shared before.

Simply pass the baskets around and give participants time to search and reminisce within themselves. When everyone has selected an item, allow time for people to jot down the memories triggered by the item. Next have everyone take turns orally sharing the memories. If the participants are not able to write, go directly into the sharing. Honor the person sharing with genuine interest and appreciation.

STEP TWO: THE DAILY CHALLENGE

Remember — ANYTHING can trigger memory!

After participants have experienced success with this memory-triggering exercise, challenge them to a daily commitment to continue the process. Start with 10 minutes a day: 5 minutes to daydream and remember; 5 minutes to write or record.

1. Daydream!
2. Select any item lying around and let it trigger a memory.
3. Let the memory lead. Listen to your heart. Look with memory-seeking eyes.
4. Write it down, or if that is difficult, record it on a tape recorder.
5. Read your writings once a week.
6. Are there more memories triggered?
7. Write or record those memories as well.

STEP THREE: FOLLOW UP

Remember, shared experiences always trigger memory. Bring the group members together again to touch base with each other and share their memory harvest. Encourage them to share their memory harvest with others as well, especially with family and friends. The harvest will trigger another crop of memories as well as create a deeper bond for the participants.

Remarkable results

Geraldine was 71. She sat in my class and looked cynical as the basket of assorted items worked its way down the row to her. It was obvious she didn't think there was anything in the basket that would affect her. When the basket came to her, she grabbed the swimming goggles and passed the basket on quickly. She told me later that she had thought she would share some silly swimming memory and be done with it. But when she took a moment to truly look at the goggles, she was stunned to discover they had triggered a memory. She remembered a summer day in her youth when she and her friends had been swimming in a canal. The day had turned tragic when one of them went under the water and didn't come back up. The body was never found. Geraldine's 40-year-old daughter was in the workshop as well. She was stunned by the story and asked her mother why she had never told her that before, because it would have helped her understand why her mother had always been so adamant that her daughter should never swim in canals when she was little. Geraldine responded that she had not remembered that day for years and years. The goggles had triggered the memory. The daughter said the memory had filled in a gap for her and helped her more fully understand the woman who had raised her.

Chad was well into his 50s when he came to my workshop. The workshop was presented out of doors, and frankly he looked like he would have been more comfortable slipping into the woods behind us than looking through a basket of anything. But he stuck it out and rummaged around in the basket. As soon as he came across the rusted, old, claw trap in the bottom of the basket, he smiled. When it was his turn to tell his memory, he told of a day in his childhood when he and his father had been setting claw traps to catch the raccoons and possums that were stealing from their farm. Later in the afternoon, they went to check the traps and discovered a fully mature golden eagle with one of its feet held tight. Their eyes filled with tears at the absolute helplessness and fear they saw in its eyes. He told of watching his father speak softly and soothingly to the magnificent bird, all the while inching toward the trap. Then he watched in stunned silence as his father released the bird from the trap. The eagle soared high above their heads and hovered above them, nearly out of sight, for a moment. Then it swooped down and flew a slow low-flying circle around their heads as if to say thank-you, and then flew away for good. Chad's eyes grew moist with the memory. He told us he and his father went home that day and got rid of all the claw traps. I asked Chad when he had last thought of that day and whether he had ever told his children that story. He said he hadn't thought of that day for years and promised to go home and tell his children.

Connie was a young mother in her late 20s when she attended the workshop. She selected an early 50s style woman's blue dress hat out of the basket. I was a little uneasy when she picked out the hat because I saw a scowl pass over her face and a tear trickle down her cheek. She brushed it away almost angrily, then started writing feverishly. I reminded myself that not every memory is filled with joy, nor should it be. My responsibility as the exercise leader was to listen and guide Connie to a place of peace, if need be, after she had shared her memory. I braced myself for what was to come. The hat had reminded Connie of her grandmother. She had always held a deep-seated resentment for her grandmother and worked actively not to remember her because most of her memories were of her grandmother being drunk. When she was drunk she was mean. Connie's most powerful memory was of being locked in a car with her sister outside a bar while her grandma got smashed inside the bar. Connie told us she had vowed never to tell her children about her grandmother. Yet when Connie picked up the hat, it had triggered a

memory of one sun-filled afternoon her grandmother had taken Connie and her sister to the park. They'd laughed and played, and her grandma hadn't had a single drink. Connie said this triggered memory had reminded her she had actually loved her grandma. She said the memory had filled her with light. She told us this was going to be the memory onto which she would hold. Her grandma was gone and she certainly couldn't alter the past, and she could never understand what demons drove her to be the way she was, but she could honor her grandma best by sharing that sunny memory and the joy of that day with her children.

Memories begin to flow

Connie's experience is not unique. I have never had a workshop participant share a dark memory and leave it there. Each time an object has triggered a memory, it has led to a positive recollection. My observation has been that the memories triggered first are usually moments of joy or discovery, sweetness or nostalgia, triumph or success. Naturally, group leaders need to be sensitive and prepared for the fact that not every memory is a pleasant one. We need to be in a healthy position emotionally ourselves to orchestrate this exercise. Yet, with that being said, we need not fear. Memories can become great wellsprings of healing and understanding when we allow them to guide us in this simple way.

Time and again I have seen this process happen. Whether a shell takes a person back to the first day he smelled the ocean, or a pink foam curler reminds someone of a sleepover or her first date, the thrill of discovery of a long-forgotten moment in our lives is the same. Each rediscovered memory opens the floodgates for more memory. Each shared memory opens a conduit for successful communication. Each moment of successful communication leads to deeper human ties.

Ruby remembered

On September 22, 2000, my Grandma Ruby passed away. She asked me to speak at her funeral. Her main desire was that I tell her stories, of which others might not be aware. This was not a simple task. She had shared her life with 6 children, 21 grandchildren, 79 great-grandchildren, and 25 great-great-grandchildren. I went back to the baskets, and now every item triggered a memory of Grandma and a story she had shared with me. I shared those stories at her funeral.

When the funeral was over, the response I heard most often was "I never knew any of that; thank you so much for taking the time to listen and share."

Storyteller and writer Ed Okanowicz once said, "Nothing is sadder than to reflect on the recent death of an older relative or friend and realize the number of experiences that also were buried inside that bronze casket." Because of my experiences with Ruby, and those baskets full of memories, we closed the lid on her casket, but we did not close the lid on her memories. Her stories will continue to be told and cherished, and we will keep her with us through those stories.

PRESERVING OUR CULTURE AND COMMUNITY: SHARING OUR STORIES

Games to teach interviewing

DOUG LIPMAN

YEARS AGO, I WORKED in a program that paired children and elders. The children were to meet with the elders and elicit some of their life stories. My job was to prepare the children for their role as interviewers.

How would I do this? I had no idea! However, I remembered my experiences of being interviewed by students for their class newspapers. Time and again, the students would appear with a carefully compiled list of questions. They might begin with a question like "How did you become a storyteller?" I might answer, "Well, I began by telling stories to my younger brother ...." Then they'd continue with the second question on their list. "Did you ever tell stories as a child?" I'd be furious! Hadn't they listened to my first answer?

Based on these experiences, I knew I wanted the students to learn to ask questions, not from a list, but from engaged listening. How could I help them learn that skill and get practice at it? It seemed that a game might be the best way. So I created a first game and tried it out. Then I brought in some elders for the children to interview. Over time, and through trial and error, I developed a series of games and tools that seemed to prepare students for the task at hand.

In the process of trying to articulate what the children needed to learn, I realized that interviewing skills are similar to story-crafting skills. In both story-crafting and interviewing, you complete the story in your mind through your own activity. In crafting a story, you decide what more to imagine; in interviewing, you ask questions to fill in what you need to make a completely imagined picture. I have taught these tools and used these games with students in Grades 4 through 8 (ages 9 through 13). All but one used me as the subject. This lets me make the games more lively and educate the students through my responses.

Closed-ended and open-ended questions

The students need to learn that a good interviewer uses two different kinds of questions, each with an appropriate purpose. Closed-ended questions require specific answers, such as "Yes," "No," or "I was 10 years old." Open-ended questions call for non-specific answers; they often invite the teller to tell more stories.

Closed-ended questions are useful for extracting particular information. If the interviewer is confused about when something happened, a closed-ended question gets the answer quickly.

Closed-ended questions can help a shy interviewee get started. Some experienced interviewers always begin an interview by asking a few closed-ended questions whose answers will be "yes." This can put the interviewee at ease enough to answer a more open-ended question.

Closed-ended questions are also useful for stopping a story that goes on too long. A series of closed-ended questions requiring only "yes" or "no" answers will almost certainly cause anyone to stop offering information freely.

Open-ended questions, conversely, start the flow of narrative. As a result, they are more useful to the interviewer who wants to elicit stories. Young interviewers, especially, tend to need instruction in the art of the open-ended question.

I provide examples of closed-ended questions:

- "Did you like school?"
- "What was your sister's name?"
- "How old were you when you got your first job?"

These, on the other hand, are open-ended questions:

- "What were some things you liked about school?"
- "What sorts of games did you and your sister play together?"
- "What was it like for you to stop school and go to work?"

What fairytale character am I?

This story-game has two goals: to sensitize interviewers to the flow-stopping effect of closed-ended questions; and to encourage interviewers to ask questions based on what they have just heard.

I begin the game with the following explanation: "This is a guessing game. I will pretend to be a character from a fairytale. Your job will be to guess who I am. You can ask me questions about

my life, and I'll answer them. But there are two special kinds of questions in this game.

"One special kind of question is the 'yes/no' question. These questions can be answered with just one word — 'yes' or 'no.' Every time you ask me one of these questions, I get a point on the blackboard. If I get five points, I win the game.

"Another kind of question is the 'follow-up' question. A follow-up question asks about something I just said. Every time you ask a follow-up question, you get a point on the board. Every time you get three points, you can make one guess about who I am."

The game proceeds with me answering questions as though I am, say, Rapunzel. My job is not only to answer the questions, but also to judge the correct amount of information to give. With younger children, I might be quite forthcoming. With older or more experienced interviewers, on the other hand, I might give evasive answers that conceal as much information as possible. In either case, my primary goal is not to fool the players, but to point out effective questions when they ask them.

The hidden mystery

As an interviewer, I have often found myself convinced that I had stumbled on a significant story, but could not quite elicit it from the interviewee. For example, I once interviewed a 10-year-old student in front of her class, as a demonstration for them of how to interview. The student was telling how she had left her home in the Caribbean some years before. The scene of her departure for the United States seemed important to me, but her description of it lacked any feeling or sense of storyline. Finally, I began to imagine the scene in detail. I asked her exactly where she was when she said good-bye to her family, and what time of day it was.

Finally I asked who was present. When she answered, I noticed she omitted her sister. When I asked, "Where was your sister," she told us her sister had gone to school already, and she never got to say good-bye to her. This was the significant part of the story, but I could only elicit it by carefully imagining every aspect of the entire scene.

To help students develop this skill, I tell them:"I'm going to tell you a story that has a hidden mystery in it. Everything about the story is ordinary, except one thing. You have to ask me questions until you get me to tell you the one unusual thing. Try to imagine the entire scene. It may help if you think about questions that start with words like 'who,' 'when,' or 'where.'"

Then I respond to their questions, gradually telling a story about a day when I had a tea party for some of my friends — and one of my friends was a pink rhinoceros. When they force me to describe the pink rhino, they have won the game. As usual, I comment on perceptive and helpful questions as they ask them.

Before and after

A good interviewer not only elicits stories, but also extends the stories by exploring themes. For example, if the interviewee has just told a story about a childhood quarrel with a brother, the interviewer might pursue the theme by asking, "Were there other times you two quarreled? Tell me about them." If that question leads to a series of stories about rousing good arguments, the interviewer might eventually ask, "Do you two still fight?" In this way, the interviewer responds to a story by extending one of its themes back to its beginnings and up to its end, or at least to its status in the present.

To help students develop this more advanced interviewing skill, I might tell them a true story from my life. For example, I might tell about the time I accidentally threw a stone through a car windshield and then was so frightened I lied about having done it. The story I tell should seem complete in itself, but should also have several possible themes that can be explored.

Then I encourage the students to ask me "before" questions or "after" questions that develop a theme in my story. Examples might include "Tell us about the first time you ever lied" or "Was there a time after that when you got that scared again? Tell us about it." For each appropriate theme-building question, I give students a point for "before" or for "after." When they have reached, say, five points in each column, I declare them the winners.

The awful interviewer

To highlight overall interview decorum once the students have played all of the other games, I will role-play being the worst interviewer I can be.

With a student volunteer as interviewee, I will ask a series of closed-ended questions without taking into account — or even waiting for — the answers. I will start to talk about my own experiences at length. I will give advice or speak judgmentally about what the interviewee says. I may even insult the interviewee or get distracted by something in the environment.

After the brief demonstration, I ask the students to describe some of awful things I did.

Next steps

After learning these games, a group will probably be ready to practice interviewing a volunteer accomplice, such as a teacher or the principal. During the interview, if necessary, I can offer reminders about a principle or two that they may have forgotten in their excitement. Later, I can offer the group appreciations about their interviewing.

After a successful interview or two with me present, the students can be sent in groups or individually to interview community or family members. Having played the above games and then applied the lessons in a supervised interview, there is an excellent chance that they will be able to treat their interviewees with respect, elicit their stories, and follow up on what they hear with perceptive questions.

The Wickenburg Way: A storytelling history play unites a community

Dennis Freeman

My adventure began with a phone call from Desert Caballeros Western Museum in Wickenburg, Arizona. Curator Sheila Kollasch explained that the museum was planning to produce a history pageant and inquired whether I would be interested in collecting stories that might possibly be used in the production. Throw me in the briar patch! I was off to Wickenburg for five years of total immersion in western history.

I soon discovered that the oral and written histories of the white residents had long been collected and archived, but the memories of the Mexican pioneers, Yavapai Indian history, and the stories of the very few African-Americans had long been ignored. I concentrated my efforts on the people of color and began to make contacts with families and descendants of pioneers.

Stalking the wily informant was an art in itself. The families had to get to know me, learn to trust me, and gain confidence that I was going to accurately portray their story as they told it. Sometimes confidence was gained through an introduction by a trusted friend. Other times I was passed along to another family after doing a good job with a first family. Sometimes I ate ice cream and drank coffee, talking about everything but family stories. Then the moment would come when family members would glance at each other and the matriarch of the clan would say, "We would be happy to tell you our stories."

I would show up at their homes with tape recorder, extra tapes, extra microphone, extension cords, outlet adapters, and extra batteries in case there wasn't any place to plug in the recorder. I also brought certain objects that were touchstones to memories in order to glean the story material from these descendants of pioneer families.

I have a "magic box," decorated and lined with soft velvet. Inside are various objects that I have used over the years to help people remember stories:

- An old dog collar elicited stories of family pets and favorite family dog anecdotes, often humorous and affectionate.

- A rusted cowbell brought out stories of ranching and humorous tales about the antics of the family bull.

- A bandage summoned stories of times when someone was hurt, was thrown from a horse, or had a serious encounter with cacti or a rattlesnake.

- My own Vietnam Air Medal elicited memories of the bravery of family members in times of challenge.
- A 100-year-old medicine bottle reminded families of sicknesses they had endured, the family doctor, and family home remedies.

I recorded the sessions, made duplicates of the tapes for the family and museum, then went through the long word-for-word transcription process. I turned over copies of the materials to the museum and contributing families for their personal archives.

My approach was different than the classic oral history interview. Of course I was interested in names, dates, places, and who was related to whom. But my real interest was the story, the dramatic element that gave spice to the sessions. I was looking for the tragedies, the triumphs, the miracles, the love stories, the struggles, the real thread of experiences that wove these lives into the tapestry of historical Wickenburg.

There was plenty of history to dig through. Wickenburg was home to the richest gold mine in the Arizona territory, Henry Wickenburg's Vulture Mine. A few miles north were the Weaver Mountains, where the first prospectors popped gold nuggets right off the top of Rich Hill with their hunting knives. Their discovery ignited a gold rush to the "Apacheria," as the locale around Wickenburg was known.

The Yavapai Indians, known to themselves as the Tolkapaya, had lived in the rich Hassayampa Valley for 600 years. The Yavapai realized that the white and Mexican miners were going to drive them from their traditional lands and watering holes if the tribe didn't take a stand. The

Wickenburg area exploded into fierce Indian wars against settlers and miners until the Yavapai people were defeated by General George Crook and the United States Cavalry.

Wickenburg is the fifth oldest town in Arizona, certainly older than Phoenix, and home to the "notorious" Hassayampa River, which runs wet, then dry as the water suddenly dives underground, leaving a sandy river bed, before it resurfaces a few miles downstream.

There's a legend centuries old,
By the early Spaniards told,
Of a sparkling stream that "lies"
Under Arizona skies,
Hassayampa is its name,
And the title to its fame,
Is a wondrous quality,
Known today from sea to sea,
Those who drink its waters bright,
Red man, white man, boor or knight,
Girls or women, boys or men,
Never tell the truth again!

A man called Andrew Downing wrote this poem during Wickenburg's territorial days, probably before the turn of the last century. Wickenburg was one of the major gold-producing areas in the state, with many mines in operation. If the gold mines were less than productive, owners were known to cut their losses by selling worthless mining stock. They greatly exaggerated the value of their mines in order to lure investors. The dubious practice became so common that the veracity of anyone living along the Hassayampa River was called into question, thus the source of inspiration for the poem.

Now that river presented a problem to this storyteller. It seems that everybody in the town had taken a sip of that river at one time or another, so trying to find a consistent version of oral history in the town was a challenge because no one could agree on what actually happened. It was also a saving element because whenever two versions of the same event were told, I could always allow for the "Hassayampa Effect," which seemed to good-naturedly reconcile everyone to their differences.

This approach was so successful that Desert Caballeros Western Museum asked if I was ready to script the collected stories into a historical pageant or a play. Thus was born *The Wickenburg Way*. The title is a play on words based on the name of the main street through town as well as the unique style Wickenburg people have of getting things done.

Due to the Hassayampa effect, this could have been a play of parallel universes. But we had to make choices. In its uncut form, *The Wickenburg Way* would have run about five hours on stage and would have flattened the bottom of even the most ardent history buff.

I extracted the choicest stories from all the families who gave me their time and family memories. I took my researched version of the Yavapai Indian wars directly to the tribe itself, and members scrutinized it for accuracy and gave me their blessing, along with our principal Native American actor, Uqualla, who also reviewed the script for accuracy and intent. That process in itself took more than a year.

I found friends who shared a passion to discover the life of Elizabeth Hudson-Smith, an African-American woman and the daughter of a slave, who, my research indicates, was educated by the Ursuline Order in New Orleans, Louisiana. In 1905, Mrs. Smith opened the first all-brick hotel in Wickenburg, the Vernetta, and was a co-founder of the Wickenburg Presbyterian Church. Hudson-Smith was an astute businesswoman,

purchasing mining properties, rental houses, and the Wickenburg Opera house, where her own repertory company staged plays for the local folks. She lived in a golden age, seemingly immune from prejudice, until the Ku Klux Klan came into Arizona in the 1920s and drove her underground. People forgot that Mrs. Smith helped to build Wickenburg. They forgot that she gave money to families to keep them going through hard times. She was not allowed to attend the church she helped to found. In fact, in order to be less conspicuous, Elizabeth finally removed the satin dresses, white gloves, and stylish hats she had worn for so long. The newcomers in town thought she was the maid in her own hotel.

Elizabeth died in 1935. How she died depends on who one talks to. Her will mysteriously disappeared, and most of her holdings were appropriated by the wealthy white men in town. The descendants of these men still live in Wickenburg, so to bring her life to the stage was a risk but a personal passion.

It was all worth it. When the actress and Arizona storyteller Mary Kelly finished the last lines of Elizabeth's story, her triumphs, her grievous disappointments, and her consoling farewell to Wickenburg, the audience leapt to its feet in a standing ovation.

Since *The Wickenburg Way* was a storytelling play about the town's history, my intention was to include as many Wickenburg community members as actresses and actors as possible, no matter their level of experience. Professional dramatists and seasoned community performers might have made for a more polished production, but it would never have had the heart and spirit created by family members portraying their own family histories. Out of a cast of 55, there were only 5 professional actors and musicians. The rest were community actors ranging in age from 8 to 88.

Three generations of Garcia women stood on stage and recounted the saga of their family struggles and their beloved grandfather's death. The Quesada family told of the heroic exploits of their vaquero father, Don José Quesada, known by other cowboys as "Iron Joe" Quesada. The name was well earned. The Quesadas related the story about the time their father was a young man working on the Cartwright family's Seven Springs ranch in Arizona. José had just caught a fast-running steer with his lariat, and as he quickly wrapped the rope around the saddle horn to stop the steer in his tracks, known as "taking dallies," the rope snapped taut, drawing in and cutting off three fingers of his right hand at the middle joints! Ouch! José wrapped the stumps of his bloody fingers in his bandana and continued to work the rest of the day without saying anything to anyone. It wasn't an act of bravado. There was a job to be done and the outfit needed every man. There was no time to stop for injuries. But when his injuries were revealed and his fingers cauterized with a red-hot branding iron, the cowboys dubbed him "Iron Joe."

Then the Macías family told of the grand barbecues held by their father, Francisco Macías. Francisco loved dancing so much that he built an outdoor cement dance floor right next to the Hassayampa River under the shade of giant cottonwood trees. They called this area of his ranch the "Down Below." Many warm family and community memories were born there amidst live music for the dancers, moms and babies under the shade trees, foot-race competitions between families, homemade ice cream, slow-cooked barbecue, hand-made tortillas, and the best beans this side of heaven. These were the days when people took the time to set aside their differences. The gatherings at the Macías ranch often lasted three days: three days to feast, dance, laugh, and take a break from the hard work of their daily lives.

The Melendez brothers — Tony, chief of police in Wickenburg, and Gilbert, a long-time Glendale, Arizona, policeman — affectionately retold the exploits of their mule-skinner grandfather, Joe T. O'Campo, who had told them the story of the Ghost of El Volcho, a headless rider who haunted the wagon road to the Vulture Mine. History buffs themselves, the brothers related the hardscrabble lives of the Mexican ranchers and prospectors who settled the Hassayampa River Valley in the later 1800s.

The Wickenburg community orchestra performed an original score written by Arizona Humanities Scholar of the Year Jay Cravath and me. Uqualla chanted a Yavapai song that he assured us had not been sung in more than 100 years.

With so many stories swirling around, I had a difficult time deciding how to end the performance. I not only wanted to portray the histories. I also wanted the audience to experience some of the ambience of old Wickenburg. My answer was in the music. Our three-piece string band — fiddle, bass, and guitar — performed the period music of turn-of- the-century Wickenburg. We had learned the favorite dances of the Macías family, "Quatro Milpas" and "Pete's Polka." As *The Wickenburg Way* band swept into these nostalgic dances, you could see the smiles of recognition on the faces of the older people in the audience. Then the cast came off the stage and into the audience. They invited audience members to dance, took their hands, and waltzed them into the open spaces in the aisles. Soon the room was full of dancing partners. For those moments, the memories of times past lived. When the music ended, we had a built-in standing ovation!

After the final curtain, the cast members were mixing with the audience when Wickenburg's oldest resident, Tony O'Brien, approached Mary Kelly, the storyteller/actress who played Elizabeth Hudson-Smith. Tony, who passed away in early 2000, had known the real Elizabeth when he was a young man. As Tony neared Mary Kelly with tears streaming down his face, he held out his arms to her and said, "Elizabeth, it's me, Tony!" Mr. O'Brien had to have one last hug with his old friend Elizabeth. Everyone within hearing felt tears well up in their eyes as we stood in a circle around them. A bit of theater magic? Perhaps, but here was a long-time, much-needed healing that took place. After so many years, Elizabeth and the town made their peace with each other.

For two glorious days, the previously untold history of Wickenburg lived on the stage for sold-out audiences. But *The Wickenburg Way* was more than a play. It was a gathering of tribes, clans, and families. Their stories were honored, their courage and determination applauded. Fifty-year-old wounds were balmed with the healing salve of recognition and respect, and the old stories came alive in the present.

Of course, there are still two families arguing about whose grandfather came first, but that came with the territory, and so did their grandfathers. We did our best to honor them all.

I am not so naive as to think *The Wickenburg Way* righted all the wrongs and erased intolerance and racism. But I believe beginnings were made, memories were jostled awake, and the possibilities of healing historic wounds were revealed through the production. Perhaps the overall effect of the play can best be summed up by a young community actress who put it this way: "You know, I always thought that this town was kind of a yuck, boring, nothing-to-do place. But now, when I look at Mrs. Smith's old hotel, the Hassayampa River, and the buildings along Railroad Street, I know their history. Now these places speak to me. It's almost as if the memories are my own, these are the memories of my *home*. Wickenburg talks to me like it never did before. It's all about the stories, isn't it?"

For me, many of the Wickenburg stories live on in my repertoire, and the family names ring out in my performances. Will there be another *Wickenburg Way?* I hope so. In another town, in another time, someone will realize the importance of the community learning its own history. When the call comes, I'll be ready.

On the trail of Judge Rabbit: Sharing tales of Cambodian refugees

CATHY SPAGNOLI

Don't take the straight path, or the winding one,
Take the path your ancestors have taken.

— Khmer proverb

STORIES SHARE THE PATHS of the past. Yet refugees suddenly coping with a strange and different setting may find it a challenge to follow their ancestors' path. When immigrants strive to adapt to their new lives in a new land, they may question or even disregard their own ethnic identity. They may find it even harder for their children to learn and understand their long and rich history. How can refugees create identities that balance two cultures and preserve valuable heritage? Storytelling can provide one way to walk this path, connecting times past with times to come.

Refugees have stories to share, from true and sometimes terrifying tales of their journeys, to traditional tales that nourish the spirit and bring back the beauty and warmth of a remembered homeland. In work with refugee and immigrant populations, I have found storytelling to be invaluable as a means to encourage cultural pride while sharing heritage, to provide for intergenerational learning and communication, to build community, and to develop oral English skills, listening comprehension, and self-confidence.

I stumbled into storytelling with refugees while telling in Seattle-area schools in the 1980s. Although many people opened homes and hearts to Southeast Asian refugees at that time, resent-ment and prejudice were found as well. When I heard name-calling and teasing too often in certain schools, I decided to try storytelling as a way to help break through this prejudice. With the assistance of several skilled volunteers and a small grant from the Washington Commission for the Humanities, I started a project, "Singing Bamboo: Through Our Stories We Continue," to collect traditional Southeast Asian tales and true stories from the recent past. Our goal was to share the stories in schools and neighborhoods. We wanted to help preserve these rich and fascinating cultures while promoting understanding and acceptance among the wider community.

Yet before I could collect stories from our new neighbors, I needed some stories to tell that would encourage the telling of more tales — "story bait." I scoured library books seeking Southeast Asian stories that could spark memories. I made countless calls to find refugees and immigrants who might know stories. Then I met with a wonderful assortment of warm people who were eager to share their stories. I heard tales of Judge Rabbit from Thom Kong in his Laundromat, giggled with Lina Mao Wall over the tales of A-Chey while eating noodle soup, sat listening to poet Luoth Yin translate the story of Vetsandon as orange-robed monks chanted it in a Seattle Buddhist temple, and shared tales with women's groups at Refugee Women's Alliance.

While collecting stories, I spent many days

with a wise young man, Putha Touch, who longs to tell tales again in Cambodia, though he may never have the chance. Putha grew up hearing stories about twice a week in school there. Later, as a teacher in Cambodia, he used folk tales often; he even remembers which tales were told to different grades. His great interest in storytelling led him to gather tales, even in the midst of a terrible war, from elders weakened but eager to pass them on. Putha came to Seattle as a refugee. In his own stories he describes the pain of so many, such as when he returned to his home during a truce:

> I came to Phnom Penh and saw the proud international bank kneeling on the ground, and next to it, a favorite temple now a garbage heap. I stopped by my former high school: trees and grass like a jungle surrounded it. I started down a road with no sign, feeling close to my house. Suddenly, a bony hand touched my shoulder. I turned and saw an old lady. I recognized my mother's friend although her face had changed, it held such a great grief. Yes, her whole family had been killed except her. I could not barricade my tears as she pointed to the empty space with broken bits of walls — that was my home. And not only my house was gone, but my brothers and relatives had disappeared, too. The pool where I used to swim every evening was a dirty pond. Neighbors used to gather to chat, tell folktales, and play at night there. Now only death, glass pieces, and sad stories remained.

Putha came to Seattle because he believed "there was no other choice," and he felt immediately vulnerable: "In Cambodia, I felt strong and capable. Here I seem so little, and Americans so big and powerful." Sharing stories, true and traditional, from his homeland was one way for him to rediscover self-respect and confidence. We spent many long afternoons in his apartment, traveling on the sound of his mother's gentle chants and the smell of her incense back to a Cambodia strong and proud, one that could boast of the great King Jayavarman VII, the magnificent Angkor Wat, and the wily national folk hero, Judge Rabbit.

From the months of collecting came various stories I shared throughout the community with exciting results. The Washington Commission for the Humanities funded programs in local libraries, schools, and museums of personal "coming over" stories and folktales told by some of the many people I had interviewed and by myself. When these stories were told in the local schools, Southeast Asian children left school assemblies walking a little more proudly. Recordings of these stories accompanied by Southeast Asian musicians were featured on local public radio to reach an even wider base of the community. In the Refugee Women's Alliance, a center in Seattle that teaches refugee women English, I shared folktales to encourage learning a new language while preserving heritage. Women juggling babies laughed joyfully at their friend Judge Rabbit. Later I wrote down some of my versions of the Judge Rabbit stories and published them so that these families could read their own stories in print for the first time. (I split royalties from the books with the Refugee Women's Alliance.) When youth groups from the Alliance began to tell, collect, and perform more of these stories for their families, their elders responded by telling more tales to young ones at home, encouraged by their interest.

I have learned so very much. Here are a few more thoughts from my limited experience, which may be useful to others seeking tales from a refugee or immigrant community.

1. **Start carefully and slowly, yet with enthusiasm.** Respect the hierarchy in the community.

Be sensitive to cultural etiquette, rhythms, and values. Introduce yourself to those acknowledged as leaders; offer evidence of your experience, interest, and care; then ask for their help. And don't be afraid to show your genuine enthusiasm for the power of story.

2. **Do your homework.** Just as I learned of Cambodia's past — about the tricksters Judge Rabbit and A-Chey, the well-known epic *Tum Teav*, and the famous kings and battles — you will need to know more about the culture you are entering.

If you work with many groups, you will obviously not be able to go into such detail with each, but use this list as a starting point for possible background research:

- **History:** Note important historical periods and key figures.
- **Modern times:** Know about recent changes, wars, and modern conditions.
- **Religions and values:** Learn about the major religious groups and religious leaders, the saints and sages, tales of miracles. Determine key values, past and present.
- **Story material:** Find the major myths and epics of the culture. Determine other major types of stories told, including popular trickster figures or fools, well-known heroes, tales of humor, and more.
- **Storytelling styles:** If possible, discover how stories are told and by whom. Find out if props are used, or music, or improvisation. See if storytelling forms have changed and which are still popular.
- **Related arts:** Discover various related art forms, folklore forms, and written literary forms that may have influenced storytelling.
- **Cultural Details:** Find images that place

the story in its cultural context for the listener, starting with this beginning list.

a) **Setting:** Smells, sights, foods, animals, housing, clothing, weather

b) **Language:** Greetings, sound words, formulas to open and close story

c) **Gestures:** Daily typical ones, forms of greeting, insulting ones to avoid

d) **Sounds:** Music, environmental

- **Stereotypes:** Determine stereotyped images that Americans might have of this culture and work against them in your story.

3. **Go graciously and build trust.** When you are ready to collect from people, bring a gift, perhaps of food, to show your thanks and to set the mood. Or send a little remembrance afterwards — the story written down and illustrated, a book, a craft, or a copy of the interview tape. Make sure beforehand that your informant feels comfortable speaking in English, and arrange for translation if necessary. Ask if you may tape, but respect a refusal if taping makes someone nervous. Be very clear with your informants about the reason for your collecting. If you may use the story in some way later, have a clear release form that states exactly how the story will be used.

4. **Use stories and more to encourage storytelling.** It is always nice to start off by sharing something, including your own work. Use story bait: tales, songs, objects, visuals, sayings, and more to jog memories. Proverbs work too, such as this Khmer proverb that might spark off various associations: *If a tiger lies down, don't say, "The tiger is showing respect."*

5. **Let the tale unfold.** It is best not to ask questions while the story is being shared, for once a person takes on the role of storyteller, they

enter into a different space. Save your questions for after the story is finished, to clear up points of interest and story details. However, if your informant is having difficulty remembering or begins to ramble far away, use your questions to help lead her further into the story or to bring her back to the plot ("What do you think did happen then?" and so on).

6. **Try group collecting.** *The wood for a temple does not come from one tree.* Take this Chinese proverb to heart after you've collected from an individual teller. Gather several people together and fish for tales. I have found this a great way to collect stories, for everyone helps each other remember, and they spark ideas and images. The story emerges as it is pieced together by several heads and hearts. Even if you don't collect from a group, you may still need to talk with several people to find one complete story, so save all the bits of a tale you discover.

7. **Prepare the tale with care.** After you have collected a tellable tale, shape it in a way respectful to the culture. It is often difficult to retell it exactly as you heard it, but you will not want to change it greatly if your wish is to share a culture through its stories. From your study, or by working with someone from that culture, see what cultural details you might add and check to make sure no inaccuracies come through. As I shaped Khmer tales, I found lovely images: "sadness followed him like a shadow." I discovered in telling *Tum Teav* that an offering of love would not be a rose, but rather a betel nut. And I liked adding a touch of language, such as saying, "when the men thanked Judge Rabbit 'akoon, akoon'" (spelled phonetically).

8. **Give the tale back.** Reach out to the refugee community as well as to its neighbors. Share the story to remind refugees of old story friends, of perhaps forgotten tales. Then tell the tale as well to introduce others, of various backgrounds, to these story pieces of world heritage and to their neighbors.

9. **Extend the telling.** After the tales are told, consider other ways for the telling to continue (through drama, art, radio, on the computer, etc.). You can also pass these stories on by creating books, although there may be challenges of accuracy when moving into print. As I turned the proof sheets of one of my first books, *Judge Rabbit Helps the Fish*, I felt quite pleased until I came to the page where the kr'an fish bumps his way out of the water and begs Judge Rabbit to help. I squinted, then stared some more at the illustration. No, it was not a kr'an fish I saw; it was a crayfish. That was wrong, very wrong. The kr'an fish is a wonderful, well-known fish in Cambodia, one that can actually walk on land. The kr'an fish had to be in the story, not a crayfish with its claws. Luckily, the publisher was concerned and asked me for a picture of a kr'an fish so that the drawing could be corrected.

This proved very difficult. I ran from friend to friend in the Cambodian community and got a number of simple sketches of generic fishes, but not enough for the illustrator to work from. Pressure mounted as the illustrator demanded details that I didn't have. Then my new editor went home to relax one evening and reached for a mystery high on her shelves. Next to it was a garage-sale find she had long forgotten, *Tropical Fish of Southeast Asia*, complete with a double-page spread on the kr'an fish. So the ending was a happy one, with the right fish drawn and a lesson well learned: gather as many images and details as possible to help share a culture correctly.

Tiger and Judge Rabbit

A Cambodian folktale retold by Cathy Spagnoli*

One who can turn the tongue can turn the world.

— Khmer proverb

This proverb well describes the power of a main trickster character in Cambodia — Judge Rabbit. Judge Rabbit is a delightful charac-ter, a special favorite with children, who not only tricked other, larger animals and humans, but who also helped. This tale shows one of his favorite tricks against Tiger, a frequent character in Judge Rabbit tales. Other tales show the judge side of Judge Rabbit as he rescues humans and animals when they cannot find human justice.

Tiger was mad.
Judge Rabbit had tricked him once again.

Poor Tiger had hurt his tail because of that trick. So, with a face of rage, he raced after Rabbit to teach him a lesson.

"I'll get you, Rabbit," he roared as he ran through the forest. Rabbit ran and ran and ran, as quickly as he could. But he heard Tiger close behind.

"Tiger runs fast," thought Judge Rabbit. "So I'll have to think even faster."

Just then, Rabbit saw a bee's nest on a tree. He climbed quickly up and sat next to it. Carefully, he took a leaf, licked it, and used it to cover the tiny doorhole.

Angry bees were suddenly trapped inside the nest. They wanted to get out. They buzzed and buzzed very, very loudly. And the buzzing sound-ed like a special kind of drum.

Judge Rabbit pulled back his paw, then swung it almost to the nest. He pretended to hit the nest, but of course he was most careful not to. Back and forth his paw waved, as if beating a fine steady sound on a drum. Tiger came up and stood under the tree.

"I've got you now, Rabbit," he growled. "And I'm going to eat you up."

"Not now, Tiger," cried Rabbit. "Later you can eat me. Right now I'm too busy."

"Busy doing what?" asked Tiger as he watched Judge Rabbit, who seemed to be hitting something.

"I'm playing the drum for the heavenly dancers," he replied. "They love this music so they'll give me grand gifts."

Tiger listened. BZZZZ BZZZZ BZZZZ. It did sound quite nice, like a finely tuned drum. He didn't think about bees. He didn't recognize the bee's nest. He just thought about all the gifts Judge Rabbit was getting. So Tiger felt jealous.

"Rabbit, I want to play the drum and get gifts," he said.

"Sorry, Tiger," said Rabbit. "It's my turn."

"Please, Rabbit," pleaded Tiger. "Please let me play."

"But if you come up here, you'll eat me," Judge Rabbit replied.

"No, no, I promise I won't," said Tiger. "Let me play and I'll be your friend forever."

"Wellllll," said Rabbit.

"Pleeeeeease," begged Tiger.

"Oh, all right," said Judge Rabbit. "I'll go find another drum. You climb up here and watch me. When I jump up and down three times, hit that drum as hard as you can. Then you'll get your reward!"

"Akoon, akoon," said Tiger, thanking Rabbit again and again. Then Rabbit came down and started to run.

Tiger climbed up slowly and sat next to the drum. He watched and waited for Judge Rabbit's signal. At last he saw the three big jumps. With a grin, he gave the drum ONE HUGE HIT!

B Z Z Z Z Z Z Z Z Z
B Z Z Z Z Z Z Z Z Z Z Z Z
BZZZZZZZZZZZZ

The nest broke. Hundreds of furious bees raced out. Tiger jumped down and tried to run, but the bees followed right behind. Those angry bees chased him for a long, long time.

As for Rabbit, he was far, far away and quite safe. He wiggled his ears, munched his favorite cucumbers, and thought about poor Tiger, tricked again. 🐾

Cathy Spagnoli has published 14 books of Asian folktales and resource guides that may be useful in working with your community.

For elementary readers/listeners

- *Judge Rabbit and the Tree Spirit* (Children's Book Press, 1991). Popular Judge Rabbit outwits a ghost in this Cambodian folk tale.
- *Judge Rabbit Helps the Fish* (The Wright Group, 1995). Judge Rabbit uses his wits to save some small fish from big, hungry mouths.
- *Kantjil and Tiger* (The Wright Group, 1995). A tiny mousedeer outwits a powerful tiger in this humorous Indonesian tale.
- *Nine in One, Grr! Grr!* (Children's Book Press, 1989). ALA Notable Book. A Hmong tale, also available on CD-ROM from Macmillan/McGraw Hill.
- *Thao Kham, the Pebble Shooter* (The Wright Group, 1995). A lovely Lao tale of a boy with disabilities who discovers a special talent.

- *A Treasury of Asian Stories and Activities for Schools and Libraries* (Highsmith Press, 1998). Resource guide with ideas for pre-K through Grade 3.

For ages 12 and up

- *Asian Tales and Tellers* (August House, 1998). Wide new selection of tales and material on Asian tellers and telling.
- *Jasmine and Coconuts: South Indian Tales* (Libraries Unlimited, 1999). Introduction to a rich region, through stories, photos, and artwork.
- *Terrific Trickster Tales from Asia* (Highsmith Press, 2001). Twenty tales of Asian tricksters, with background notes, resources, and telling tips.

Credits: Putha Touch's life story used courtesy of August House, from *Asian Tales and Tellers*. Judge Rabbit story collected during several sessions with Cambodian women at Refugee Women's Alliance, Seattle, and used courtesy of Highsmith Press, from *Treasury of Asian Stories and Activities for Schools and Libraries*.

Growing Up in East Los Angeles: An Immigrant Story

Olga Loya

In many immigrant families there is a conscious decision not to speak the language of their native land with the children. The message the children can and often do get is that their own native language is "not good enough." As an extension of that belief, they may come to believe that their own culture is not good enough either.

Keeping one's family language and customs alive contributes to one's sense of self-worth and direction. A common theme in storytelling interventions is that it is important to know where you came from in order to understand where you are and where you want to go.

I come by my Spanish naturally, but not easily.
You see, I was in a family that wanted its children to "make it."
In our family, that meant that no adult spoke Spanish to the children.

Oh, all the grown-ups spoke Spanish to each other, but they never spoke it to us. Whenever I tried to say something in Spanish, they would say, "No, don't speak Spanish. You must speak English because this is your country and English is your language!" It wasn't because they were mean or wanted to deprive us of our culture. They wanted us to fit in! They wanted us to speak without an accent.

It didn't take much to convince me. When I was growing up in the 50s, if someone spoke Spanish in school, the teacher would scold, "No, speak English!" If they kept speaking Spanish, the teacher would send them to the office. I even saw some kids get hit on the hands for speaking Spanish. All the other kids would make fun of the kids who spoke Spanish. I thought to myself, "Hey, no way am I speaking Spanish, it's too dangerous!"

We grew up in East Los Angeles, California. People called this part of the city "Little Mexico" because there were so many Mexicans living there. We children were growing up in the middle of a Spanish-speaking population, being raised by Mexican families that were making every effort *not* to speak Spanish to us. The message was very clear — speak English, not Spanish; be American, not Mexican.

Fortunately for me, I had two grandmothers and one grandfather who only spoke Spanish.

My two grandmothers talked all the time. My grandfather didn't talk much in Spanish and he couldn't speak English. All my aunts and my grandmother would be talking and talking and my grandfather would quietly go out and work in his garden. My grandmothers didn't speak much English. My maternal grandmother could only say "sheet" and "son of a beech." My paternal grandmother could say "hello" and "sheet."

I was madly and wildly in love with my paternal grandmother, Grandma Loya. She was about five feet tall and would always dress in those shiny dark garbardine dresses with buttons in the front. She wore old-lady shoes with the little heels and she always wore her long gray hair back in a *moño* (bun). She was very small-boned and fragile-looking. She had high cheekbones and deep-set brown eyes with thick black eyebrows. She was gentle and kind and she ran the family with an iron fist.

She would call my father and say, "*¿Sandy, puedes venir a cortar el zacate?* (Can you come and cut the grass?)" No matter what my father was doing he would say, "*Si, mama,* I will go this Saturday and work on the garden." He would be there that next Satuday even if the grass was up to our knees at our place. When she said to do something, all the grown-ups jumped to do whatever she wanted. I could never figure out how she made them move so fast. Oh, I knew why I did things for her. I wanted to please her. I loved her because she was kind and gentle. I especially loved her because she never scolded me about being too rough and being a tomboy. Everyone else was always after me.

My mother always said, "Why can't you stay clean? You are always so messy!" My aunts said, "*Ay, niña,* why do you have to run around so much?" My *abuelita,* grandmother, liked me the way I was. I'd arrive at her house all dusty and dirty and she would just laugh and say, "*Mijita quieres una taza de cafe?* (My little one, would you like a cup of coffee?)" She was the only one who ever gave me coffee. She would give me a cup with a little bit of coffee and lots of milk. Then I would sit down with her and she would ask me about my day.

When my family asked me what I had done that day, I would usually answer, "*Nada.* (Nothing.)"

My *abuelita* would say, "*Olgita, pues qué hiciste hoy?* (Little Olga, what did you do today?)"

"Oh, *abuelita,* I played dodge ball with my friends."

She'd say, "Who is your best friend, Olgita."

"My best friend today is Lola. We played together all day."

"What are you studying?" she'd ask.

"We are studying our letters. I can write your name." Then I would write her name "Grandma Lòya." I would tell her every detail of the day. Then she would tell me what she had been doing that day. She went every day to the *mercado* to visit with her friends. I loved to hear about Lola, Maria, and Lupe.

I spent as much time as I could with her. I ran over to her house after school, and if we got baby-sat, it had to be my Grandma Loya or no one. I never spoke Spanish anywhere else except when I was with my Grandma Loya. I would go and sit with her. She would put her arm around me and she would tell me stories. Sometimes she would say things like, "*No debes de salir con tu cabello mojado.* (You shouldn't go out with your hair wet.)" Somehow it never dawned on my parents or me that when I was with my *Abuelita* Loya, I was speaking Spanish. As far as I could tell, I was speaking Grandma-talk. I understood everything she said and I could talk with her quite easily.

My *abuelita* died when I was 12 years old. It was as though my Spanish died with her. From the age of 12 to 19, I almost never spoke Spanish. If I did speak at all it was *poco*, you know, "*Cóhmo aysta ustaaad?*" I would run into the *ancianos*, old ones, and they would say, "*¿Por qué no hablas español, qué no eres Mejicana?* (Why don't you speak Spanish; aren't you Mexican?)" I would feel soooo embarrassed. Oh, I knew I was able to understand Spanish, but I was absolutely sure I could not speak it!

I graduated from high school and went to the local college. In my last year of college, I decided to take a Spanish class. Around the middle of the semester the teacher came over to me and said, "I thought you said you couldn't speak Spanish."

I said, "I can't."

She said, "Well, why do you always answer correctly?"

I thought about it for a while and finally I said, "I don't know. When I speak Spanish, it just sounds right!" Suddenly I remembered those cartoons where a light bulb goes up over the person's head and she has a realization or idea. I realized I *did* know Spanish. I had all the Spanish locked up in my head. I knew I wanted to find the *llave*, the key, to open up all the Spanish inside me.

Not long after, I graduated and moved to Northern California. For the first time in my life I was not working full time. I decided to go to junior college to take Spanish grammar because I wanted to know how the words went together. It was like an explosion in my mind. I would be walking along and suddenly a word would pop into my mind like *madrugada* (dawn) or *rompecabeza* (puzzle). Soon I was dreaming in Spanish. One day I woke up and thought, "Hey, I am going to go home and talk Spanish with my family."

The next time I was visiting in Los Angeles, I walked into my family house and said, "Hey,

guess what! I can speak Spanish. Let's talk Spanish." My mother and father gave me that fish-eyed look that families can give to their children so well. We had the weirdest, most stilted conversation I had ever had. I went back home and tried to decide what had gone wrong. I finally figured it out. I couldn't talk about speaking Spanish. I just had to do it.

When I went to Los Angeles again, I walked into the house and said to my father, "*Hola, papa, cómo estás?* (Hello, father, how are you?)"

He looked up, and without blinking an eye he said, "*Muy bien, mija, y tú?* (Fine, my daughter, and you?)" Ever since that time, we always spoke Spanish rather than English when we got together.

Unfortunately, my younger brother and cousins don't speak Spanish because they missed out on the *abuelitos*. They all can understand Spanish, but they don't speak it. My older cousin Eddie can speak it, though, because he was very close to our maternal grandmother, Grandma Goya. He discovered he could speak Spanish when he was in the Air Force, hanging around with Cubanos. One Christmas I was down to East Los Angeles from Northern California and he was home on furlough.

I said, "*Hola, Eddie, cómo estás?* (Hi, Eddie, how are you?)"

Eddie's eyes got real big and then he said, "*Muy bien, Olga.* (Fine Olga.) I didn't know you could speak Spanish."

"*Sí*, I can speak Spanish. Why don't we speak Spanish tonight?" The next few hours we delighted in our new/old language. The rest of the family looked at us, shaking their heads. There we were being different again. Except this time we were speaking Spanish.

For the last 15 years I have been working as a professional storyteller. One of my specialties is bilingual storytelling. Because I am paying so much more attention to language, I have made some discoveries. It's very easy for me to go from Spanish to English and English to Spanish because where I grew up, people said things like "*vamos a la* house" or "let's go to the *casa*." I also found out that my family failed completely as far as accents go. Not only do I have an accent when I speak English, I also have an accent when I speak Spanish!

I am very happy to be speaking Spanish again and telling stories from my life and *familia* and from the *folklorico* of Latino America. It all feels like an adventure to me, as if I am traveling through my *cultura* and my Spanish language, and it's a road that I want to travel for a long, long time. 🐾

Many times when I write a story, I will have trusted friends listen to the story and provide feedback. The first time I told this story to a friend, I read it to her with my back to her. I was new at all of this and it embarrassed me to be reading the story. I finished it and turned to her. She had her head in her hands and was shaking her head back and forth and saying, "No, no." I thought, "Geez, it wasn't that bad!" I leaned over and heard her saying, "No, no, the same thing happened to me with Yiddish."

I have discovered this is an immigrant's story. When I perform this story, I have people from many different cultures come to me and tell me their stories of the grandmothers they had or the grandmothers they did not have and the language they did not learn. I always encourage everyone to speak their native language as well as English so they don't have to find their language late, like I did. When I wrote this story, I was describing my experience, but when I began to tell it, I came to realize that the story is more than just my experience.

Tales from the heart and spirit

JOSEPH NAYTOWHOW AND CHERYL L'HIRONDELLE WAYNOHTÊW

THE GOAL OF THE Meadow Lake Tribal Council of Saskatchewan is to strengthen its members' health and self-reliance by ensuring a balance of the spiritual, physical, and emotional well-being among the nine communities of the Meadow Lake First Nation. In keeping with this goal, the Office of Education of the Tribal Council created a storyteller-in-residence position in the fall of 1995. Joseph Naytowhow, a Cree speaker, singer, and storyteller from Sturgeon Lake First Nation of Saskatchewan, became the first storyteller-in-residence.

The storyteller's half-time position was divided between going to Meadow Lake First Nation (MLFN) schools to tell stories to students, and visiting with elders recommended by principals, teachers, Meadow Lake Tribal Council Elder's Helper, and other community members. The initial reason for visiting the elders was to find people interested in accompanying Joseph during these school visits to tell their own stories.

On Joseph's first visits he found several elders reluctant to go to schools due to previous unhappy visits where they found the classroom setting disheartening and the children inattentive. Equally distressing at the time was the high ratio of Cree and Dene youth in these classrooms who did not speak their native language. The elders were still interested in having students hear the stories and, they hoped, be influenced by the values their life experiences exemplified. The next step then became to collect stories that Joseph would tell to the youth on behalf of the elders. In northwest Saskatchewan, outside of the nine Meadow Lake First Nation communities, there are many Métis (mixed blood) and people in townships who are in some way related to tribal members.

In this area, First Nation elders are well-versed in several languages due to pre-treaty trapping, hunting, and travel routes. Hence, Joseph was able to interact with Cree and Dene elders in either Cree or English. Many elders preferred oral transmission of the story instead of being audio- or videotaped, so Joseph would visit an elder and then return home to immediately begin the process of transcribing the visit from memory. The transcriptions were edited by Cheryl L'Hirondelle Waynohtêw, a Métis/Cree interdisciplinary artist and storyteller, who changed Cree and Dene sentence structure to an English format and worked with Joseph to ensure the original intent of each thought was not lost or misunderstood.

After four years of school and elder visits, with several thousand kilometers traveled, many stories were gathered and edited. Each story has been given a moral value based on what the underlying message of the story appears to be. Normally, if an elder shared a story directly, the individual hearing the story would analyze it for his or her own specific need, whether it was for an emotional, spiritual, physical, or mental difficulty one was experiencing on the journey through life at the time.

But for the purposes of a bimonthly newsletter distributed to 500 teachers in northwestern Saskatchewan (as well as for a newly created website), Cheryl began to recognize patterns, seeing that each story represented a particular moral value that could be imparted by teachers in the classroom setting, adding it into their regular activities and curriculum when appropriate.

Moral values were presented as 15 poles of a teepee, a model originally put forth by the family of the late Mr. Smith Atimoyoo, an esteemed elder of Little Pine First Nation, Saskatchewan. In the 1970s, Smith, who was working with what was then the Saskatchewan Indian Cultural College, brought together elders from the five Nations in Saskatchewan — Dene, Cree, Saulteaux, Dakota, and Nakota — to discuss the idea. As a result, the teepee concept was endorsed by these elders, to be introduced into First Nation schools throughout Saskatchewan.

The 15 poles of the teepee represent the following values:

- **Obedience:** Learning by listening to know what is right or wrong
- **Respect:** Honoring each other's basic rights
- **Humility:** Understanding our relationship with the Creator and creation
- **Happiness:** Acting happy makes our ancestors happy in the next world
- **Love:** Living in harmony, with kindness and goodness
- **Faith:** Believing in a power greater than ourselves
- **Kinship:** The roots that tie us to the lifeblood of the earth
- **Cleanliness:** Good health habits reflecting a clean mind

- **Thankfulness:** Giving thanks for others' kindness and the Creator's gifts
- **Sharing:** Providing for each other
- **Strength:** Accepting difficulties and tragedies and having patience to endure
- **Good child rearing:** Recognizing that children are unique and blessed with the gift of life
- **Hope:** Hoping for better things to make life easier for us
- **Ultimate Protection:** Taking ultimate responsibility to achieve healthy balance of body, mind, emotions, and spirit
- **Control Flaps:** Acknowledging the connection of all things that controls and creates harmony in our lives

The stories in the collection match each value. In addition, a few different titles/values have been added, such as "Nêhiyâwin: The Cree Way," that help emphasize the importance of our heritage and language. It is also recognized that facets from each story themselves represent each value, making the story a complete set of values in itself

On the website is a short biography of each elder with a photograph, and information about the nine Meadow Lake First Nation communities they represent. There are also short commentaries that either set the scene for when the story was gathered or give additional information about the elder and his or her relationship with the storyteller-in-residence.

Each story is written in English and in the language of the contributor, either Cree or Dene. Cree is one of 14 languages that make up the Algonkian family. Some of the other Algonkian languages are Blackfoot, Saulteaux Ojibway, Odawa, and Micmac. Cree settlements and reservations are scattered throughout Canada from Quebec to the foothills of the Rocky Mountains. A few settlements in northern British Columbia also speak Cree. Dene is one of numerous Athapaskan family languages in North America. Within the Dene Nation there is: Slavey, Dogrib, Loucheaux, Gwichin, Navajo, Apache, Chipewyan tribes of Saskatchewan and Alberta, as well as possibly some tribes in Siberia and South America. Dene settlements are scattered throughout Canada from Saskatchewan into the Northwest Territories and into northern Alberta and Manitoba.

Stories bring us back home to ourselves

About Joseph Naytowhow: Listening to stories happened to me one day as my inner voice, the innermost part of my being, cried out for someone to fill a void I was feeling. It was Winter 1976. A very strong yearning to find out who I was, to discover what it meant to be Cree, emerged as I was taking a course at the University of Regina in Saskatchewan. I met a resident Cree elder from the Saskatchewan Indian Federated College in Regina who sparked my interest and desire to know what it meant to be of Cree heritage. In grassroots terms, at that time I was an "apple" Indian: red on the outside and white on the inside, a Cree Indian without language, culture, or history.

I spent hours with the elder, Mr. Mosquito, as he spoke to me in English and Cree. He was very polite. After all, my Cree was at the level of a two- or three-year-old Cree child who has been raised strictly within the Cree tradition, and I am probably bragging at that. The storyteller within was being fed by this wise old man. He would talk and I would skip classes just to listen to him. Since that time, I met elder after elder from various language and cultural backgrounds. They would share stories and rituals willingly when I presented them with an offering of tobacco and gifts. Slowly, without really knowing it, I was being prepared to be a storyteller.

On becoming a storyteller, I quickly learned the importance of visiting elders, attending ceremonies and cultural camps. All of these activities fed into the pot of ingredients needed to tell a good story. One Cree elder said to me one day, "You know the way of the white people. It is up to you to inform them about our traditions, the Cree way of seeing, knowing, and living."

About Cheryl L'Hirondelle Waynohtêw: I wasn't born into, nor did I ever live in, a traditional cultural Cree community until recently. I also grew up without the presence and influence of grandparents. However, I am from a large mixed-blood (Métis — Cree, French, and German) family where storytelling and making music was a daily event.

From 1983 to 1993 I was actively involved in the performance art scene in Calgary, Alberta. I was trying to say something — something intelligent, something true — but I couldn't find the words. I also sang with a few musical groups, but was never satisfied with what I was singing. It didn't express who I was, and I wasn't pushed to any insights about my existence nor about making any real connections to the contemporary human experience of being mixed blood, female, and urban.

I then moved to acting and was fortunate to co-write a play and have it produced on a Calgary stage. I was writing and performing poetry at this time, and making some of my first songs. There was still something I couldn't articulate — something I didn't know, couldn't quite grasp — and it was very frustrating.

Now here I am a few years later, and somehow I've managed to get myself invited into the homes of Cree and Dene elders in northwest Saskatchewan. And I'm re-telling some of these wonderful stories offered to me with others: youth in schools, at conferences and festivals, and, importantly, to my own family back in Alberta. For the past seven years I've been singing traditional and hybrid songs, and I am hearing the sounds so long submerged within my being. I'm also learning Cree, and I am realizing that my inability to articulate, to say something, was directly linked to my lack of understanding and insight into my language and worldview.

This is why I think these stories are so important for communities and youth. They come from the experience of those who live on the land, who speak, eat, breathe, hunt, and dream a worldview that is so undervalued in this pop-motivated world. These stories provide so many layers of understanding of who we are, where we come from, and how to proceed to ensure our distinctive position as original people of the earth.

Tapahtêyimowin: Humility

AS TOLD BY PHILOMENE CORRIGAL*
OF THE CANOE LAKE FIRST NATION (CREE)

The following story is about respecting the laws of nature. It is also about proper conduct. The pelican is one of nature's most beautiful and majestic creatures. The wind spirit is the pelican's ally and a mighty wrathful force at that.

The story I am about to tell you happened one time when I, my mother, and other family members had been out on a hunting trip. The hunt was successful. It happened by a lake where many tree-lined islands could be seen.

We were on our way home when we caught sight of some pelicans. This was one of their favorite locations in the area. At the edge of the island where the pelicans had gathered, it was well packed down from use by other animals and birds. The beautiful birds were easily visible as they were silhouetted against the dark green background of the island's tree line. Without really thinking about what he was doing, my uncle began to shoot at them. Being an excellent marksman, he easily hit five of the pelicans, killing them instantly.

Surprised by my uncle's actions, my mother turned to him and using a firm voice, told him that he had tampered with the law of nature. Needlessly killing pelicans, she said, would bring the wind to answer this desecration.

Later that afternoon, we could see the clouds gathering in the distance to the west. By the time evening arrived and we were on our way home, the wind really began to blow. At one point, a window of a nearby cabin was blown right out of its casing. Standing trees were blown over by the force of the wind, spread over the ground like a roughly woven blanket. This intense wind also brought rain.

We rushed into the house and began to board up the windows with canvas frames. Rain pelted against the house and seeped in under the door. During the night, after we had already gone to bed, my father had to leap from his bed to grab a white canvas board so he could nail it quickly against another window blown apart by the continuing fury of the wind. We all awoke to help my father brace the other windows with yet more canvas frames.

When morning arrived, the whole area adjacent to our cabin was covered with a thick blanket of grass, sticks, leaves, and branches.

That was how strong the wind blew. 🐾

159

Beghąnuwétą HHéø Bets'édie: Love and Support

AS TOLD BY GABRIEL LARIVIERE*
OF THE ENGLISH RIVER FIRST NATION (DENE)

This story is about survival, compassion, and harmonious coexistence with the natural world. Hearing a story of this type, where a man is able to communicate with a bear, shows people that we are capable of interacting with the world around us, and that it is inseparable from us. We are shown, through the spirit of a four-legged being's acceptance, that gifts are available to us as long as we are open to receive them. Lastly, we are shown that gifts given to us must be valued and shared with others who will respect and honor them.

No part of this story about a man cared for by a bear is untrue.
It really happened.

In this story, a man had gotten lost.

He must have searched and searched for his way back home, but no matter how hard he tried, he always saw the same misleading landmarks. He was definitely lost. So after finding a bear's den, this man decided to rest for the night.

The bear who the den belonged to eventually returned from foraging. According to the way this story is told, bears and humans could talk and understand each other, although it was on a higher level than plain speech. So this bear took pity on the lost man and cared for him. The bear told him that he would need to live off the bear in the future and then proceeded to teach him all about bear nature. The bear also reassured the man that he would never go hungry. This was the bear's gift to the man.

When winter set in, both the bear and the man went into hibernation. While inside the den, the bear continued to teach the man. When the man got thirsty, the bear instructed the man to lean forward and drink in fresh, cool water where a river flowed from between the bear's legs. From this same river the man received enough minerals to keep his body strong and healthy throughout the long cold winter.

When it reached midnight of the winter sleep, the bear turned over to its other side. The man did the same. In the spring, which to the bear's world is really the next morning after a long, long night's sleep, the bear awoke and said to the man, "I'm getting tired of your relatives worrying about you. It's time for you to go home now." The man agreed. He also sensed his family was missing him terribly.

The bear told the man to extend his hand outside the den to check if any snow remained. Amazingly, it had all melted. It was spring. The bear guided the man back to his village. Arriving at the edge of the village, the bear departed.

The following winter this same man went hunting — for bear. He was not successful on the first hunt. On the second hunt, the memories of what the bear had taught him returned, and this time he watched for signs of warm breath escaping hidden dens along hillsides; its contact with the cold winter air formed a misty cloud. From that day on, every time he went hunting he was successful.

The other hunters from the village quickly recognized this man's ability to hunt bears. They became jealous and told him that it was not the Creator's will for him to have such luck all to himself. Although the man tried to explain the gift of hunting bears was only meant for him, the hunters kept harassing him. Finally he gave in. The man knew he had betrayed the bear who had cared for him, and all for a moment of weakness. This feeling of betrayal saddened him deeply. He vowed never to tell another person after that. 🐾

Edenílʔa: Self-Reliance

AS TOLD BY MRS. VERONICA TOBAC*
OF THE BIRCH NARROWS DENE NATION

This story has several delightful moments in the free-flowing manner in which it is told. To generalize and say it is a "feel good" story is to trivialize these moments in our lives when life is showing us the true nature of our existence as loving, happy, and sharing beings. The Self-Reliance tale presents an opportunity to learn from longstanding survival-based traditions of fishing, hunting, and gathering how to appreciate life at its fullest. As we read about the interaction between adults, and between children, we can see the definite roles each had within the community. There is no question as to who takes care of whom, when it is appropriate to have a good time, and when it is time to be responsible.

My story goes back to a time when my friends, relatives, and I lived at Clear Lake. I was just a girl at the time and attended the Beauval Indian Residential School.

We stayed at school for ten months, and by springtime we were anxious to go home. Our parents would come to pick us up in Buffalo Narrows and take us home by boat. Then, when we got back to Clear Lake, everybody was getting ready to go on a fishing trip that would last for the whole summer.

Everyone would be busy helping one another getting things ready, like making dried fish and smoked meat and, in the evenings, mending tents. The teenage girls would look after the children. We would take them all over with us, keeping them playing so we wouldn't be in the way of our parents. People would be rushing from one person's place to another, lending each other stuff needed to prepare for the journey. If somebody was short of paint for their boat, they would go and find somebody who had some, so their boat would be ready.

There was a big fishing boat that came from Buffalo Narrows. There was a barge already tied to the fishing boat with the Hudson's Bay store on it. They'd have supplies on board to sell. The old guy's name was Magloire Morin and his wife was Alexie Morin — they were the ones that used to look after the store.

Everybody would tie their boats behind the barge, one after another, if they didn't have a motor. Anyone with boat motors would travel alongside the barge and fishing boat until we'd get to the first camp where the men were going to start fishing. On the way, people would get hungry. If we couldn't stop, people would share food, and if somebody didn't have any, they'd just pass food from one boat to the other, sharing with the kids and everyone. It was like one big family traveling together. People enjoyed themselves. I remember it was a very good time because I was part of a big family. It made me feel good because I knew at the time, I had seen my future. I would

never be alone. I had the feeling there would always be somebody there, whenever I needed help.

When we got to the fishing camp, people helped, even if it was late at night. The young boys would help the elders pitch their tents. Then everything would settle down. The next day when we woke up it looked like a big fishing camp. There were tents all over. In the morning, people would be laughing, chopping wood, and getting breakfast ready. You could smell bacon, eggs, and whatever people had to cook. You could hear the kids laughing and babies crying. It was a good sound in the morning and a really good feeling that I grew up with. This good feeling kept up from one place to another, all summer long.

The first fishing camp was at a place we called Matsins Island. From there we'd go sometimes to Jackpine and then to a place with the flat stone, where we'd then end up at the rapids. We would go through the rapids to come to Turnor Lake, and then from there people also used to fish at Wasakemew, Turnor, and Little Turnor Lake. They used to take the fish down the rapids. There was lots of fish and we got a good price for it, too.

All summer long people would hunt and fish. The women made dried fish. Kids did our own thing, like enjoying helping out with wood, hauling water, and washing clothes. We made our own games. We made swings. We went swimming and played ball. We even made balls out of moose hide. We'd stuff the moose hide with rags and grass, pack it really good, and sew it up. Then we made bats and played ball. We did everything. We also made tents. But the best part of it was everybody enjoyed themselves all summer long.

People enjoyed what they were doing, and when one person was making moose hide, others helped out. When people saw someone having a difficult time, they helped out, and if a moose was killed and somebody went and asked for meat, they'd give meat to that person. Even when you went to visit a woman who had dried meat or dried fish hanging up on a rack, you'd just help yourself and nobody never said anything about it, never gave it a second thought. That was the way life was in those days.

In those days, we worked to get the things we needed. If we needed something, we'd ask the person who had it. They'd make us haul water, haul wood, or even help with laundry. It was fun for us, even washing clothes. We young girls would have competitions to see who would wash their clothes the fastest, who would haul and warm the water first and put the clothes on the clothesline. When it was time to cook bannock, we would see who could make the best bannock and find different ways to cook it quickly.

Yes, we did all sorts of things. We tried all sorts of ways to see who was good at doing things. Even when we made camp, we would see who could haul the biggest bag of spruce boughs. We'd laugh at one another because a lot of times the younger ones would try and com-

pete with us, and they would have a hard time. And we would climb trees. We would even have competitions with boys, and we'd play-fight with spruce cones. The boys would try to chase us away. We just kept on fighting them. We would make bows and arrows and slingshots. Yes, it was lots of fun.

People had a hard time making a living, but nobody ever had hard feelings about it. Nobody took time to be miserable. They just did what they had to — to make the best of everything. If the older adults were telling stories they didn't want us to hear, they would tell us to go and play or do something. Today, there are so many things said in front of kids, and they take it all in. Kids get all that anger within themselves, and that's what they grow up with. In those days we never grew up that way. The older people took care of things and kids weren't involved. That is why, as young children, we learned to have more fun. We enjoyed nature. I remember going out sometimes with just a blanket. I would go along the shore to find a good spot, a beautiful spot where I could lie back and listen to the birds or look at clouds. It was so amazing for me. I was only about 10 or 11 years old at the time. ❧

Nêhiyâwin: The Cree Way

AS TOLD BY HARRY BLACKBIRD*
OF THE MAKWA SAHGAIEHCAN FIRST NATION (CREE)

The following story deals with the spirit world and our relationship with that world. In the dream, the boy meets an "Oskapêwis," one who passes on traditional knowledge. This word translates as "helper" and is also used to describe the relationship between teacher and student.

Some other Cree words used in the story are: Nêhiyawêwin, meaning Cree Language; Nêhiyawak, Cree people; Nêhiyâwin, Cree worldview.

> *One day while sleeping, an elderly man was awakened by his deceased wife, who had died six years earlier. She came in spirit form.*

The elderly man had mixed feelings about this visit, but nevertheless managed to remain calm and sat up, curious, wondering why she had come to visit him.

She began to speak, "Listen very carefully...I have been sent by the Creator to tell you about a boy who passed away recently.

"Upon entering the spirit world he was greeted by an Oskapêwis, who led the young man down an easy road to follow. At a certain point, the road forked, going in two directions. They first traveled down the road to the right. This road was also easy to follow. After walking for some time, they came to a village. A number of young people about the same age as the youth came running towards him. The group of young people stopped to observe the new boy who'd been brought to them by the Oskapêwis.

"The young people then began to speak in the language of his ancestry — Nêhiyawêwin. Unfortunately, the young man could not make out what they were saying, even though he was of the same nation, Nêhiyâwin. He even had the two long braids of hair, common trademarks for Nêhiyawak who were following the Nêhiyâwin way. Confused and feeling lost, the young man was quickly whisked away by the Oskapêwis towards the other road at the fork.

"This new road was also easy to follow. They came upon a cluster of houses, and another group of young people came towards him. Only this time these youth kept their distance, with disappointment written all over their faces upon viewing his aboriginal features. Listening to their conversation as they whispered among themselves, the young man could only make out a few words.

"He was able to understand these youth because they spoke English, but their behavior showed they obviously weren't interested in this new boy. He felt betrayed, alone, and wondered why he didn't fit in.

"The Oskapêwis once again whisked him away, and this time left the young man at the fork of the road. His spirit is lost and wandering now because while he was alive, he hadn't learned to find his way.

"Now, my husband," the deceased wife's spirit added just before she vanished, "it is up to you to make certain that young Indian children are told this story I have been sent here to tell you."

The idea of including storytellers within the Office of Education of the Meadow Lake Tribal Council demonstrates that storytelling is still very much a part of our social, psychological, and cultural makeup as a people. Our heritage and language need to be respected and learned. It is our deep hope that through gathering and sharing the stories of our Cree and Dene elders, the First Nation worldview will be preserved among our people and understood by others who wish to know and understand us. It is important that our youth learn of the past their ancestors have shared in order to walk into the future supported by this knowledge — this is their birthright. The vision of the Meadow Lake Tribal Council — the shared vision of healthy people, families, and communities — continues to guide what we do and also serves as a constant reminder that much work still remains.

Visit the website "Dene/Cree ElderSpeak: Tales From the Heart and Spirit" (www.aboriginalcollections.ic.gc.ca/tales/About.htm). ❧

PROTECTING OUR ENVIRONMENT

Storytelling nature:
Story speaking and listening in the information age

Susan Strauss

I HAVE OBSERVED THE degeneration of a skill that I believe is essential to healing the rift between human society and the natural world — namely, the art of listening. Listening is at the core of the storytelling art and is essential to all perception. Deep listening can help us avoid the extensive pain and suffering that are often by-products of limited perception. The fast-driven pace of modern life plus the lure of television and computers are greatly responsible for the degeneration of listening. The victims will first be the natural world and then ourselves. In *The Passionate Fact* I wrote that if a storyteller does nothing more than create an atmosphere of listening for an audience, he or she has helped the earth. Now I will add that if we don't become practitioners and models of deep listening, there will not be any soil in which to plant our stories. Here is a story about a storytelling experience to illustrate some of what I mean.

Once I was in a rural California school giving a performance of my program "The Bird's Tale." This is a collection of myths and fairytales that focus on the bird as a symbol. As a preparation for the myths, I tried to elicit qualities that the children in my audience would associate with bird life, such as freedom, grace, or fragility. At one point, I asked, "When you see a bird soaring in the wind, how does it make you feel?" A devilish look streamed into the eyes of a boy in the front row. He shouted out, "Like shooting it!"

I felt in that moment that he was judging me as some gentle nature lover he had learned to despise. He seemed to take special delight in the prospect of upsetting me with his comment. I was taken aback, but consciously did not show it. I said, "Hmm, yes, shoot it …. Hmm … yes, kill it. Well, I suppose it's so beautiful up there flying around that you'd want to pull it down … have it in your hand … something that is so out of our reach."

I don't think the boy knew what to make of my response; he was somewhat stunned. I realized at that moment I would begin with the story I usually couch in the middle of the program because of its tragic weight. This was the perfect story for one who would kill a creature, alive and beautiful, as easily as opening a soda pop can — or at least one who wanted someone to believe he would. So I told him "The Hundredth Dove."

This old English fairytale is about a gentle fowler who is commissioned by the king to capture one hundred doves for the royal wedding feast. The king is marrying an extremely beautiful woman whose manner and appearance resemble a dove. When the fowler meets the prospective queen, he is so taken by her soft beauty that he trembles as he reaches to kiss her hand in respect.

The fowler is determined to be a good servant to the king and manages to capture a few doves each day in the meadow. But each day, one white dove slips from his net. This doesn't disturb him until he discovers that this white dove is the last of the flock and the hundredth dove. Finally, he manages to grasp the dove as she slips from his net. He holds her in his hand and she speaks. She begs the fowler for her freedom in exchange for all sorts of treasures. None shake the fowler's profound sense of duty to the king. Then the dove offers the love of the queen. In a desperate confusion between duty and love, the fowler breaks the dove's neck.

The next day he returns to the castle with the one hundred doves, ninety nine in a cage and the limp white one in his hand. He discovers that the wedding has been canceled because the queen has mysteriously disappeared. Knowing his part in this, the fowler gives up his service to the king and lives out his life in sorrowful solitude.

The brash boy in the front row sat with eyes as deep as a dove's throughout the telling of this story. In his eyes, I saw something of transformation. Who knows what might have been going on in his mind, but he sat in perfect stillness for the rest of the performance, just as he had for "The Hundredth Dove." 🕊

It was out of a deep listening to that boy that I happened to find, in the moment, the best way to receive his "speak" and respond to him by choosing a story that would serve. In the Jewish Hasidic tradition, "storytelling" is not a performance. It is a kind of feeding. Often a story is told from one Hasid to another in a moment when the one hears that his or her friend needs the story. In this audience of one, the story is born out of a listened-for need, not out of scheduled program or entertainment. Here is another important illustrative story.

Once I was at a public hearing that would set regulations on land use within a quarter-mile range of sensitive bird species, including golden eagle nesting sites. The room was filled with angry landowners who didn't want "some bird" regulating when they could run a chain saw or build a new barn. Several government biologists and Audubon Society folks testified about the massive decline of these bird populations since the 1960s. They spoke about data and government mandates to protect species before they became eligible for the Endangered Species list. Nothing seemed to move these irate landowners from their conviction that this was a government "taking" and that they should be able to do whatever they wanted to do, whenever they wanted to do it, on *their* land.

Then naturalist Jim Anderson spoke. He spoke in rhythms and pictures. "If there's an 'X' signifying a nest on your property map, I guess you can be angry with me because I'm the one who put it there. I've been studying the eagles of central Oregon for more than 40 years, and I've seen how they're disappearing. What I'm trying to tell you is that you don't know how lucky you are to have a nest on your land. Those eagles out at Smith Rocks have been there for about 30 years ... and so have those eagles that nest over near your place, John. There used to be a nest out at Pine Mountain. It's gone. There used to be a nest out on the upper canyon. It's gone. Two men shot the adults. There used to be a nest out on ..." By the time Jim was on his third "There used to be a nest," the pioneer-faced elderly lady in the second to last row stopped making her snide comments and joined the stillness that was spreading across the room. 🕊

In the heat of the hearing, Jim was deeply listening, and out of that listening he found the "dark heart" of ignorance and fear. He was willing to go and stand in that "dark heart" with his first statement, "If there's an 'X' on your map, I'm the one who put it there." When he essentially said to the angry crowd "You can get angry with me," everything became personal. It wasn't the big, bad, removed government anymore; it was Jim. Jim's story is a clear example illustrating one of my two primary truths about storytelling natural history — *story creates relationship*.

Jim continued creating relationship between the audience and the subject by telling the personal story of each eagle. Jim's speaking was a perfect example of what I like to call "storytelling speak." There was no narrative line, but there was rhythm and detailed pictures. What had been "some bird," all at once became a specific bird with a name for its home and a life story. By personifying the information, he enacted my second truth about storytelling natural history — he *transformed the information into image*. While both

the Bureau of Land Management biologist and the speakers from Audubon spoke in terms of statistics and abstract concepts (such as ecology, biodiversity, endangered species, Class 2 species, etc.), Jim spoke in pictures ("That eagle that used to nest near your house, Bob, hasn't come back").

We need to become elegant and sophisticated in our skill of personification or telling "the peoples' story" if we hope to educate human beings who are able to listen to nature's tale. One can begin imagining how to tell natural fact as story by imagining the various beings of the natural world as various "peoples." This concept first came into my experience through my work with Native American mythology and culture. It is a way of seeing the world that can be found among the indigenous cultures of many lands. One merely thinks of the various creatures as a separate tribe or people with a different culture, just as we think of the French being different from Americans, Arabs, or Japanese. All are respected as sovereign peoples with their own particular lifestyles and language. Thus, the story begins:

Bottle Brush Squirrel Tail Grass People know how to survive in the desert. Well, they've lived here much longer than we have. So you can figure that they've gotten their act together. You see, they live in one bunch so they can trap and hold water in their communal root system. They don't miss a drop of opportunity to conserve water. You can see it even in their dress. That fur on their leaves gathers and holds every drop. As natives to the desert, water conservation runs deep in their traditional way of life.

This way of speaking about non-human creatures does not anthropomorphize them. They are not living in brick houses like the Three Little Pigs. They retain their natural ways. Only our way of speaking about them has changed, and thus our way of seeing them has changed. As "a people," they are seen as unique beings with varied and fascinating ways of interacting with the world.

Just as our constructs of reality are broadened and enriched when we learn about the ways different cultures think about time, perform courtship, educate their children, or care for their elders, so we will be broadened by learning about the various beings of our landscape. In human culture, a dead person may be referred to as a corpse; in the communities of Ancient Forest Peoples, a dead Tree Person is a "nurse log." It has not left its community, but lives on into the next generation, which it feeds. Is it not equally true that elderly humans are rich with experience with which they can feed a younger generation? Is the judgment that an ancient forest is "degenerative" (timber industry term) because the trees grow slowly an accurate description of an ecosystem that supports a rich variety of life, or is it the projection of an impatient and impulsive culture that does not appreciate the virtues of age? The cultural point of view of the person telling the story can change the science. We must take time to reflect on how we are reading the book of nature. What wisdom might we lose in translation because of our human point of view?

Stories excite our imagining of place. In 1979 I moved out west from Virginia to work for a traveling outdoor school — a sort of academic version of Outward Bound — called the High Country School. The administration, maintenance crew, kitchen staff, and teaching staff consisted of three teachers and me. We were teachers of geology, history, natural history, and language arts. When our bus, loaded with students, library, and camping gear, barreled over the mountains into the deserts of eastern Oregon and Idaho, the staff became suddenly ecstatic about landscapes that to my Virginia eyes seemed barren and dull. When I had traveled days to sit at the shorelines of what was once a great prehistoric inland lake that helped the Spokane flood carve a good portion of the Northwest, or looked out to the horizon and imagined strangers coming into my homeland in trains of heavy wagons like a foreign army of invading tanks, or pictured a time when there were so many salmon in the Columbia River that I could walk across the river on their backs, I came to realize that story is a gift that humans can give back to the earth.

Natural facts are in themselves fantastic images. The tree of life. The apple. The rose. The maggot. These images are already telling a meaningful story. They dress up a world of myths and become the special imagery of fairytales just by being so fully what they are. A rose is a flower like no other, and the dove can never play the hawk's part.

Once, a colleague in one of my workshops was working on a story about bears. She wanted to leave her audience with two main ideas about bears in the national parks: One, bears aren't bad, they just have their own habits and priorities firmly established; and two, if you feed bears, they will learn to raid your camp, and if they raid your camp, they will probably end up being destroyed by Park Service staff. She translated these ideas into image by telling one bear's story through two points of view: a Park Service employee's and the bear's. Telling the story through the two contrasting points of view made her first idea clear. Since she had spent many long hours observing bears, she had a fantastic ability to take on the bear's mannerisms ever so subtly in her gaze and in hip and hand movements. In addition to the structuring of her story, the way she became the bear was absolutely riveting. At one moment in the story, the bear came back to a camp where it remembered finding unlocked coolers the year before. Telling the story from the point of view of the bear, she said, "I raised up to get a better look at the things on the table. This human came running in front of my view and was waving his arms around and screaming. I looked to the side of him. The cooler was on the table."

Here the teller becomes, actually embodies, the bear's point of view. She created the park management point of view by juxtaposing the bear's telling with walkie-talkie conversations between park employees who refer to the bear by a tag number. Her second message is conveyed by juxtaposing the image of the bear as a number and as a personality or a living, thinking being.

Such a telling is testimony to the gift we humans can give to the world through our attentiveness. With our personal experiences, research, and scientific observations of the world, we are constantly building a body of potential story material. Our skill as story makers is directly proportional to the degree of our attentiveness. When the average person comes to a museum, park, or nature center, you, who have spent those 20-some hours a week looking at bears or bugs or birds, can provide through story the knowledge and experience that most people in contemporary culture lack. After all, what is story really but a field trip without the bag lunch?

For those to whom nature begins to reveal her secrets, there is an irresistible yearning for her most worthy interpreter, Art.
— Johann Wolfgang von Goethe

Books by Susan Strauss featuring stories of the natural world

- *Coyote Stories for Children: Tales from Native America* (Beyond Words, 1991).
- *The Passionate Fact: Storytelling in Natural History and Cultural Interpretation* (North American Press/Fulcrum, 1996).
- *When Woman Became the Sea: A Costa Rican Creation Myth* (Beyond Words, 1998).
- *Wolf Stories: Myths and True-Life Tales from Around the World* (Beyond Words, 1994).

Gaura Devi Saves the Trees

DAVID H. ALBERT*

Gaura Devi is eight years old. She lives in India, near very high mountains called the Himalayas. The tops of the mountains are covered with snow all year round. When the sun hits the mountaintops, they shine like diamonds.

Gaura Devi lives on a hillside below the mountaintops, in a house made of stone and slate. It is a good house. In summer, when the sun is hot, the house is cool. In winter, when the snow is very deep, the house is warm. Gaura Devi is poor, but she is happy.

Every morning, Gaura Devi takes her two goats down to the valley so they can eat grass there. On some mornings she goes to the forest above her village with her aunt. The forest has many big trees. In the forest they pick special plants and flowers and berries. Gaura Devi's aunt uses the plants, flowers, and berries to make medicines. She takes care of all the people in her village when they are sick, and she usually makes them well again.

In the afternoons, Gaura Devi goes with her mother to collect broken branches and twigs and dried grass. They use branches and twigs to make a fire for cooking. The fire also keeps the house warm in winter. The cow eats the dried grass and gives them milk every morning and evening. Gaura Devi and her mother walk very far every day to collect enough for the family.

Gaura Devi wondered why her mother did not go up to the forest nearby and cut down the trees. She asked her mother, "Why do we walk so far for wood every day, but leave the trees in the forest?"

Her mother replied, "Gaura Devi, you listen to me. The trees are our brothers and sisters. They provide shade for the plants and flowers and berries that your aunt makes into medicine. They are houses for the birds and animals."

Gaura Devi's two goats stood still as if they were listening, too.

"The roots of the trees are like hands. They hold the earth to the side of the mountain. They also hold the water from the big rains and from the melting snow. If anyone ever cuts down our brothers and sisters, our village will be washed away."

Gaura Devi told all her friends what her mother said.

One day, Gaura Devi and her two goats walked up the mountain trail toward the forest. She saw a truck parked by the side of the road. Many men, wearing caps and carrying axes, were walking toward the forest. Gaura Devi went up to the leader. "Why are you going to the forest?" she asked.

The man said, "We are going to cut down the trees."

"My mother says the trees are our brothers and sisters. They are not to be cut down," Gaura Devi said.

The man replied, "We have orders from the people in the city to bring the wood to them. Now we have to go to work."

Gaura Devi thought. She began to walk down the mountainside. Then she began to run. She ran as fast as her legs would carry her. The goats ran behind.

She ran to the big gong in the open space in the middle of the village. She picked up a stick and beat the gong as loud as she could. Again and again she beat it until her arms got tired. All the women in the village came to the open space. The men were away working. Gaura Devi told them what she had seen. The women began to walk quickly up the mountainside. Gaura Devi's mother was the leader. Gaura Devi ran behind. The goats followed.

Soon they reached the forest edge. They saw the men preparing to cut down the trees. The women ran up to the trees and began to hug them. Gaura Devi's mother said to the leader, "We come as your friends and do not wish you any harm, but we cannot let you cut down the trees."

"Get out of the way," said the leader of the men.

"The trees are our brothers and sisters," replied Gaura Devi's mother. "If you cut down the trees, our village will be washed away when the rains come. We are hugging the trees. If you cut the trees down, you will have to hit us with your axes first."

The men looked around at the women hugging the trees. They knew they shouldn't cut down the forest, even though they were told to do so by the people in the city. They were ashamed. The leader said, "You have taught us a lesson. We will not cut down the forest. We will go back home with our axes."

The men walked slowly back to the truck. Some of the women ran back to the village and brought tea. The men were thankful, for they were thirsty. "We will tell others not to cut these trees down," they promised.

That evening, Gaura Devi's father and the other men from the village returned. When they heard what the women had done, they were very happy. The whole village had a big celebration. They ate fruits and sweet cakes and sang songs and danced.

Gaura Devi was a hero! Her friends put a necklace of sweet-smelling jasmine flowers around her neck. The village women gave her a string of little silver bells.

Gaura Devi was happy. Her two goats jumped to and fro as if they were dancing. The birds sang beautiful songs as the sun went down. The snow on the mountaintops glistened.

Soon Gaura Devi felt tired, so she went to sleep. But in the nighttime, the forest was not asleep. The animals whispered about what had happened and how brave Gaura Devi and the women had been. Her sisters and brothers, the trees, did not talk. But they too were happy. They did not sleep. They smiled. 🍂

Hugging trees: The story behind the story, and beyond

DAVID H. ALBERT

BEDBUGS MADE ME do it.

You see, I had just come out of the foothills of the Indian Himalayas, where this story "Gaura Devi Saves the Trees" takes place, and where my wife and I had helped build stone walls to prevent the little mountain cows — smaller than many goats — from getting to our newly planted trees. I was on an overnight train from New Delhi to Mumbai (Bombay for those of you still equipped with old gazetteers). I always travel second class because that's where you see the *real* India, complete with children hanging from luggage racks, betel nut shells covering the floors, and barefoot railway wallahs hawking "toMAAToSooop" from portable metal samovars. But the only berths available were in first class, with sleeping mattresses six inches wider and compartment doors that almost actually closed, only not really.

I might have gotten a good night's sleep, this June 13, 1981, but the bedbugs (perhaps they only travel first class?) had other ideas. They goaded me into composing "Gaura Devi," the first "children's story" I ever wrote. There was to be no sleeping that evening — the bedbugs, who, I believe, must have had some communication with their brethren to the north, made sure of that — and by morning, when the train pulled into Victoria Station (the largest train station in the world), with the hawkers shouting "pinAYpulLATE, pinAYpulLate" (pineapple plate) at the top of their lungs, "Gaura Devi" had made it to paper.

I was totally exhausted by the time I got to the home of my friends, two social workers, who worked among the slum-dwellers living directly in the flight path of the airport. I quickly found out that I was a promised attraction and away we went into the 110-degree urban oven of flimsy tent-like overhangs made of burlap and cardboard shacks. After a round of introductions and songs from the children, they all turned to me, as they wanted to know something about America. I agreed, but only if they'd listen to my tale of their northern neighbors, whom I had traveled more than 10,000 miles to visit. I think the tale went over fine, but I didn't speak enough Hindi or Gujarati or Marathi to be able to find out.

"Gaura Devi Saves the Trees" is based on an actual event that took place in the village of Reni in India near the Tibetan border on March 26, 1974 (the one change is that Gaura Devi was the name of the little girl's mother — I was never able to track down the name of the little girl). It is part of a much larger story of the Chipko ("Hugging Trees") Movement in the mountainous region of Uttarakhand in northern India, of village men, women, and children stopping big lumber companies from clearcutting mountain slopes by issuing a call to "hug the trees." The Movement grew as people began to collectively realize that deforestation was instrumental in causing devastating floods and landslides, as well as destroying the trees that people depended on for the material of their daily lives: fodder, fruit, and fuel; flowers and medicinal plants; even water and soil.

Stories become history, and history becomes folk history, and sometimes it is difficult to unravel the threads. By 1980, although anthropologists universally disagree, the people of the Chipko Movement had adopted a group of villagers from Rajasthan, 800 or so miles to the southwest, as their literal ancestors, because they had become aware of another story.

September 12, 1731: Maharajah Ajit Singh of Jodhpur, a princely kingdom in what is now Rajasthan, the westernmost state of modern India, decided to build a new palace. His ministers sent an army of men into the desert reaches to bring back wood for burning lime, necessary for construction.

Included in the Maharajah's domain was Khejare, a small village among several in the desert, surrounded by a small forest. The villagers, members of a reform Hindu sect known as the Bishnois, included in the 29 tenets of their faith the protection of trees and wildlife, and thus had been able to nurture the forest for generations. The Bishnois consider the black buck antelope and the chinkara (Indian gazelle) sacred, and the latter to this day is generally found around Bishnoi settlements. Community-accepted legend has it that Bishnoi women would suckle the young of a chinkara if its mother deserted it or was killed.

When the Maharajah's man approached, an elderly woman named Amrita Devi (not to be confused with Gaura Devi who lived 250 years later) pleaded with him, telling them that the felling of trees was not only against the Bishnois faith, but that trees provided the village with food and fodder and were the protectors of the villagers' water supply, vital to their desert existence. Seeing the axeman unmoved, Amrita Devi grabbed the tree in her outstretched arms and hugged it. The axeman threw her to the ground. She got up and hugged the tree once more, begging the axeman to chop her down first before destroying the tree. The axeman hacked through her body, only to have Amrita Devi's three daughters come forward to hug the tree and meet the same fate. On September 12, 1731, 363 people went to their death hugging trees.

After hearing of the incident, the Maharajah, seeking to make amends, declared a permanent injunction against the felling of trees or the killing of wildlife in the area, and permanently exempted the villages from all land taxes. To this day the villages around Amrita Devi's home remain a green and wildlife-filled preserve amidst the sandy isolation of the Rajasthan desert, and Amrita Devi's village itself has now been declared India's first national environmental memorial.

On my first visit with participants in the Chipko Movement in 1977, I collected folksongs by a (then) young folksinger named Ghyanshyam Sailani. It was a laborious process, as the songs had to be translated first from Garhwali into Hindi, and then from Hindi into English. Well before publishing them, I circulated the songs to friends involved in budding ecological movements in the U.S. They were picked up a young folksinger and storyteller in New England named Sarah Pirtle who (without any knowledge on my part) set them to music. When Sunderlal Bahugana, a leader of the Chipko Movement, visited the United States for the first time, he was greeted at his presentation at the University of Massachusetts with a song setting of Ghyanshyam's words (the music can be found in the book *Spinning Tales, Weaving Hope: Stories of Peace, Justice, and Environment*, edited by Ed Brody, et al., and published by New Society Publishers):

> Where will we go if the green trees fall?
> What will we eat? What will we wear?
> Where will we go if the green trees fall?
> Where will the poor go then?
>
> (chorus)
> Come with me now and embrace the trees,
> Feel their heart beat next to yours,

> Come with me now and embrace the trees,
> Feel their heart beat next to yours.
>
> Where will we go if all India is flood?
> Where will we walk? Where will we live?
> Where will we go if all India is flood?
> Where will the poor go then?
>
> (chorus)

I later found out that Bahugana, greatly moved, took the song and words back with him to the Uttarakhand, song and story now having completed an around-the-world journey.

June 5, 1981: From the tiny hamlet of Bemru, 5,600 feet high and only 100 very treacherous miles from the Tibetan border, it is easy to see why the Chipko Movement had to be a women's movement. During the week I spent with the 39 families of Bemru, where I helped prepare the ground for the planting of young mulberry and walnut saplings, I met exactly one male villager between the ages of 16 and 35.

"They're all down on the plains or in the military," said the village headwoman, proudly surveying her small terraced vegetable garden below her sturdily built stone and slate house. "They pull rickshaws or wash dishes or haul rocks or do whatever they get paid for. There's no work for them here." And it was indeed clear that the fate of their families, culture, traditions, domestic economy, and natural environment were totally in the hands of these rugged and beautiful women.

Living five miles from the nearest road and from the mighty Alaknanda River (all, the memory in my legs and lungs reminds me, uphill!), their lot is a hard one. Each square yard of terraced farmland represents the work of generations and had to be lovingly preserved and cultivated. Young children scramble about on the dangerous rock-strewn slopes, looked after by barely older children removed from school for that purpose and also to tend the miniature mountain cattle. The nearest medical station is a tough three-and-a-half-hour journey away.

Bemru is lucky: it is one of the villages in the sub-district closest to the only road, and it has a school to which young children trek from more than five miles away. The women of Bemru are fortunate in another way. They have to spend only four or five hours daily scouring the woods for fodder for the cattle and fuel for cooking and for the little heat that helps take the edge off the chill brought by the stiff Himalayan winds. In some areas to the south and west, women are not so fortunate. Fuel and fodder is so scarce on the mountain slopes that women travel for two whole days, sleeping out in the open on the intervening night, in order to collect wood and fodder to sustain the family for the next three days. This pattern of two days of foraging followed by one day at home cooking, farming, and caring for the children, the elderly, and the animals, wreaks havoc on what is left of a culture once built around a strong family life, but already virtually bereft of able-bodied men.

The women of Bemru are also more fortunate than their counterparts to the east. There the forest springs have dried up, as the earth, depleted of humus, refuses to hold water anymore. Nightly, the women leave their families and journey to places where underground springs once gushed up through the earth, in order to catch the few trickles of water that collect before morning.

The songs of the women of Bemru, which I collected, are evocative and bittersweet. In one song they plead with their fathers to marry them to men from the plains so that they can leave behind the backbreaking tasks that have been allotted to them. In the next song they will beg to be married to men from the neighboring village so as not to lose touch with the wisdom that comes from a life lived precariously amidst the wild grandeur of the mountains, where living beings, human and animal, are locked in a harmonious natural balance with the earth.

Sisters! Join this crusade to protect our forests.
We have to embrace the earth, full of life!
— Ghyanshyam Sailani

February 1, 1978: Five hundred people, mostly women, gathered at the foot of the Advani Forest, Tehri District, Uttar Pradesh. As the dawn sun rose and three police jeeps and two trucks approached, the slogan-shouting became more intense:

The Himalayas will awake today,
The cruel axe will be chased away!

By the side of the road, their axes and saws piled on the ground, squatted two dozen contract laborers brought from far away by a labor contractor. The labor contractor, in turn, had been hired by a timber company that had purchased 640 trees from the state forest department.

The forest department had marked the trees to be felled, but every time the contractor and his men approached the forests with axes, the local people ran up to hug the trees, forcing them to return empty-handed. Weeks earlier, the women had marched on the same forest, singing, pulling out the iron blades used by the forest department for resin tapping. They bandaged the wounded pines and tied "sacred threads" around the trees. These sacred threads marked the trees as their children and signified the women's pledge to save the trees even, if need be, at the cost of their own lives. This time, district officials agreed to send an armed constabulary force to assist in the felling. A hundred men, armed with rifles and bayonets, arrived a day in advance and paraded publicly up and down the road leading to the forest, hoping to instill fear in the women.

After consultations with the police, the contractor beckoned to the laborers to begin their operations. As they moved toward the forest, so did the villagers, now formed into groups of three or four and including young children. They encircled each marked tree as the laborers approached, chanting, "If the axe falls on the trees, it will fall on our bodies first." As the laborers moved on, so did the tree huggers. The police could not possibly arrest the villagers; there was no place to put them, no way to transport them, and no method short of physical violence to separate the villages from the trees they embraced. After several hours of fruitlessly seeking an unprotected marked tree, the contractor, laborers, and police gave up, the contractor complaining about the growing undependability of doing business with the state government.

Prior to the first publication of "Gaura Devi Saves the Trees," I published the story of the then-young Chipko Movement in a small magazine. A friend of mine gave a copy to his friend, an Indian-born, American-trained engineer named Ravi Chopra, whom I had never met, but whose American wife Jo I had known some years earlier. Only 18 years later did I learn of its

impact. Chopra, headed back to India but with no clear direction regarding what he was to do next, apparently read my article while on the plane. Soon he moved his family to the foothills of the Himalayas, to a town named Dehradun, where he formed the People's Science Institute (PSI). Chopra became keenly aware that the future of the area was dependent on the development of small-scale agriculture and industry. This would free people from dependence on production of timber for the cities on the plains and make it possible for men who left their families for months or even years at a time seeking employment in the overcrowded urban areas to remain in their ancestral homes.

Chopra also understood that all the development schemes of the government were geared toward large infrastructure projects: improperly built roads that scarred the mountainsides and brought rocks and silt down upon the rivers below; huge dams that displaced tens of thousands of people to produce electricity for the cities; water projects for the plains; timber for, among other things, the manufacture of tennis rackets! So Chopra and others that he recruited to PSI set to work, building small solid-waste-management businesses; teaching people how to dig and maintain their own wells and irrigation projects without any government support; supporting community-based forestry; and training people how to retrofit their homes, using local materials and traditional methods, to make them earthquake-proof. This proved critical, as a large earthquake hit the region in 1999, destroying more than 10,000 homes, but proving the efficacy of PSI's methods. Following the earthquake that struck Gujarat to the southwest the next year, PSI found itself in a position to train international relief agency workers in these approaches. At the same time as Ravi was building PSI, Jo set up what is probably India's most progressive school for children with mental disabilities.

I think the bedbugs must have been biting them, too.

By 1981, after untold numbers of scientific studies and surveys, the Chipko Movement had won a complete ban on commercial felling of trees on hills above 1,000 meters high or with slopes with gradients greater than 30 degrees. Only dead, dying, and diseased trees could be removed, and only after local demands for timber and fuel were met. The villagers also were guaranteed the plantation of the "5F" trees — food, fodder, fuel, fertilizer, and fiber — up to a distance of three kilometers from every village. Plantation, protection, and upkeep of these areas, even if they fell within the boundaries of reserve forests, were entrusted to the village communities themselves.

Still, the victories of the Chipko Movement remained fragile. The demand for electrical power, water, and timber in the major urban areas of the plains continued unabated, the lure of possible employment remained, and political power was still concentrated in the major cities.

When I returned to India in the fall of 1998 with my family, I had hoped to visit my friends in the Chipko Movement, but my way was blocked by landslides caused by recent heavy rains that washed out roads and bridges all the way up to the Tibetan frontier. Instead, having been introduced as the man who (unwittingly) brought Ravi Chopra to the north, I got to sit in at a meeting of a "shadow" environmental cabinet in Dehradun, examining new bioregional forms of planning. ("Bioregionalism" is a way of thinking about a regional "commons" in which political

units and decision-making are oriented around the natural carrying capacity of a biologically regenerative community — say, a watershed — in which human beings are only one part. For an excellent introduction to the idea see *Home! A Bioregional Reader*, edited by Van Andruss et al. and published by New Society Publishers.)

On November 9, 2000, after 20 years of ecological and political strife, the flag of the new Indian state of Uttaranchal was raised over Dev Bhoomi (the land of the Gods), presided over by the 25,000-foot-high Nanda Devi and other Himalayan peaks, its rivers — the headwaters of the Ganges — swelling with pride. With an interim capital at Dehradun and a population of more than 7,000,000 people (Ravi Chopra, last I spoke with him, was trying to figure out an accurate way to count the mountain cows in order to calculate the value of potential milk production against the carrying capacity of the land), Uttaranchal may be the first large political entity in history to be formed as a result of environmental struggle.

I almost forgot. On a more modest scale, these two volumes of *The Healing Heart* would not have existed except for those bedbugs. You see, my co-editor Allison Cox contacted me for the first time for permission to use "Gaura Devi Saves the Trees" in her swan song of a public health project (see "Once Upon a Time There Was and There Was Not …" in the first volume of this set, *The Healing Heart: Storytelling to Encourage Caring and Healthy Families*). Little did she know that I lived only 40 miles away, worked for the state board of health, and would play a role in convincing the local health department to hire her to do health promotion through storytelling, would end up "overseeing" her graduate school practicum (which was collecting the material for these volumes), and that the bedbugs would have me sign on as co-editor.

But once you've been bitten …

Gaura Devi's legacy lives on. Following a visit to environmental sanctuaries north of Dehradun, my then 11-year-old daughter Aliyah Shanti (which means "Pilgrimage of Peace") wrote the following poem:

The trees speak,
But their language is hidden deep inside their bark,

They must trust us,
Before they reveal it.

The wind speaks,
But in so many different languages
That it is hard to pick one out.

The stars speak,
But their fiery flares
Make us afraid to know what they say.

All things in the universe have a language.
It is not they who must learn to speak,
It is we who must learn to listen.

I think the bedbugs should be very proud. I am learning to listen. And the trees are still smiling.

Storytelling to speak for the heart of a place

JANA DEAN

WHEN STORYTELLERS LISTEN — at street corners, in wetlands, in parking lots, at the beach, on mountaintops — the stories they hear speak for those places. When storytellers in turn tell those stories of place, they weave culture and nature together, connecting people to one another and to their physical surroundings. Stories of place can galvanize community members, providing common ground and a locus for belonging. The sentiment stirred by these stories can sustain the collaborative work essential for building and maintaining healthy communities.

The ability to speak for a place has become increasingly rare as people have become more mobile and as the non-regional world powerfully enters our lives through the media. And yet, a sense of place — knowing the moods and rhythms of a locale — provides a feeling of belonging. Call it "feeling at home."

So where do we find these stories of place? They surround us. We just need to take the time to listen. Marching out with the focused intent of finding a tale and learning it may result in a story, but the story won't likely speak the truth of the place. Instead, the teller must slow down and take in the landscape at the body's pace. To know by heart rather than to seize with the mind requires that we step back and allow ourselves to come to know things slowly. This kind of intimate knowing is born of a commitment to paying attention.

The act of receiving challenges us as storytellers. So often we see ourselves as givers and keepers of tradition; yet to carry and hold the stories of a place, we must stop talking and instead pay attention.

Several years ago I undertook a project, the goal of which was to encourage a sense of place and thereby increased stewardship and responsibility among the people in my Puget Sound neighborhood. After conducting dozens of oral history interviews, I realized that the Nisqually River figured large in my community's historic sense of place. I sought a way I could speak for the river. I found that to build a full imagination of the Nisqually, I didn't need to limit myself to a specific river, but could pour all of my river experience into a vessel from which to draw.

I used to live near a river that, even a half mile away, was louder than the sound of the highway. The river was a compass and a gauge. Even though it changed its course every year, it still mostly ran north and south. By the river I could point to Seattle, 1,000 miles west, and to New York, 2,000 miles east. Spring banks told how warm it had been and how much snow remained on the mountains. Winter banks told of night's ice. During the summer, waters ran higher after thunderclouds hovered over nearby peaks. And in spite of all its activity just half a mile from my house, 30 miles to the south the river seeped quietly into cracked basalt and never flowed to the sea.

How different was the Nisqually River! It doesn't run with the compass; it meanders from volcanoes to the sea. It begins not in a mountain range, but on The Mountain: Mount Rainier. I went to the river. I walked the delta. I found the public fishing and swimming holes. I took off my clothes and dove in. I listened to the sound of the river. I smelled its trees. I ran my fingers through its gravel. I sat still by the banks of the river and imagined where it had come from and where it

might go. I asked myself, "What stories did these waters tell?" and "How are these stories the same and how are they different from my wild and disappearing river to the east?"

Then I sought out others who knew the river far better than I. I found people who had fished the river and walked the river and floated the river. I listened to them, and while listening, I let myself suspend my own vision so that their stories could become my own. I saw the river as they saw it. I smelled the river as they smelled it. I touched the river as they touched it. I let go of my ideas and experience of the river to embrace theirs. All of this story gathering left me with choices to make. How could I shape it into a tale that would inspire others to a passion for place?

Saturated with my own experience and the experiences of others, I stepped back and considered what story the river might have to tell. I had to decide what really mattered and find the truth of the river's story. I knew it had to do with the changes the river had undergone: the arrival of strangers from the east; the depletion of the salmon; thundering Highway I-5 meets the river where it opens to the sea; the dyking of the estuary; and the endurance of the Nisqually Indian Tribe.

To structure the story, I turned to folklore. The story "Magpie" follows the format of a how-and-why tale. A how-and-why story, which almost always involves animals, explains how things came to be the way they are today. Much of the appeal of how-and-why stories, for both children and adults, is the way the animals mirror us. Salmon and magpie are much better teachers than a didactic human moralist. We see ourselves and our own silly, imperfect behavior. We can laugh at ourselves, rather than feeling defensive that we've been caught with our guard down. This indirect teaching is the core of the wisdom of storytelling. The tighter the story-teller holds to the idea of the moral behind the story, the more didactic the telling. Telling some-one straight out "You've got to fall in love with your neighborhood" is likely to be far less effec-tive than indirectly giving them a new way to love it through a story. My hope is that "Magpie" will give people a new way to fall in love with their river that runs to the sea.

Magpie

Jana Dean*

Eagle saw him first. Magpie came hopping and flying and hopping westward, looking for a place to live. Now I must tell you that Magpie is a bird who can sing the song of any bird in the forest. He's that good of a singer.

But this was before Magpie had learned anyone else's song. He knew only his own song, and you'll see that's what he'll sing when he took his place by the river. Magpie was very tired and very hungry. He stopped not far from the salt water.

Raccoon was the first to greet him. Raccoon had come, as usual, with something to eat. Today he held a mass of worms in his fist. Raccoon greeted Magpie and set to washing his worms. Then Magpie said, "Ooooh, I am sooo hungry." That's when Eagle first thought to himself, "This noisy fellow might mean trouble."

Raccoon, on the other hand, makes himself at home just about anywhere, and he didn't see why Magpie shouldn't do the same. He looked at his worms, shrugged his shoulders, split them into two parts, and offered half to Magpie. Magpie cackled and crowed his appreciation, making so much noise that Beaver popped up to see what was the commotion.

Beaver climbed out of the river and stood there leaning on his heavy tail, squinting at Magpie. Beaver extended a welcome by inviting Magpie to tour the riverbank — from the water, of course. Magpie was so busy eating that he declined. So Beaver solemnly took Magpie's wing into his hand as a sign of welcome and thought to himself, "Well, we'll see how well this one builds his house."

Ant was the next to greet the stranger. He stood at Magpie's feet and had to shout to get his attention. Ant, like Beaver, was skeptical. This newcomer seemed none too observant.

Next, Bee came buzzing around. She caught Magpie's eye and then settled in on a branch to keep an eye on the bird.

Bear was there, too, but she watched and lis-tened from a distance.

Magpie made himself right at home in no time. He had a proud, invincible attitude, even though, being new to the river, he had much to learn. Between you and me, he would have starved that first season had it not been for Raccoon. Raccoon brought Magpie food every day, whether it was frogs, worms, or fish. Magpie grew stronger and stronger all through the season. Magpie told Raccoon tales of faraway lands. Raccoon was fascinated and invited Magpie to the annual animals' council.

Eagle called the meeting to order. As was their custom, each member of the council shared the year's observations. Beaver noted changes in the river's course while Magpie arranged his tail feathers. Raccoon gave a report on the night world as Magpie intently compared one of his feet to the other. Eagle made note of the tides while Magpie admired the sheen of his white feathers against his black ones. Bee spoke of the buds and flowers all up and down the river, and Bear noted where trees had fallen and where springs ran the freshest as Magpie counted his wing feathers. Ant had something to say about the year's crop of seeds, and he reminded everyone that he could move a mountain if they gave him time. When all had been heard, it was Magpie's turn to speak.

"As far as I reckon, I have been here all this season," he said. "And I have decided where I will build my nest." All the animals listened, but Magpie said nothing more. The animals exchanged stories far into the night. Then everyone went home, including Magpie.

Now what the animals hadn't understood was that Magpie intended to hold his spot on the river all for himself. In fact, he would make the river his own by making more noise than the river itself. After all, he was the most important creature on the river because he had the most to say!

So Magpie set up house and started singing his only song. "The River is Mine! The River is Mine!" he called over and over again, strutting along the riverbank and flying back and forth over his piece of the river. He guarded it for himself. Every once in a while, Magpie would stop on

a stone by a still pool and admire his own image. The water so beautifully reflected his black and white feathers that he took it as a sign that the river indeed was his.

Raccoon had taught him enough that Magpie no longer had any use for Raccoon, so he did not allow Raccoon near his stretch of the riverbank. Magpie couldn't keep Eagle from casting his shadow on his piece of the river, but Magpie was making so much noise that Eagle could barely concentrate. Eagle didn't come around much anymore. Beaver grumbled about all the racket. Ant was furious about Magpie's noise and stood not far from the bird, shouting until he was red in the face. But Magpie didn't hear him or anything — except himself.

When Bee saw Magpie ignoring Ant, she became indignant. She decided she would give Magpie a message he couldn't ignore. She buzzed around Magpie's head and then stung him right below the eye. Now you and I know what happens to Bee when she stings. She loses her stinger — and part of her body, for stinging is a great sacrifice. Yes, Bee died. As for Magpie, he hardly noticed, except that his reflection was a little less comely for a while. Bear saw it all and quietly kept her distance.

When the animals met again in council, Magpie was not invited. They had already heard enough from him. As usual, they went around and traded news and observations. And you know what happened? Magpie and his noise were everywhere. Magpie had found his way into every river story they told. Magpie was in all of them, with all his noise.

"I am sorry," said Raccoon. "I taught this noisy bird to survive here."

Year after year, Magpie kept it up: "The River is Mine. The River is Mine." The animals continued to watch the river, and they listened as best they could above Magpie's din. And they continued to gather each year to share their stories.

Then, one late summer, the river disappeared. Raccoon went to the water that morning to rinse his breakfast. The river was gone! Only drying rocks lay exposed to the sun. Beaver came out of a hole in the riverbank and blinked in the dry hot sun. Ant came out of his hill and said to himself, "I knew it! That Magpie!" Eagle flew high in the sky and looked up and down the river basin. The riverbed was as dry as bones. Bear ran from spring to spring. The fresh flowing pools were quickly drying up. Then, one at a time, they realized that not only had the river disappeared — so had Magpie's clamor.

You see, Magpie, that morning, had just set about making his racket when he, too, realized that the river was gone. It no longer gave back his reflection. Then for the very first time, Magpie tried listening — and he heard nothing.

Eagle called a council. When the animals gathered, Eagle said to them, "I have flown and I have seen that the river has stopped flowing close to its source."

Ant said, "I can move a mountain, if you give me time."

"I'm afraid we don't have time, Ant," said Bear gently. "Even the springs are drying up. We will die without the river."

As they stood in silence, Magpie approached them. They could see by the way he was standing that he was very worried. "The river no longer throws back my reflection," said Magpie. "I listen, and I hear nothing. Can anyone here speak for my river?"

The animals were silent for a long time. Then Bear answered, "Until you came, Magpie, everyone living on the river listened to the river, and we all spoke for the river. The river brought a different message to each of us. We all speak for the river, Magpie. Since you came, it has been much harder for us to hear what the river has to tell us."

Magpie looked at his toes and said, "I guess that's what Bee was trying to tell me. I will try to listen."

Then Eagle spoke. "Magpie, it will not be so easy as you think. You must go and find Brother Salmon, who swims in deep water. You must go and pay him a visit. He will tell you what to do."

Magpie went. He went to find Deep Water Salmon. Brother Salmon was waiting for him in his deep water house. Magpie stood nervously in front of Salmon and said, "Eagle sent me. Eagle said you would know what to do."

"Indeed," replied Salmon. "What seems to be the trouble, Magpie?"

"Well, you see," explained the black-and-white bird, "my river is gone."

"Yes, I know," replied Salmon. "And it is almost too late. With all the racket you've been making on the banks of the river, the river has not been able to hear my song. And so it does not know to come to the sea. And now I cannot even swim to its headwaters to tell it to come." Then Salmon was silent.

Magpie paced back and forth. He felt just awful. This was not what he had intended. Magpie tried to get Salmon to tell him more, but Salmon was silent. As Magpie paced back and forth in front of Deep Water Salmon's house, Salmon began singing. Magpie stopped pacing. For the second time in his life, Magpie stopped to listen. He listened to Salmon's song for a little while. Then he began tapping his foot and he started singing with Salmon. Oooh, he had to concentrate to learn that song, for it was long, and complicated. Salmon was patient. Magpie spent a l-o-o-o-n-g time in Salmon's house.

Finally, Magpie was ready. He knew what to do. He would fly to the headwaters of the river and sing Salmon's song so that the river would hear it. He would stop at every spring the length of the river basin and sing Salmon's song. Then the river would know to come to the sea.

Well, Magpie did just that. He flew far up the river basin, all the way to the mountain. He found the river just a trickle that seeped into the gravel not far at all from the glacier. Magpie stood there and sang Salmon's song. Slowly, the river began to flow more freely. Magpie followed the tongue of the reborn river as it lapped against dry rocks and gradually gained momentum. All the while, Magpie flew from stone to stone and sang Salmon's long and complicated song. He sang it just right until the river met the sea. Then he went back and visited the springs and one at a time sang them back to the river until once again the river flowed full and strong.

Then Magpie took his place by the river. And from that day onward, he sang not only his own song, but he also sang for all the creatures of the river and the forest. 🐦

HABITAT KITS FOR CREATING HOW-AND-WHY STORIES

SHARING STORIES

While telling stories can encourage deepened commitment to community and place, encouraging others to build their own stories can strengthen existing connections. Stories could be personal narrative, or community members might build tales based on natural habitats in the how-and-why story format. Even without spending months contemplating a place, people can enhance their relationship to place, particularly to its non-human inhabitants, through a simple exercise in building how-and-why stories.

The exercise described below involves melding direct observation of specific habitats with bits of natural history to create a story that describes how things came to be the way they are. For example, the crab must shed its shell to grow. Each time it does so, it pumps itself up until its new shell hardens. Then it shrinks back down to size with room to grow in the new shell. Imagining this quality of a crab into a story resulted in a beautiful and insightful tale about how crab learned to grow at a "Sense of Place" storytelling workshop I once gave.

Prepare participants for this activity by reading or telling and then discussing how-and-why stories. In the how-and-why story, a character, usually an animal, moves through its habitat and undergoes some change that has become one of its lasting traits. For example, in the Oneida tale "Why Crayfish has his Eyes on a Stalk," Crayfish tries so hard to see through the mud on his eyes that his eyes pop out of his head to wave around on stalks.

ACTIVITY

Assemble one habitat kit for each group of four or five participants. As you assemble the kits, be sure to include something that can represent the protagonist. (For example, a bird nest or feather would represent a wren.) Making the kits will require some outings, which could also be incorporated into the activity itself. Generally speaking, animals make better main characters than plants.

Some examples of kits and their contents are:

Urban City Lot
Crow
Ant
Dandelion
Horsetail

Forest
Salamander
Robin
Steller's jay
Filbert tree

Stream
Coho salmon
Mosquito
Willow
Dragonfly

Beach
Sand dollar
Crab
Starfish
Western gull

Wetland
Bog water
Pacific tree frog
Muskrat
Owl

Direct each group of participants to:
1. Discuss the possible relationships between the objects in their kit. (It is helpful to assign each person to an object in order to structure discussion and encourage participation from the whole group.)
2. Read from the prepared natural history cards about each object (see below).

3. From the pieces of the kit, decide on a main character who could move through the habitat. Brainstorm about the characteristics of that character. What is special about him or her? What could your story explain?
4. Build a how-and-why story from what the group knows about the main character and the pieces of the habitat in the kits.

Encourage participants to keep their stories simple. Emphasize that they are building a story based on what they already know and can embellish about a habitat. In this activity, using the imagination is more important than scientific accuracy. This helps keep them from being overwhelmed by the prospect of making up a story from scratch.

NATURAL HISTORY FACTS FOR THE HABITAT KITS

Urban City Lot

Crow
Often an older male will apprentice a yearling male to help protect young and defend territory. This allows the elder more time for mating and feeding young.

Ant
Ants are farmers. They raise and harvest aphids to eat.

Dandelion
In spite of their reputations with lawn growers, dandelions offer edible flowers and leaves and roots with medicinal qualities. In French, dandelion means "tooth of the lion."

Horsetail
The horsetail can crack its way through up to an inch of asphalt. After the 1980 eruption of Mount

Saint Helens, it appeared before any other vegetation in the mud-scoured landscape.

Forest I

Salamander
Some species of salamanders lack lungs and breathe through their skin, while others lack eardrums and "hear" by feeling vibrations with their feet.

Robin
Pairs of robins generally raise two clutches at a time. The male takes care of the first while the female sits on the nest of the second brood.

Steller's jay
Jays that breed in the spring remain together in family groups through the season.

Filbert tree (Hazelnut)
The filbert grows in the shade of the woods and is one of the first trees to turn color in the fall.

Forest II

Moss
Moss that has completely dried up can return to a verdant green with the first drizzle or dew set.

Robin
Pairs of robins generally raise two clutches at a time. The male takes care of the first while the female sits on the nest of the second brood.

Mosquito
Females need one big blood meal, greater than their own weight, for nourishment to lay eggs. Males don't eat blood at all. They just buzz around our ears in expectation that that's where the girls are.

Owl
Many species of owl can locate their prey by sound alone. They do this by detecting the minute difference in time that it takes the sound to reach each ear.

Stream

Coho salmon
While some chinook and sockeye salmon migrate up to 2,000 miles in fresh water, coho or silver salmon often spawn just a few miles from salt water in tiny urban creeks.

Mosquito
Females need one big blood meal, greater than their own weight, for nourishment to lay eggs. Males don't eat blood at all. They just buzz around our ears in expectation that that's where the girls are.

Willow
The willow grows where few plants will, often in soil-less gravel right on a stream bank, with its feet perpetually wet.

Dragonfly
The dragonfly gets its name from its ferocious nature as a larva. These little aquatic creatures are known to devour even tadpoles.

Beach

Sand dollar
The sand dollar, relative of the starfish, has tubular feet that operate by hydraulic pressure. Rather than grabbing food, the sand dollar undulates its feet to draw detritus to the mouth on its underside.

Starfish
The starfish eats by ejecting its stomach and

inserting it into the shell of its prey, which it has opened with its tremendously strong arms.

Western gull

The gull lays its eggs in the open, near water, and must cool them by soaking its belly and then wetting the eggs by lying on the nest.

Crab

The crab must shed its shell to grow. Each time it does so, it pumps itself up until its new shell hardens. Then it shrinks back down to size with room to grow in the new shell.

Wetland

Bog water

Most bog water is actually under the vegetation. A thick floating mat of vegetation covers the water. In some places you can actually walk on it and feel the "ground" move beneath your feet.

Pacific tree frog

This little frog spends less time on trees than in water and on the ground. During mating season, the male amplifies his voice by blowing up a throat sack to three times the size of his head.

Muskrat

Muskrats can take enough breath in a few seconds to last them 15 minutes under water.

Owl

Many species of owl can locate their prey by sound alone. They do this by detecting the minute difference in time that it takes the sound to reach each ear.

COMMUNITY DEVELOPMENT IN OUR NEIGHBORHOODS AND ACROSS THE MILES

The Learning Center

WENDY WELCH

THE LEARNING CENTER, tucked inside a Housing Authority apartment complex, was an experiment in on-site literacy work. We were there to "break the double chains of poverty and illiteracy in order to help people attain their chosen place in society." Ostensibly.

In reality, we were the place where people came for help in filling out forms; to beg a quick ride to the doctor's office; to ask for homework assistance; to share their boredom; or to borrow needles, glue, thread, scissors, staples, and other paraphernalia of life. More than 100 people of all ages flowed through the Center's doors in any given month.

They took classes in parenting, women's rights, assertiveness, sewing, computer skills, typing, jewelry making, and building model rockets. They read books in the library, played games on the computers, fingerpainted in the "wreck" room, had snacks in the kitchen. Sometimes they just dropped in to talk something over with Gina or me. As the director, Gina's job was to oversee the chaos; as the children's programs coordinator, mine was to create it.

We did everything we could think of to expose these kids to as many positive influences as possible — including their own parents. Society in general, and the government agency involved in particular, had decided the residents of this 128-apartment block were "Bad Parents." It

was a non-negotiable given, and when our grant funding was handed out that year, along with it came a *mandate* to "offer educational opportunities designed to enhance, reinforce, and otherwise promote family cohesiveness, and proper parenting." Or something like that. "Proper" never really did get a thorough explanation.

But inside the complex was much like outside. Some parents spent time with their kids; some didn't. But even the more reluctant parents often turned out for our monthly storytelling plays. As "resident storyteller," I held monthly auditions in the wreck room after copious advertising throughout the complex. At these events I would tell the kids a couple of folktales, favoring those with repetitious plots featuring animals. Then we would agree on a fairytale that we all knew well enough to perform and chose a silly song from the kids' own vast repertoires. Then we divvied up roles. Everyone got a part; we once had a child playing a potted plant, but everyone got a part.

After a quick run-through of each piece, I sent the kids home and filled out the paperwork: documentation of the activity, how it was intended to increase literacy skills, goals and motivations, etc. The kids returned the next day, bringing a welcome reality back to this project that looked so flat on paper. Rehearsals had a way of getting delightfully out of hand, particularly if the kids were having fun (something we tried to encourage, although it was not in the program's stated goals).

Following a last rehearsal on the third day, Gina and I turned the Center into a theatre while the kids rounded up their parents. Gina would spend hours during the day preparing special foods with which to entice the community out for the evening: fresh fruit and vegetables, homemade pizzas, special desserts. I once watched her saw a watermelon into decorative halves, scoop it out, and fill it with honeydew melon and cantaloupe.

This was not mere decoration, nor was it coincidence that these story events were produced during the last week of the welfare check cycle, a time when food was scarce for several residents, fresh fruit an undreamed of luxury. A "typical" monthly check in 1992 for this region was $156.81 to feed a family of one adult and two children, not to mention covering incidentals such as clothing or school costs. By the third week, the money was usually gone, and people lived off what they could. Our storylets were often popular for more than one reason. We never had fresh fruit left over.

With our food in place and our actors prepared, we would present the stories with gusto, if not grace. It wasn't the National Storytelling Festival, but flashbulbs blinded the children whose proud parents had come to watch, and even neighborhood curmudgeons sometimes had a smile for a particularly cute fire-breathing dragon. The community spirit these events evoked, and the connections they established between parents and children, made even the paperwork that followed seem worthwhile.

In fact, it was the paperwork and an overdue plane that gave us one of the Center's best breakthroughs in cultural literacy. As a professional storyteller, I often produced story events for the larger community in addition to my work with the Center. After one festival, I took balloon artist/storyteller Jeanne Donato of Rhode Island to the airport, where we discovered her plane was two hours late. Jeanne promptly produced two balloon pumps and a bag of #360 balloons, the type of balloon most commonly used to mold animals.

"Here," she said, handing me a pump. "It's gonna be a long wait." Two hours later, the lobby about us was filled with misshapen mice and dogs (mine) and incredible winged horses, dragons, and butterflies (hers). Balloon shreds and curious onlookers littered the room. My doggies were just beginning to look passing fair when her flight was called. As she headed toward the gate, Jeanne handed me a pump and a fistful of balloons. "You'll need these," she said enigmatically, and disappeared.

She was right. Balloons, I quickly discovered, were addictive. Molding them helped reduce the stress of the Center; things were not going well there. We had run out of fairytales known to all the kids after only three performances. The kids knew only those tales that had been reproduced in media entertainment (usually Disney); they had Cinderella down cold, but they had never heard of Rapunzel. This might seem an unfortunate but minor loss to some, but think about it. Aside from the more sentimental considerations of lost childhood and aesthetic lack, think how much information you would have missed in school if you had not understood who and what the Ugly Duckling was. Consider how often in your daily routine you hear references — subtle, simple references — to ideas espoused in the major fairytales of the western canon.

If you don't know who the Third Little Pig was, let alone what he or she represented, how can you internalize the idea that hard work will take you to safety? If you have never heard of Rapunzel, are you prepared for the War of the Sexes? Granted, fairytales were not originally meant for children; however, in the sophisticated modernity of our world, children are ready for the concept of a Big Bad Wolf in Granny's bed long before parents are prepared to tell them the truth about wolves and grannies. And when the other kids know, and you don't, it matters.

So at the next story session, I took my group of 20 kids (ranging in age from 4 to 13), sat them down, and started telling them about The Pigs. Although the young ones liked the rhythm of the story, the older crowd was yawning by the time the houses were up. They began to cut capers and push the rules until I had to stop. "That's a baby story," they said. "We don't wanna do that one."

Explaining the importance of lazy vs. industrious pigs to a sexually active 11-year-old who is the functional mother in a family of four can be a difficult task. These kids were mixed bundles of sophistication and ignorance; if they said it was a baby thing, you could kiss it good-bye.

All this was bubbling just below the surface of my brain as I shaped balloon hats, flowers, and ducks in the privacy of my home. It was the day I invented a crown balloon that the two concepts fused. Next rehearsal I entered the wreck room armed with multiple pink balloons. The kids eyed me with interest.

"I have an idea," I said. "Today let's act out a story as I tell it. I'll tell you what the character thinks, and you decide what the character will do in that situation. Okay?" The kids were enthusiastic, so I put pig-ear balloons on three kids, wolf ears on the fourth, and we set off.

It was not storytelling as a professional performer would know it. It was glorious chaos. It was balloons bursting and kids clamoring and a hoarse-voiced narrator shouting, "No, Pig Two!

The one with the stick house!" But it was the story, start to finish, actions, thoughts, words — and meanings. By the time Pig Three had graduated from night school with a nursing degree, the kids had the message down cold. They presented it on performance night with great enthusiasm.

The next month we did "The Emperor's New Clothes"; the following production featured "Rumpelstiltskin." The balloons continued to hold the interest of the older crowd in "babyish" stories and, conversely, allowed the younger kids to participate in more sophisticated tales, such as "Rapunzel." The stories and the storytelling kids were flying high.

But this program was not the only thing going. It is a phenomenon well known to those working in public social service facilities: as Christmas approaches, so do the volunteers. Church groups, civic organizations, and troops of Scouts converge from the four corners of the earth, looking for good to do. So it was that Gina found herself on the phone with a church from the other side of the tracks. This upper-middle-class establishment had chosen our Center as its first mission field for their puppet team. The team, consisting of children between 10 and 14, wanted to perform for us in December. They would also provide pizza for the entire facility. We were thrilled.

So were the parents who formed our core group of volunteers. Three moms and one dad sat down with me to discuss how to organize the visit. Tiffany,* one of the most timid mothers, suddenly spoke up. "You know, if their children are coming and performing for us, shouldn't we have our kids do something too? As a kind of welcome, or an exchange, you know, something like that." The other moms agreed. But Tiffany continued, "And maybe we grown-ups could do one, too?"

*All names of parents appearing in this article have been changed.

Ever since storytelling programs had been running at the Center, Gina and I had cherished the idea of an adult-cast performance. The stories we produced always featured morals relevant to life around us; we did "The Ugly Duckling" following some teasing trouble, and "Three Billy Goats Gruff" after suspending a bully from the Center for a week. We had always nurtured hopes that some parents might come forward with suggestions or even volunteer for participation; then we could state with pride on the governmental form that the objective of "increasing family values" had been met.

The only successful adult production thus far had been "Little Red Riding Hood." This was done after rumors circulated of a green station wagon in the area, its driver allegedly trying to entice children into it with pleas for help in finding a lost dog. The police called to the scene never came. Concerned parents asked me to do "Riding Hood" the next month. They thought its moral, "Kids! Don't talk to strangers!" was timely.

I knew an opportunity when I saw one. Shamelessly, I said, "Don't you think it would be even more effective if their parents did it?"

Certainly the sight of that month's production, when six grown men and women made adorable idiots of themselves before a larger-than-usual group of children, left a lasting impression. The laughter was so loud, people not normally interested in the Center had come down to see what was happening; we staged an encore for their benefit.

Despite this rollicking success, an adult performance had never happened again, which made Tiffany's follow-up suggestion startling. But it, too, was greeted with interest, so we cast about for a suitable story we all knew. One of the moms suggested "The Three Little Pigs."

"I like the version the kids did. It's funny, most of us saw it, and we could pull it together in a hurry. Let's do it," said Sarah. One of the women hadn't seen it, so we rehashed the plot for her: the first little pig dropped out of high school, pregnant, and never went back. The second little pig dropped out, got her general equivalency degree, but didn't look for work. The third little pig finished high school and became a nurse's aide while she went to college and got her degree. The big bad wolf was rehabilitated, and the whole menagerie wound up volunteering at the Center.

When we'd gone over the plot, Tiffany said, "The first little pig, that's me." I started a cast list: Tiffany, first little pig.

"No," she said, "I mean, that's me. I never finished high school because I got pregnant."

Embarrassed, I started to cross her name out, but she laughed. "Nah, I think that's good. I think I want to do that." The other women began to choose and redesign characters to fit their circumstances (except that the third little pig hadn't finished her night courses yet because her daughter had been ill). The only male present didn't want to be the big bad wolf, so another community member was recruited. We had only one rehearsal; even that was probably unnecessary. These people were playing out their lives.

So the day came. A crowd of about 30 well-dressed people huddled at one end of the courtyard, looking nervous yet trying to appear friendly, bellowing greetings at passersby in the too-hearty voices of the truly frightened. In the kitchen, some of the church women had become busy with the Learning Center women; oven mitts were handed round and names exchanged in a frenzy of activity as the pizzas were placed in warming ovens to await the close of the show. When all was in readiness, the puppeteers began. A charming rendition of a Bible tale, complete with cute modernizing twists, was well-received by the audience of about 100 residents (an unheard-of response from a complex of 300 or so people). We were ecstatic.

Next our story kids did their stuff. Although not the most inspired effort — the smell of pizza was beginning to waft from the kitchen — it was nevertheless politely applauded. Then "The Three Little Pigs" began.

As the first little pig explained her life circumstances, the huddle of outsiders at the back began to look pained. By the time the second little pig had opened the door to the big bad wolf so she could buy drugs, the guests did not know where to put their eyes. The third little pig's success as a nurse's aide left them looking confused. But they loved the part where the big bad wolf reformed.

It was an interesting insight into just how divided two groups can be. The home crowd was roaring with laughter and recognition. The visiting group was confounded. Perhaps some of them were beginning to realize that they knew only the most basic of stereotypes about why a person might be living in subsidized housing, not the subtleties parodied here. They had no concept of walking clean from a drug rehabilitation program straight back into apartments where drugs flow like water because you haven't got enough money for a bus ticket to your sister's in Phoenix. They had never been turned down for a job because they had no transportation or could not work afternoon shifts because leaving the kids with family members would result in abuse. They had absolutely no concept of a 2 a.m. desperate flight from a drunken, enraged monster, leaving clothes, cash, credit cards, everything but the children behind. And they were totally unprepared to cope with the ability of Those Less Fortunate Than Themselves to have a sense of humor about the situation.

Credit should be given the visitors, though. They rallied admirably, trying hard to be friendly and act natural. If their attempts were rather obvious, they were also genuine, and the groups parted with mutual goodwill. Individuals from that group later plugged into our tutoring program and become beloved volunteers.

But the pigs-cum-parents were the stars of this event. When it was over, no one spoke much about what had happened. Perhaps we didn't want to admit what we had done; perhaps we wanted to savor it. I'm really not sure. All I am sure of is this: every pig has its day, and these women knew they had had theirs.

⌒ Sun and Rain ⌒

A CHEROKEE STORY RETOLD BY WENDY WELCH*

This is a favorite story of the Learning Center kids and always involves creating balloon costumes for each character.

Sun: Use a yellow #360 balloon inflated to within half an inch. Wrap it around the character's head in a simple bonnet, making one twist under her chin. Be sure not to twist the balloon in place under her chin; take it off after measuring, make the locking twist, and then put it on her.

Rain: Inflate a blue balloon to within an inch. Make a leaf twist near the top of the balloon.

Flowers: Inflate two green balloons to within an inch. Make a leaf twist in each balloon. If you like, attach Geo-blossom balloons or simple round balloons to the leaf twist by wrapping the knot around the twist. (If you get a boy to be a flower, discard the blossom on top and tell him he is poison ivy. Boys like this.)

Mother Nature (the storyteller) stands with Sun and Rain on either side of her.
Sun and Rain were brother and sister.

They did what all brothers and sisters do: fight. (The audience will say this if you encourage them.)

Mother Nature would be taking them on a car trip somewhere, and Sun would say, "You're on my side of the car. Scoot over!"

Rain would say, "Am not!"

Sun would say, "Are too!" (*Encourage the kids to pick this up.*)

"Am not!"

"Are too!"

"Am not!"

"Are too!"

"Am not!"

"Are too!"

"KIDS!" Mother Nature would roar. "Don't make me pull this car over ...." and they would quit. For at least a minute. Then it would all start over again ....

"Am not!"

"Are too!"

"Am not!"

"Are too!"

"Am not!"

"Are too!"

"KIDS!"

And so it went. Sun and Rain argued about everything, everywhere. Finally, Mother Nature snapped. She walked in on an argument in progress.

"Am not!"

"Are too!"

"Am not!"

"Are too!"

"Am not!"

"Are too!"

And she said, "That's it! I am separating you two! Sun, you go live on that side of the world (*point to edge of performance area*). Rain you go live on that side of the world (*other side of performance area*). And don't come back until I tell you!"

So off Sun and Rain went, to live on opposite sides of the globe. (Don't you mothers wish you could do that sometimes?)

Well, when the flowers on the east side of the world — that's all of you in the audience — saw Rain coming, they got very excited. After all, Rain makes things grow. So the flowers sat up very straight, with their bottoms on their chairs (*or the floor or whatever*) and their hands on their knees. And when it started to rain (*child shakes blue balloon*), the flowers started to grow (*cue Flower 1 to begin rising*). And the flowers grew like this (*hands going slowly up in the air*), getting taller and taller until they stood up out of their seats (*it helps if the storyteller is also seated like the kids, and stands*) and got taller and taller, reaching up on their tiptoes, even.

But the rain kept raining. (*Kids will drop flower pose; keep yours.*) And all the flowers began to say, "Okay, that's enough, thanks." But it kept raining. And raining. And the flowers began to say (*make swimming motions with hands*) "Help! W-blub-we can't swim-glub! Help!" And all the flowers began to drown under all that water, until they had withered down into their seats with their bottoms on the floor and their hands on their knees.

(*Cross performance area*)

Meanwhile, on the west side of the world, Sun began to shine. And all the flowers — that's you guys — got very excited, with their hands on their knees and their bottoms in their seats. Because they knew that the sun makes things grow. So when the sun began shining (*encourage child to smile brightly*) the flowers began to grow. (*Repeat growing sequence.*)

But the sun kept shining. And the flowers began to get hot (*wipe forehead with "leaf" hand and sniff own underarm*) and ew! smelly. But the sun kept shining. And the flowers said, "Help! I'm melting!" and began to wither under that hot sun until they had withered back down into their seats with their hands on their knees.

When Mother Nature saw what was happening to all her lovely flowers, she said, "SUN! RAIN! COME HERE!" When your mother uses that tone of voice, you should do exactly what she tells you to.

And Mother Nature said, (*When kids are standing on either side of you*) "Now look, kids. See what's happening to the flowers? It takes the Sun AND the Rain to make flowers grow. And when you two fight and fuss and argue, you don't just hurt yourself; you hurt everyone around you. See what's happened to the flowers? You have to learn to get along. Now shake hands and make up."

So Sun and Rain shook hands. When they did, a rainbow formed. Now we know the rainbow is a symbol of peace. So the next time you see one, remember: Don't fight with your brothers and sisters! 🍂

Jack Fury and friends

DAN YASHINSKY

STORYTELLERS LIVE IN THE REAL WORLD. We vote, we participate in public affairs, we join the debate. In 1996 there was a referendum held in Quebec, a vote to determine if it should remain a province of Canada or establish a new relationship with the country. In the days leading up to this historic event, Canadian politicians became more and more hysterical in both of our official languages.

Thinking that storytellers could build the bridges that the politicians were destroying, I invited three Quebecois tellers to Toronto. They joined four English-speaking storytellers for a bilingual night of storytelling in front of a full house at Tallulali's Cabaret.

So it was that two days before the referendum, instead of watching the CBC news, I was listening to Jocelyn Berube play a lightning fiddle and whinny like a horse. He was telling the story of Alexis "le Trotteur," an extraordinary speedster from the Gaspe region of Quebec. Jocelyn had heard the legend from his father, who'd heard it from his father, whose best friend had been there on the fateful day back at the turn of the century when Alexis had run the world's first — and perhaps only — three-minute mile. Fueled by nothing more anabolic than *poutine* (an indescribable delicacy eaten in Quebec made of French fries covered with cheese and gravy) and perhaps maple syrup, this greatest of all Quebecois marathoners broke every record held by human or beast.

He had already beaten all the local racehorses when a new challenger came to the Gaspe: a locomotive. His race against the "iron horse" was, alas, the last he ever ran. Trying to outsprint the train, the mighty heart of Alexis "le Trotteur" burst. He died by the side of the tracks, the locomotive steamed past oblivious of its mechanical victory, and his glorious career fell to the storytellers to celebrate. According to Jocelyn, whose telling is paced by fiddle, neighing, and dog-dancing, the spirit of "le Trotteur" is still alive. Alexis continues his exuberant mad dash beyond all earthly orbits, out past the planets, happily chasing shooting stars and romancing the comets.

Jocelyn came to Toronto with Michel Faubert and Marc Laberge. They told in French, we — Itah Sadu, Bob Barton, Lynda Howes, *et moi* — told in English, and for one brief and bittersweet evening, I understood what Canada could be. The storytellers were doing what our politicians had been unable to accomplish. We weren't trading lists of grievances, arguing over constitutional amendments, effusing over or shunning our neighbors. We were simply listening to each other's stories. A wise writer, stating her philosophy of teaching, said, "Put your play into formal narratives and it will help you and your classmates listen to one another. In this way you will build a literature of images and themes, of beginnings and endings, of references and allusions. You must invent your own literature if you are to connect your ideas to the ideas of others." This is Vivian Gussin Paley describing how storytelling helps her class act like a community (in *The Boy Who Would Be A Helicopter*). She's talking about three-year-olds.

If this works for her preschool class, why not for the citizens of Canada or any other troubled land?

What stories were told that night? What "images and themes" were part of the literature we were trying to invent together? Marc Laberge told about the time a whole flock of ducks got caught by a sudden drop in temperature and were frozen in a pond. He and his father were out in the woods when they discovered this strange sight. They got in the middle of the ice and cut away the edges. Sure enough, when the ducks flapped their wings, the iceraft rose into the air. That's how they got home (luckily the ice didn't melt until they reached their own yard). It must have been a remarkable experience. Marc went on to become one of Quebec's most renowned adventure photographers, still gazing at the world through a lens made not of ice, but of finely ground glass.

Michel Faubert's story was about Ti-Jean, that notorious French trickster. When some bullying, bragging thieves steal his prize pig, Ti-Jean exacts a very thorough, rough, and comical revenge (it features cross-dressing, impersonating a physician, and a very big stick).

As for the English storytellers, Bob Barton told a creation myth about how earthworms came to be (God had some extra clay and wasn't sure what to do with it). Lynda Howes told about a Russian innkeeper who is plagued with mice until he shows kindness to an impoverished traveler (who turns out to have miraculous powers for herding both large and very small cattle). Itah Sadu told a Caribbean-inflected yarn about a boy who tried on lots of identities and names until he came back to Christopher, the one he started with. And I told the story of Jack Fury, a tale I heard from the late Cape Breton storyteller Joe Neil MacNeil.

Jack Fury works for two stingy bosses. Like all good folklore tricksters, Jack Fury turns their greed against them. I won't tell you all he does, but at the end of the story these two fools are begging Jack to throw them into the river so they can round up some of the fat cattle Jack has told them live under the water. He obliges, of course, and inherits their farm.

"Invent your own literature," as Paley says. Seven stories in two languages. Not much, perhaps, but surely a beginning. For one thing, the stories were told by word-of-mouth, and, as Joe Neil used to say in Gaelic and English, "What the ear does not hear will not move the heart." So these stories passed directly from the tellers to the listeners, there to be, one hopes, remembered and retold. Secondly, the stories evoke seven important ideas: speed and lightness; gazing through a new lens; using your wits; being creative with the clay in your hands; showing kindness to chance travelers; searching hard for your identity; and having the fury of Jack when the bosses show surpassing greed and criminal stinginess. I suspect all of these seven qualities were worth remembering on the eve of the referendum.

Over a beer late one night we did end up talking politics. The visiting tellers said that nobody they knew wanted to break the country up. They also said that change is necessary and urgent. I suspect they planned to vote *"oui"* to the idea of Quebec's sovereignty (in fact, a majority of

Francophones voted to separate from Canada and were outvoted by less than one percent of the vote). I also know they had a fine time in Anglophone Toronto and were astonished to find so many eager listeners for their stories. They went back up the highway to Montreal vowing to build stronger bridges between our two cultures.

Jocelyn made up this French proverb: "Life is a pair of pants held up by the suspenders of hope." Perhaps the greatest value storytellers bring to the world of politics is our love of listening. My country is still in a state of uncertainty, still trying to know and claim its proper destiny. My hope is that change can begin by listening to each other's stories.

Storytelling on the path to healing in Northern Ireland

Liz Weir

IRELAND IS KNOWN WORLDWIDE as a country with a strong oral tradition, and yet often this rich heritage is appreciated much more by those who live outside the country than by its own people. For many in Ireland, storytelling belonged in the past, and it is only in recent years that a genuine revival has taken place. This revival has been set against a backdrop of 30 years of violence and civil unrest in Northern Ireland. Storytelling has proven to be a force to bring people together regardless of religion or cultural background.

Shortening the road

The Belfast Public Libraries Summer Storytelling Program, which began in 1975, brings storytelling to children at up to 80 venues per week in the city. These are children who have been forced to grow up too quickly because of the unrest going on in the streets around them. In the early years of the program, tellers visited community centers. Word would spread that the storytellers had come to town. In spite of all the trouble, fires burning, overturned cars — we may have had to take the long way around to get there safely — tellers always did their best to arrive, for

we knew that the children would be waiting to hear our stories.

All the tellers involved had to be willing to go anywhere, whether they were Protestant or Catholic. Some of the tellers even changed their names so people wouldn't know their background right away, though the pronunciation of certain words in Ireland is an immediate giveaway. We made sure that we had storytellers representing both sides appearing at all our venues.

When I told stories to children, I noticed that the adults gathered and listened, too. Sometimes even the army foot patrols would stop at the edges of the gathering and listen to the stories. It seemed to me that the adults should also have a venue for sharing their own tales. In 1985, the formation of the first community storytelling group, The Yarnspinners, gave adults in Belfast the opportunity to meet and share stories in a neutral city center venue.

Since then, storytelling for adults has continued to spread its web, with clubs in Dundonald, Derry, and Newry, and has also spread south to the Republic of Ireland, with groups in Dublin, Cork, and Limerick. The Ulster Storytelling Festival started in 1989 at the Ulster Folk and

Transport Museum in Cultra, Holywood, County Down, and since then festivals have sprung up all over Ireland, in Derry, Dublin, Cape Clear Island, Omagh, and Courtmacsherry.

Stories in the schools

Educators soon realized the value of bringing young people together, and two new cross-curricular strands were added to the Northern Ireland curriculum — Education for Mutual Understanding and Cultural Heritage. Since the vast majority of children in Northern Ireland are educated in segregated schools, with Protestants attending state schools and Catholics going to schools run by the Catholic Council for Maintained Schools, it is all the more vital to give young people the opportunity to meet and share experiences. There were projects in which pupils from these two school systems listened to stories together and then collected and shared family stories and local legends. The aim was to enable them to appreciate other people's stories and to realize that history itself can be interpreted differently depending on whose story we hear.

Once, before the first cease-fire, storyteller Billy Teare was telling stories to the school children of Castlederg, on the border between Northern Ireland and the Republic of Ireland. Billy had just spent one week at the local Catholic primary school and was about to begin telling at the state school the following week. The children from these two schools rode the same bus — Catholics on one side and Protestants on the other — never talking to each other during these daily bus trips throughout the school year. But the bus driver reported that one day he heard one of the children from the Catholic school call across the aisle, "Hey — you're going to have that storyteller coming to your school this week, aren't you? See if he tells you this ..." and then the student went on to recount the entire story that Billy had told at his school!

Story projects for peace

There are many examples of storytelling being used as a vehicle to bring people together to express their sincerely held views. During 1999, an award-winning BBC radio program, "Legacy," broadcast daily accounts of people's memories of the troubles: a mother whose son was shot by a policeman, a policeman who lost his wife — everyone knew someone who was lost among the one-and-a-half-million inhabitants of Northern Ireland. This five-minute slot, right before the main nine o'clock morning news broadcast, gave a voice to many who had previously bottled up their pain.

An Crann (The Tree) is a project that helps people tell their own stories of the last 30 years of conflict. WAVE, an organization set up to offer support for victims of trauma, participated in the project. Prisoners' wives, policemen's widows, bomb victims, and more all come together to share the stories of their pain and move a step closer toward recovery.

There have also been initiatives in the Maze Prison, where political prisoners have had the chance to work with a professional storyteller to gain storytelling skills and prepare themselves for release. In any situation where violence has caused deep hurt, the needs of victims must be taken into account, and yet it is impossible to move forward without considering those who have been involved in the conflict and their place in any solution. I shared stories with the inmates that they could later tell to their own children at visiting time. Some of these men intended to work in community service placements with troubled youth. Since stories help produce intimacy, the former inmates found that sharing stories with young people was a good way to get to know them. We worked on a mixture of stories springing from creative writing, oral history, and traditional tales.

Telling secrets never told

When the Verbal Arts Center in Derry asked if I would be interested in working with residents of the Simon Community, which provides accommodations for homeless people, I immediately said "Yes!" I was eager to embark on what sounded like a fascinating project combining photography, video production, journalism, and storytelling. Everyone in our society has a story to tell, yet sometimes certain groups of people get overlooked, so this seemed to be an excellent way to give a voice to homeless people who may not have had a chance to put their stories forward before.

All the participants were men — of the sort who didn't usually talk about themselves. Some of the people were staying in short-term residential hostels and others in long-term apartments. Over time, I learned that some had come to the Simon Community due to changes that had occurred in their lives. Some were going through divorce, others had jobs but no transport, some were in recovery from alcohol addiction, and some had lost their jobs. Each person's story was different. I had known of the work of the Simon Community in the past and always reckoned that it would be foolish to stereotype "homeless" people; every individual is different and everyone has a different tale to tell, and the group in Derry was no exception.

The way I approach storytelling is to meet people, tell them stories, and try to encourage them to tell whatever sort of story they want. From our initial meeting at the Bonds Hill Center, I was struck by the richness of material available: everything from jokes, riddles, supersti-

tions, personal memories, folktales, ghost stories, creative writing, even traditional sayings such as the rhyme for counting magpies:

> *One for sorrow*
> *Two for joy*
> *Three for a girl*
> *Four for a boy*
> *Five for silver*
> *Six for gold*
> *Seven for a secret never to be told.*

We met on a weekly basis to talk, laugh, share food, and of course drink tea together, and as the evenings wore on we swapped tales and grew comfortable with each other. Humor was big and we heard such funny tales. One member of our gatherings told of a local who had seen a vision of the Virgin Mary by a bush. The man stripped and jumped into the bush. His faith thus tested and proven also left the man with prickles in extremely tender places. A regular named Stan told us of the time he was going to join the French Foreign Legion. Stan was so drunk at the time that he was thrown out of the Foreign Legion office, for which he is now forever grateful because he has since learned that it is near to impossible to get out once you are in. There were stories of the troubled times as well. One resident spoke of someone who had shot at the British Army and then run into his family's living room to escape. Everyone just moved over on the couch to make room for the intruder, and they all watched TV together as the soldiers ran through the room in pursuit.

I had to be flexible and patient for this work. These folks didn't have to be there and they would vote with their feet if they lost interest. The content and direction of a project like this is very much up to the participants, and we agreed that we should produce a book of some kind to preserve the stories and celebrate the sharing of them. There was real storytelling talent in this group, and also creative writing ability that deserved a wider audience. We made links with the local creative writing group, and members of the Simon Community group have also attended the monthly Yarnspinning evenings of storytelling in Derry's Central Library.

Through this process I have seen individuals become less reserved and readier to speak up, and really enjoy both telling and listening to stories. Storytelling gives people confidence — it is important for people to feel that others are valuing their stories. In today's fast-moving society there are fewer opportunities for people to spend time really listening. This project was a learning experience for me and for all the members of the group as we came to understand each other better and made the decision to move on and take the stories out to a wider audience. One of the members of the Simon Community is now a regular weekly teller on BBC radio.

The people who initiated this project weren't sure how it would be received or what would evolve from the process. Our experience not only validated that this was a worthy effort, but also underlined that it was a needed outlet for the residents to gain self-esteem and to create a closer sense of community. There is great potential to expand this project to other centers and to develop it in terms of publication and also as a radio feature.

Sharing tales between generations

"Sharing Tales" was a storytelling project undertaken for the Verbal Arts Centre based in Derry.

The project involved three primary schools in Derry, Strabane, and Limavady; three hospitals for the elderly, Waterside, Strabane, and Roe Valley; and the collaboration of storytellers, teachers, and health professionals. Our aim was to bring together seniors and elementary school pupils to share stories. We hoped to encourage the seniors to reminisce and share their own stories with the children. The nursing staff would be involved in storytelling activities with elderly patients as well. We conducted introductory sessions with teachers, nursing staff, children, and seniors to prepare everyone for this project.

After the preparation, Billy Teare and I told stories to the young people and the older people separately. Then the school classes visited the hospital on a number of occasions to hear stories with the seniors and to have the chance to talk and share their own experiences. The older people's stories were recorded. The young people also collected stories from their own families and neighbors, and drew illustrations for some of the experiences.

Memories of these events were preserved and shared. A booklet of stories from young and old was launched at a huge celebration attracting extensive press, radio, and television coverage. The nursing staff added their own evaluation from evidential changes in their patients. Elders who didn't talk at all at the hospital before were suddenly speaking up! Relatives and friends were amazed at what they hadn't known about their community. To sum up, one boy said, "My granddad died before I was born, but stories he told have been retold to my generation. This has made me feel I knew him."

A Wee Lift

AN IRISH FOLKTALE RETOLD BY LIZ WEIR*

The following story is one that I have shared with many of the audiences I have written about here. Sometimes all we have to do to give others a start toward their own healing is to share a bit of time and listen closely as they tell their story.

> *Once there was a farmer who lived with his wife in Ireland,*
> *on a hill farm in the Glens of Antrim.*
> *He had a run of bad luck.*

His fences needed mending, the cow wasn't milking so well, the hens were off the lay, and he was feeling pretty low. He just hadn't the energy to get up and fix things. One evening, as the couple was getting ready to eat supper, there was a knock at the door. On the doorstep stood an old tramp, filthy dirty, clothes ragged and torn, who asked them for shelter for the night as there was a storm coming. Of course the farmer was a kind man at heart, so they welcomed the stranger in and shared what little food and drink they had with him, just potatoes and buttermilk.

Conversation flowed over the supper table, and the farmer started to talk about all his misfortunes while the old man ate and listened. The tramp slept the night by the open fire. When he was leaving in the morning he said, "You have helped me, maybe I can help you," and from under his coat he took a bar of purest gold and handed it to the farmer. "Keep this and maybe it will be a help to you. I'll come back next year and see how you've managed." Without another word he was gone.

The farmer and his wife stared in wonder and didn't know what to do with the gold, so they buried it beside the fire in the earthen kitchen floor for safekeeping. As the days passed, they wondered.

"Maybe we could get a new cow," said the wife.

"No," the farmer said. "That old girl will come back to her own."

"What about some more hens, then?"

"I think they'll settle down — we won't rush to get rid of them."

"Do you need some posts for fencing?"

"Haven't I had posts and all in the barn for when I get round to doing it?"

And so the talk went on.

A year passed and when the tramp returned to the farm, the place was flourishing. The farmer and his wife greeted him like an old friend. They set up a fine meal on the table and soon the talk came round to the farm.

"Well, the place is looking grand!" said the tramp. "What did you spend the gold on?"

The farmer and his wife exchanged a smile. "Well, to tell you the truth," said the farmer, "we didn't spend it after all — it's still where it was buried in the kitchen. Once I started to work on things, we soon got the place going again. You gave us just the wee 'lift' that we needed."

"Well," said the tramp, "if you don't mind, I'll take the gold with me on my way because there might be someone else along my road who could do with a wee 'lift' to help them through life!"

And so it is for all of us — sometimes that's all it takes — a friendly word or action to give us a "lift." &

The Two Warriors

DAN KEDING

The following story by Dan Keding has been a favorite among the Irish audiences who are working to heal the rift in their country.
— Liz Weir

Once there was a war and two armies came together in battle.
They fought from the time the sun came up in the east till it set in the west.
When the day was at a close, only two warriors remained, surrounded by
their dead comrades covered in the blood and gore of war.

They stood facing each other, so exhausted from death that they could barely move. Finally one said, "It will do us no honor to continue this way. Let us rest till dawn and then finish this fight and only one will go home." The other warrior agreed.

And so they took off their dented helmets and unstrapped their shields and sheathed their swords. They lay down among their fallen comrades only a few feet apart from each other. But they were so weary that they could not sleep. It was the weariness that comes with too much killing. Finally one turned to the other and spoke.

"I have a son at home in my village and he plays with a wooden sword. Someday he wants to grow up and be like me."

The other man listened and finally replied, "I have a daughter at home and when I look into her eyes I see the youth of my wife."

The two men started to tell each other stories. Stories of their families, their villages, their neighbors, the old stories that they learned at their grandparents' knees when they were young. All night long they told stories till the sun started to creep to life in the east.

Slowly they stood and put on their helmets. They buckled on their shields and drew their swords. They looked deep into each others' eyes and slowly sheathed their swords and walked away, each to his own home.

Grandmother always said you cannot hate someone when you know their story. &

PASS IT ON!

The Endangered Stories Act in action

BOB KANEGIS

If you don't know the trees,
you may become lost in the forest;
But if you don't know the stories,
you may become lost in life.
— Siberian proverb

THE ENDANGERED STORIES ACT was proclaimed after hearing the all-too-familiar lament, "Grandpa used to tell such wonderful stories. I wish I'd paid more attention or recorded them. Now they're gone." Sound familiar? These stories of our families and friends are a great source of wealth, along with traditional tales, myths, legends, and folktales. They enrich our lives. They make us more fully known to each other. The loss of these stories, just like the loss of habitat or the disappearance of an endangered species, erodes the wealth of our living heritage. Act Now ... Save the Stories!

Some time ago I went about asking people to share with me a story about a special gift that they had either given or received. One young woman, a waitress in a local coffee shop, offered this tale: Her family had fallen on hard times. Her father had literally been run over by a truck and had not been able to work for several years. Christmas was approaching and her grandmother was feeling sad because there was little money for gifts. But after further thought, she realized that she had something that she very much did

want to and could give. She offered her granddaughter three days alone together, during which time she gave the gift of her life story, telling of things that she had not spoken of for many years. She told these stories to this granddaughter because she had been the one who had in the past asked and shown interest. With tears in her eyes, this fortunate granddaughter said that this was absolutely the best gift she had ever received.

You can begin by asking a friend, a parent, a child, or even a stranger to tell you something about themselves or their family that you have never heard before. A Grade 3 class took this on as an assignment and returned to class bursting with enthusiasm at their new discoveries. A library in New Mexico presented an evening of family storytelling and created a beautiful endangered stories talking stick to commemorate the event. The possibilities are endless. What is guaranteed is that the activity of asking, listening, and telling deepens understanding and strengthens relationships.

The Endangered Stories Act is an invitation to a story, the seed of an idea. It is offered as a tool to enliven the oral tradition. In keeping with the request that people commit to becoming the Caretaker of a story, it is our intention at Tales & Trails to act as the caretaker for the "story" of the Endangered Stories Act. We would love to hear from anyone who is sparked to put it into action.

There are myriad ways that people are already doing this work, and we would love to hear your suggestions so that we can pass them on. We encourage you to make and distribute copies of the Act and to implement it in your own way, in schools, libraries, family gatherings. Behind all

this is the conviction that as we are more and more known to each other through the stories we tell, we can create more possibilities for understanding and community in this world. We hope to hear from you as you put the ESA into action!

THE ENDANGERED STORIES ACT

An Act of the People, not of Congress

Proclamation

In Order to Honor the rich heritage of oral traditions that exist in all cultures and among all people; and

Recognizing the Power of Stories to enrich individuals, families, and communities; and

Aware of the Power of Stories to transmit values that help make life sustainable to our own and future generations; and

Conscious of the Power of Stories to link us to each other through the recognition and celebration of both diversity and our common heritage; and

Whereas a Story told for the last time and not passed on will become irretrievably extinct, lost forever to the people and the future;

Therefore, We The People create the Endangered Stories Act and acting on its behalf:

Promise to ask our Elders to tell us their Stories, to share with us stories of their origins, accomplishments, hardships, and their hopes and dreams for the future;

Pledge to strengthen our listening and our voices; to find and tell our own Stories; and

Commit to find a tale that speaks to us and to become the Caretaker of that Story.

We will tell and retell that Story and find another person to pass it on to, thus preserving it for posterity.

We hereby ratify the Endangered Stories Act and add our voices to begin its implementation today!

Bibliography

Recommended by our Authors and Friends

MANY STORYTELLERS HELPED to shape this collection of recommended reading and stories. Thanks go to the authors of the articles and stories in both volumes of *The Healing Heart*. We also received recommendations from members of the Healing Story Alliance and their Healing Story listserv (www.healingstory.org), the Storytell Discussion List sponsored by Texas Women's University (www.twu.edu/cope/slis/storytell.htm), members of the National Storytelling Network (www.storynet.org/index.htm) and the Storytelling and Diversity Discussion Group listserv. We extend our gratitude to the tellers and listeners we have met along the way who shared their experiences, favorite books and the special stories that provide pathways to healing.

Please respect the copyright of the books recommended in this bibliography. The literary stories can be used as a guide for shaping your own stories or you can seek permissions for oral retellings from the author or publisher.

Abuse and Domestic Violence

Abuse and domestic violence — Selected stories

Barchers, Suzanne I., ed. "The Tale Of The Oki Islands" in *Wise Women: Folk and Fairy Tales from around the World*. Englewood, CO: Libraries Unlimited, 1990.

Chase, Richard. "Like Meat Loves Salt" in *Grandfather Tales*. Boston: Houghton Mifflin, 1990.

Czarnota, Lorna. "Moth To A Flame" in *Crossroads*. New York: Self published, 1999. Phone: 716-837-0551.

Estes, Clarissa Pinkola, "Skeleton Woman," "Sealskin, Soulskin," "The Red Shoes," and "The Handless Maiden" in *Women Who Run With The Wolves*. New York: Ballantine Books, 1992.

Evetts-Secker, Josephine. "The Waterfall of White Hair" in *Mother and Daughter Tales*. New York: Abbeville Press, 1996.

Justice, Jennifer., ed. "The Story Of A Pumpkin" in *The Ghost and I*. Cambridge, MA: Yellow Moon Press, 1990.

Martin, Rafe. *The Rough Face Girl*. New York: G.P. Putnam's Sons, 1992.

Minard, Rosemary., ed. "Cap O' Rushes" in *Womenfolk and Fairy Tales*. Boston: Houghton Mifflin, 1975.

Monaghan, Patricia. "By the Fountain at the Edge of the Sky" in *Wild Girls: The Path of the Young Goddess*. St. Paul, MN: Llewellyn Publications, 2001.

Ransome, Arthur. "The Stolen Turnips" in *Old Peter's Russian Folktales*. Toronto: Thomas Nelson and Sons, 1967. As the author suggests, you can switch the roles of the husband and wife.

Stone, Merlin. "Hina," "Songi," "Lia," and "PoHaha" in *Ancient Mirrors of Womanhood: A Treasury of Goddess and Heroine Lore from Around the World*. Boston: Beacon Press, 1979.

Wolkstein, Diane. "I'm Tipingee, She's Tipingee, We're Tipingee Too" and "The Magic Orange Tree" in *The Magic Orange Tree and other Haitian Folktales*. New York: Schocken Books/Random House, 1997.

Yolen, Jane. "The Boy Who Drew Unicorns" in *The Faery Flag*. New York: Orchard Books, 1989.

———,ed. "The Spirit of the Van" and "The Seal Skin" in *Favorite Folktales From Around The World*. New York: Pantheon Books, 1988.

———. "The Tree's Wife" in *Dream Weaver*. New York: Philomel Books, 1989.

———. *The Boy Who Had Wings*. New York: Ty Crowell Co., 1974. A father shuns his son due to the boy's unique qualities.

Abuse and domestic violence — Personal stories

Wood, Wendy, and Leslie Ann Hatton. *Triumph Over Darkness: Understanding and Healing The Trauma of Childhood Sexual Abuse*. Hillsboro, OR: Beyond Words Publishing, 1993. Poetry, art, and personal stories of 70 women recovering from childhood sexual abuse.

Adoption and Foster Families

Ashabranner, Brent, and Russell Davis. "The Lion's Whiskers" in *The Lion's Whiskers and Other Ethiopian Tales*. North Haven, CT: Linnet Books, 1997.

Burch, Milbre. "Odilia and Aldaric" in *Saints and Other Sinners*. Chapel Hill, NC: Kind Crone Productions, 1990. (Audio recording) Contact author for purchase. See website <http://www.kindcrone.com>.

Estes, Clarissa Pinkola. *Warming the Stone Child: Myths and Stories About Abandonment and the Unmothered Child*. Boulder, CO: Sounds True, 1997. (Audio recording)

MacDonald, Margaret Read. "The Bear-Child" in *Look Back And See*. New York: H.W. Wilson, 1991.

Minard, Rosemary. "The Stolen Bairn and the Sìdh" in *Womenfolk and Fairy Tales*. Boston: Houghton Mifflin, 1975.

Ransome, Arthur. "The Little Daughter of the Snow" in *Old Peter's Russian Tales*. Toronto: Thomas Nelson and Sons, 1967.

Spellman, John W. "The King's True Children" in *The Beautiful Blue Jay and Other Tales of India*. Boston: Little, Brown & Company, 1967.

Synge, Ursula. "Odilia and Aldaric" in *The Giant at the Ford and Other Legends of the Saints*. New York: Atheneum, 1980.

Wolkstein, Diane. "One, My Darling, Come to Mama" in *The Magic Orange Tree and other Haitian Folktales*. New York: Schocken Books/Random House, 1997.

Wyndham, Lee. "Once There Was and Once There Was Not" in *Tales the People Tell in Russia*. New York: J. Messner, 1970.

Yolen, Jane. *Greyling*. New York: Philomel Books, 1991.

Books About Storytelling

Baker, Augusta, and Ellin Greene. *Storytelling: Art and Technique*. New York: R. R. Bowker, 1987.

Barton, Bob. *Tell Me Another*. Markham, ON: Pembroke, 1986.

Dailey, Sheila. *Putting the World in a Nutshell: The Art of the Formula Tale*. New York: H.W. Wilson, 1994.

de Vos, Gail, Merle Harris, and Celia Lottridge. *Telling Tales: Storytelling in the Family*. Edmonton: University of Alberta Press, 2003.

Livo, N. and S. Rietz. *Storytelling: Process and Practice*. Littleton, CO: Libraries Unlimited, 1986.

MacDonald, Margaret Read. *The Storyteller's Start-Up Book: Finding, Learning, Performing, and Using Folktales, Including Twelve Tellable Tales*. Little Rock, AR: August House, 1993.

Pellowski, Anne. *The World of Storytelling: A Practical Guide to the Origins, Development, and Applications of Storytelling*. New York: H.W. Wilson, 1990.

Yolen, Jane. *Touch Magic: Fantasy, Faerie and Folklore in the Literature of Childhood*. New York: Philomel Books, 1981.

Community Building Resources

Kretzmann, John P., and John L. McKnight. *Building Communities from the Inside Out: A Path Toward Finding and Mobilizing a Community Assets*. ACTA Publications, 1997.

Mattessich, Paul, and Barbara Monsey. *Community Building: What Makes It Work? A Review of Factors Influencing Successful Community Building*. St. Paul, MN: Amherst H. Wilder Foundation, 1997.

Some, Malidoma Patrice. *Ritual: Power, Healing and Community*. Portland, OR: Swan Raven and Company, 1993.

Taylor-Ide, Daniel. *Just and Lasting Change: When Communities Own Their Futures*. Baltimore, MD: Johns Hopkins University Press, 2002.

Zipes, Jack. *Creative Storytelling: Building Community, Changing Lives*. New York: Routledge, 1995. Creating community in the classroom.

Coping With Illness

Coping with illness — Selected stories

Aardema, Verna. *Who's In Rabbit's House? A Masai Tale*. New York: Dial, 1990. Talking back to fears.

Hodges, Margaret. *Buried Moon*. Boston: Little, Brown & Company, 1990. Importance of a support system.

Holt, David and Bill Mooney., eds. "Little Burnt Face" in *Ready-To-Tell Tales: Sure-Fire Stories from America's Favorite Storytellers*. Little Rock, AR: August House, 1994.

MacDonald, Margaret Read. "Let's Go On A Bear Hunt" in *The Parent's Guide to Storytelling: How to Make Up New Stories and Retell Old Favorites*. Little Rock, AR: August House, 2001. Great participation story for children who are going through difficult experiences.

Coping with illness — Personal stories

Remen, Rachel Naomi. *Kitchen Table Wisdom: Stories That Heal*. New York: Riverhead Books, 1996.

———. *My Grandfather's Blessings: Stories of Strength, Refuge and Belonging*. New York: Riverhead Books, 2000.

Rybarczyk, Bruce, and Albert Bellg. *Listening to Life Stories: A new approach to stress intervention in health care*. New York: Springer Publishing Company, 1997.

Coping with illness — Additional resource

Kuner, Susan, Carol Matzkim Osborn, Linda Quigley, and Karen Leigh Stroup. *Speak the Language of Healing: Living With Breast Cancer Without Going to War*. Berkeley, CA: Conari Press, 1999. Describes stages of breast cancer as "impact, chaos, choices, community, and spirit."

Deconstructing Prejudice

Deconstructing prejudice — Selected stories

Bryan, Ashley. "Why the Frog Never Plays with the Snake" in *Beat the Story Drum, Pum Pum*. Minneapolis, MN: Econo-Clad Books, 1999.

McKissack, Patricia. "The Woman In The Snow" in *The Dark Thirty*. New York: Knopf, 1992.

Rylant, Cynthia. "Slower Than The Rest" in *Every Living Thing*. New York: Aladdin Books/Macmillan, 1985.

Surat, Michele Maria. *Angel Child, Dragon Child*. Milwaukee, WI: Raintree Publishers, 1983. A Vietnamese girl in the U.S. is tormented by a boy at school because she is different.

Swope, Sam. *The Araboolies of Liberty Street*. New York: Random House, 1989.

Wilkes, Sybella. "The Party" in *One Day We Had To Run*. Brookfield, CT: Millbrook Press, 1994. Refugee children tell the story of the bat who just wants to find somewhere to belong.

Deconstructing prejudice — Personal stories

O'Halloran, Susan, Antonio Sacre, and La'Ron Williams. *Tribes and Bridges at the Steppenwolf Theatre*. Chicago: Angels Studio SVD and O'Halloran Communications, 2000. Available through the website <www.race-bridges.net/sue>.

Elder Tales

Elder tales — Story collections

Chinen, Allan B. *In The Ever After: Fairy Tales and the Second Half of Life*. Wilmette, IL: Chiron Publications, 1989.

Meade, Michael. *The Second Adventure of Life: Reinventing Mentors and Elders*. Pacific Grove, CA: Oral Tradition Archives, 1998. (audio cassette).

Thomas, Ann G. *The Women We Become: Myths, Folktales, and Stories About Growing Older*. Rocklin, CA: Prima Publishing, 1997.

Yolen, Jane. *Gray Heroes: Elder Tales from Around the World*. New York: Penguin, 1999.

Elder tales — Encouraging remembrance

Akeret, Ed, and Robert U. Akeret. *Family Tales, Family Wisdom: How to Gather the Stories of a Lifetime and Share Them With Your Family*. New York: Henry Holt and Company, 1992.

Crimmens, Paula. *Storymaking and Creative Groupwork with Old People*. London/ Bristol, PA: Jessica Kingsley Publishers, 1998.

Greene, Bob, and D.J. Fulford. *To Our Children's Children*. New York: Doubleday, 1993.

Kaminsky, Marc. *The Uses of Reminiscence: New Ways of Working with Older Adults*. New York: Haworth Press, 1984.

Kindig, Eileen Silva. *Remember the Time?: The Power and Promise of Family Storytelling*. Downers Grove, IL: Intervarsity Press, 1997.

Meyerhoff, Barbara. *Remembered Lives: The Work of Ritual, Storytelling and Growing Older*. Ann Arbor, MI: University of Michigan Press, 1992.

Rainer, Tristine. *Your Life as Story: Discovering the "New Autobiography" and Writing Memoir As Literature*. New York: J.P. Tarcher/Putnam, 1998.

Elder tales — Working with Alzheimer's disease

Bridges, Barbara J. *Therapeutic Caregiving: A Practical Guide for Caregivers of Persons with Alzheimer's and Other Dementia Causing Diseases.* Mill Creek, WA: BJB Publishing: 1995.

Feil, Naomi. *The Validation Breakthrough: Simple Techniques for Communicating with People with "Alzheimer's-Type Dementia."* Baltimore, MD: Health Professions Press, Inc., 1993.

Mace, Nancy L., and Peter V. Rabins. *The 36-Hour Day. A family guide to Alzheimer's disease, related dementing illness and memory loss in later life.* New York: Warner Books, 2001.

Environmental Tales

Environmental tales — Story collections

Altman, Nathaniel. *Sacred Trees.* San Francisco: Sierra Club Books, 1994.

Brody, Ed, Jay Goldspinner, Katie Green, Rona Leventhal, and John Porcino., eds. *Spinning Tales, Weaving Hope: Stories, Storytelling, and Activities for Peace, Justice and the Environment.* Gabriola Island, BC: New Society Publishers, 2002.

Caduto, Michael. *Earth Tales from Around the World.* Golden, CO: Fulcrum Publishing, 1997.

Caduto, Michael, and Joseph Bruchac. *Keepers of the Animals: Native American Stories and Wildlife Activities for Children.* Golden, CO: Fulcrum Publishing, 1991.

———. *Keepers of the Earth: Native American Stories and Environmental Activities for Children.* Golden, CO: Fulcrum Publishing, 1988.

Dean, Jana. *Sound Wisdom: Stories of Place.* Olympia, Wa: Puget Sound Water Quality Authority, 1993. Available from the author at deanjana@hotmail.com.

DeSpain, Pleasant. *Eleven Nature Tales: A Multicultural Journey.* Little Rock, AR: August House, 1996.

Elliott, Doug. *Wildwoods Wisdom: Encounters with the Natural World.* New York: Paragon House, 1992.

———. *Wild Roots.* Rochester, VT: Healing Arts Press, 1995.

Gersie, Alida. *Earth Tales: Storytelling In Times Of Change.* London: Merlin Press, 1992.

Hamilton, Virginia. *In the Beginning: Creation Stories from Around the World.* San Diego: Harcourt, 1988.

MacDonald, Margaret Read. *Earth Care: World Folktales to Talk About.* North Haven, CT: Shoe String Press, 1999.

McVickar Edwards, Carolyn. *Sun Stories: Tales from Around the World to Illuminate the Days and Nights of Our Lives.* New York: HarperCollins, 1995.

Milord, Susan. *Tales of the Shimmering Sky: Ten Global Folktales With Activities.* Charlotte, VT: Williamson Publishing, 1996.

Moroney, Lynn. *Moontellers: Myths of the Moon from Around the World.* Flagstaff, AZ: Rising Moon, 1995.

Pellowski, Anne. *The Hidden Stories In Plants.* New York: Macmillan Publishing, 1990.

Strauss, Susan. *Coyote Stories for Children: Tales from Native America.* Hillsboro, OR: Beyond Words, 1991.

———. *Wolf Stories: Myths and True-Life Tales from Around the World.* Hillsboro, OR: Beyond Words, 1994.

Yep, Laurence. "We Are All One" in *The Rainbow People.* New York: HarperCollins Juvenile Books, 1992.

Environmental tales — Selected stories

Arkhurst, Joyce Cooper. "How Spider Got a Thin Waist" in *The Adventures of Spider: West African Folk Tales*. Boston: Little, & Company, 1992.

Frankel, Ellen. "Ibn Ezra's Bad Luck" from *The Classic Tales: 4000 years of Jewish Lore*. London: Jewish Publication Society, 1998.

Gillham, Charles E. "How the Little Owl's Name was Changed" in *Beyond the Clapping Mountains: Eskimo Stories from Alaska*. New York: Macmillan, 1944.

Ginsburg, Mirra. "Which Eye is Blind" in *Three Rolls and One Doughnut: Fables from Russia*. New York: Dial Press, 1970.

Heady, Eleanor B. "The Big Fire" in *Sage Smoke: Tales of the Shoshoni-Bannock Indians*. Chicago: Follett Publishing, 1973.

Parker, Arthur C. "The Owl's Big Eyes" in *Skunny Wundy: Seneca Indian Tales*. New York: Syracuse University Press, 1994.

Rohmer, Harriet, and Octavio Chow., eds. *The Invisible Hunters: A Legend from the Miskito Indians of Nicaragua/Los Cazadores Invisibles: Una Leyenda De Los Indios Miskito De Nicaragua*. San Francisco: Children's Book Press, 1987.

Seuss, Dr. *The Lorax*. New York: Random House, 1971.

Shannon, George. "The Frog" in *More Stories to Solve: 15 Folktales from Around the World*. New York: Greenwillow Books, 1990.

Strauss, Susan. *The Passionate Fact: Storytelling in Natural History and Cultural Interpretation*. Golden, CO: North American Press/Fulcrum Publishing, 1996.

———. *When Woman Became the Sea: A Costa Rican Creation Myth*. Hillsboro, OR: Beyond Words, 1998.

Martinez, Alejandro, and Rosalma Zubizaretta-Ada. *The Woman Who Outshone the Sun: The Legend of Lucia Zenteno/La mujer que brillaba aún más que el sol: La leyenda de Lucia Zenteno*. San Francisco: Children's Book Press, 1991.

Exploring Alternative Sexual Identities

Exploring alternative sexual identities — Story collections

Cashorali, Peter. *Fairy Tales: Traditional Stories Retold For Gay Men*. San Francisco: HarperSanFrancisco, 1995.

———. *Gay and Fairy and Folk Tales: More Traditional Stories Retold for Gay Men*. Boston: Faber and Faber, 1997.

Donahue, Emma. *Kissing The Witch: Old Tales In New Skins*. New York: HarperCollins Publishers, 1997. Literary retelling of 13 fairy tales, told through the eyes of the unique women in these stories.

Thomas, Marlo. *Free to Be, You and Me*. Philadelphia: Running Press, 1998. Stories, poetry, songs, dialogues, essays that introduce the more serious realities of sexism to young children, but will be enjoyed by all ages.

Exploring alternative sexual identities — Selected stories

Chinen, Allan B. "The King has Goats Ears" in *Beyond the Hero*. New York: Tarcher/Putnam, 1993. The power of secrets.

DeHaan, Linda, and Nijland Stern. *King and King*. Berkeley, CA: Tricycle Press, 2002. A prince searches for his perfect match and finds another prince.

Exploring alternative sexual identities — Additional resource

Connor, Randy, Mariya Sparks, and David Hatfield Sparks. *Cassell's Encyclopedia of Queer Myth, Symbol and Spirit: Gay, Lesbian, Bisexual and Transgender Lore.* Continuum International Publishing Group, 1998.

Grahn, Judy. *Another Mother Tongue: Gay Words, Gay Worlds.* Boston: Beacon Press, 1990. Combines history, folklore, and personal stories to offer a history of gay culture.

Grief and Loss

Grief and loss — Story collections

Estes, Clarissa Pinkola. *Radiant Coat: Myths and Stories About the Crossing Between Life and Death.* Boulder, CO: Sounds True, 1993. (Audio recording)

Gignoux, Jane Hughes. *Some Folk Say: Stories of Life, Death and Beyond.* New York: Foulketale Publishing, 1998.

Henderson, Joseph L., and Maud Oakes. *The Wisdom of the Serpent: The Myths of Death, Rebirth, and Resurrection.* Princeton: Princeton University Press, 1963.

Livo, Norma. *Who's Afraid...? Facing Children's Fears with Folktales.* Greenwood Village, CO: Teacher Ideas Press, 1994.

Rosen, Gail. *Darkness and Dawn: One Woman's Mythology of Loss and Healing.* Pikesville, MD: Self published, 1997. 721 Howard Road Pikesville, Maryland 21208. (Audio recording)

———. *Listening After The Music Stops, Stories of Loss and Comfort.* Pikesville, MD: Self published, 1998. 721 Howard Road, Pikesville, Maryland 21208. (Audio recording)

Simms, Laura. *Stories To Nourish The Hearts Of Our Children In A Time Of Crisis.* New York: Holland and Knight, 2001.

Williamson, Duncan, and Linda Williamson. *May the Devil Walk Behind Ye!* Edinburgh: Cannongate, 1989. Traditional stories reflecting a Scottish outlook on death.

Grief and loss — Selected stories

Alexander, Sue, and Jim Trelease., eds. "Nadia the Willful" in *Hey! Listen to This: Stories to Read Aloud.* New York: Penguin Books, 1992.

Ashabranner, Brent, and Russell Davis. "The Lion's Whiskers" in *The Lion's Whiskers and Other Ethiopian Tales.* North Haven, CT: Linnet Books, 1997.

Cavanaugh, Brian. "A Cure for Sorrow," "Telling One's Own Story," "The Sorrow Tree," "Story to Heal," "The Face in the Window," "I Created You," "Grains of Caring," "Heaven and Hell," "Attitude at Work," "Merchant of Death," and "Find Someone in Need" in *The Sower's Seeds.* New York: Paulist Press, 1990.

Courlander, Harold, and George Herzog. "The Cow Tail Switch" in *The Cow Tail Switch and Other West African Stories.* New York: Henry Holt and Company, 1986.

DeSpain, Pleasant. "Grizzly Bear Feast" in *Eleven Nature Tales: A Multicultural Journey.* Little Rock, AR: August House Publishers, 1996

Estes, Clarissa Pinkola. *The Gift of Story: A Wise Tale About What Is Enough.* New York: Ballantine Books, 1993. Triumph of love over loss.

Feldman, Christina, and Jack Kornfield, eds. "The Mustard Seed" and "Blessings and Disasters" in *Soul Food: Stories to Nourish the Spirit and the Heart.* San Francisco: Harper, 1996.

Holt, David, and Bill Mooney., eds. "La Muerta: Godmother Death" in *Ready-To-Tell Tales: Sure-fire Stories From America's Favorite Storytellers*. Little Rock, AR: August House, 1994.

McVickar Edwards, Carolyn. "Kali, Dancer On Gravestones" in *The Storyteller's Goddess: Tales of the Goddess and Her Wisdom from Around the World*. San Francisco: HarperSanFrancisco, 1991.

Schram, Peninnah, and Jacob Aaronson. "Elijah's Mysterious Ways" in *Jewish Stories One Generation Tells Another*. Northvale, NJ: Jason Aronson, 1987.

Stone, Merlin. "Mawu" in *Ancient Mirrors of Womanhood: A Treasury of Goddess and Heroine Lore from Around the World*. Boston: Beacon Press, 1990.

Williamson, Duncan, and Linda Williamson. "Death in a Nut" in *A Thorn in the King's Foot: Folktales of the Scottish Traveling People*. Harmondsworth, England: Penguin, 1987.

Yolen, Jane., ed. "The End Of The World" in *Favorite Folktales From Around The World*. New York: Pantheon Books, 1988.

Grief and loss — Personal stories

Ajjan, Diana. *The Day My Father Died: Women Share Their Stories of Love, Loss and Life*. Philadelphia: Running Cliffs, 1994.

Canfield, Jack, Mark Hansen, Patty Aubery, and Nancy Mitchell. *Chicken Soup for the Surviving Soul*. Deerfield Beach, FL: Health Communications, 1996.

Grief and loss — Therapeutic storytelling

Cameron, Julia. *The Artist's Way: A Spiritual Path to Higher Creativity*. New York: G. P. Putnam's Sons, 1992. Methods for recovering your creativity when blocked by limiting beliefs, fear, self-sabotage, jealousy, guilt, addictions, and other inhibiting forces.

Gersie, Alida. *Storymaking and Bereavement: Dragons Fight in the Meadow*. London: Jessica Kingsley Publishers, 1991.

Harvey, John. *Embracing Their Memory: Loss and the Social Psychology of Storytelling*. Needham Heights, MA: Allyn and Bacon, 1996.

Rooks, Diane. *Spinning Gold out of Straw: How Stories Heal*. St. Augustine, FL: Salt Run Press, 2001.

Young-Eisendrath. Polly. *The Gifts of Suffering: Finding Insight, Compassion, and Renewal*. New York: Addison-Wesley, 1996.

Grief and loss — Additional resources

Callanan, Maggie, and Patricia Kelly. *Final Gifts: Understanding the Special Awareness, Needs and Communications of the Dying*. New York: Bantam Books, 1992. A study of the symbolic language of the dying.

Kubler-Ross, Elisabeth. *The Wheel of Life: A Memoir of Living and Dying*. New York, Simon and Schuster, 1997.

Levine, Steven, and Ondrea Levine. *Who Dies? An Investigation of Conscious Living and Conscious Dying*. New York: Doubleday, 1982. Personal stories illustrate the immensity of living with death while participating fully in life.

Miller, Sukie. *After Death: How People Around The World Map The Journey After We Die*. New York: Simon and Schuster, 1997. A cross-cultural overview on death.

Rico, Gabriele. *Pain and Possibility: Writing Your Way Through Personal Crisis*. New York: G.P. Putnam's Sons, 1991. Using creativity to achieve healing and growth.

Health Promotion

Health promotion — Story collection

Livo, Norma J. *Story Medicine: Multicultural Tales of Healing and Transformation.* Englewood, CO: Libraries Unlimited/Teacher Ideas Press, 2001. Forty tales from all over the world on healing the self, relationships, the community and the earth.

Health promotion — Selected story

MacDonald, Margaret Read. "Not Our Problem" in *Peace Tales: World Folktales to Talk About.* Hampden, CT: Linnet Books, 1992.

Homelessness

Vanderstaay, Steve. *Street Lives: An Oral History of Homeless Americans.* Gabriola Island, BC: New Society Publishers, 1992.

Wild, Margaret. *Space Travelers.* New York: Scholastic, 1992. A boy and his mother live in a jungle gym in the park while they search for a home.

Wilkes, Sybella. "The Party" in *One Day We Had To Run.* Brookfield, CT: Millbrook Press, 1994.

Lap Rhymes, Lullabies, and Finger Plays for Babies through Toddlers

Brown, Aaron J. *A Child's Gift Of Lullabies.* Nashville, TN: Someday Baby/JABA Records, 1987. (Audio recording)

Carpenter-Davis, Sandra. *Bounce Me, Tickle Me, Hug Me.* Toronto: Parent-Child Mother Goose Program, 1997.

Defty, Jeff. *Creative Fingerplays and Action Rhymes: An Index and Guide to Their Use.* Phoenix, AZ: Oryx, 1992.

Denton, Kady MacDonald. *A Child's Treasury of Nursery Rhymes.* Toronto: Kids Can Press, 1998.

Jaeger, Sally. *Lullabies and Lap Rhymes.* Toronto: Self-published, 1993. Write: Sally Jaeger, 105 Voctor Ave., Toronto, ON Canada M4K 1A7. (Audiocassette) This tape teaches rhymes, songs, and lullabies to play and say with babies.

———. *Mr. Bear Says Hello.* Toronto: 49 North Productions, Inc., 1997. Write: Sally Jaeger, 105 Voctor Ave., Toronto, ON Canada M4K 1A7. (Audiocassette) Rhymes, fingerplays, songs, games, and lullabies to play with children from one to four.

———. *From Wibbleton to Wobbleton.* Toronto: 49 North Productions, 1998. To order, call 49 North Productions, (416) 461-4327. (Video) Forty minutes of 38 rhymes, tickles, bounces, gallops, and lullabies.

Lee, Dennis. *Jelly Belly.* Toronto: Macmillan, 1983.

Lines, Kathleen. *Lavender's Blue.* New York: Oxford University Press, 1991.

Lottridge, Celia. *The Moon is Round.* Toronto: Parent-Child Mother Goose Program, 1992.

———. *Mother Goose: A Canadian Sampler.* Toronto: Groundwood Books, 1994.

Opie, Iona. *My Very First Mother Goose.* Cambridge: Candlewick Press, 1996.

Opie, Iona, and Peter Opie. *The Oxford Nursery Rhyme Book.* New York: Oxford University Press, 1955.

———. *The Puffin Book of Nursery Rhymes.* Baltimore: Penguin Books, 1999.

———. *Tail Feathers from Mother Goose.* London: Walker Books, 1988.

Stetson, Emily, and Vicky Congdo. *Little Hands, Fingerplays and Action Songs: Seasonal Activities and Creative Play for 2 To 6-Year-Olds*. Charlotte, VT: Williamson Publishing, 2001.

Men's Issues

Men's issues — Story collections

Bly, Robert. *Iron John: A Book About Men*. New York, Addison Wesley, 1991.

Bruchac, Joseph. *Flying With Eagle, Racing With the Great Bear*. Mahwah, NJ: Troll Medallion, 1993. Many stories of boys from Native American folklore.

Campbell, Joseph. *The Hero With A Thousand Faces*. Princeton, NJ: Princeton University Press, 1972.

Chase, Richard. *The Jack Tales*. Boston: Houghton Mifflin, 1993.

Chinen, Allan B. *Once Upon a Midlife: Classic Stories and Mythic Tales to Illuminate the Mythic Years*. New York: G.P. Putnam's Sons, 1992.

Chinen, Allan B., and Dan Keding. *Beyond the Hero: Classic Stories of Men in Search of Soul*. Little Rock, AR: August House, 1993. (Audio recording)

Hillman, James, Michael Meade and Robert W. Bly. *Men and the Life of Desire*. Pacific Grove, CA: Oral Tradition Archives, 1998. (audio cassette).

Meade, Michael. *Off With the Rat's Head: Tales of the Father, Son & King*. Boston: Yellow Moon Press, 1990. (audio cassette).

Meade, Michael. *Men and the Water of Life: Initiation and the Tempering of Men*. San Francisco: HarperCollins, 1993.

Men's issues — Selected stories

Holt, David, and Bill Mooney., eds. "The Black Prince" in *Ready-To-Tell Tales: Sure-Fire Stories from America's Favorite Storytellers*. Little Rock, AR: August House, 1994.

Wolkstein, Diane. *The Red Lion: A Tale of Ancient Persia*. New York: Ty Crowell Co., 1977.

Zolotow, Charlotte. *William's Doll*. New York: HarperTrophy, 1985.

Men's issues — Additional resource

Pollack, William. *Real Boys: Rescuing Our Sons from the Myths of Boyhood*. New York: Henry Holt and Company, 1999.

Oral History

Baker, Holly Cutting, Amy J. Kotkin, and Steven J. Zeitlin. *A Celebration of American Family Folklore*. Cambridge, MA: Yellow Moon Press, 1992. Includes section about collecting your own family stories.

Brecher, Jeremy. *History From Below: How to Uncover and Tell the Story of Your Community, Association, or Union*. New Haven, CT: Advocate Press. 1986.

Ives, Edward D. *The Tape-Recorded Interview: A Manual for Field Workers in Folklore and Oral History*. Knoxville, TN: University of Tennessee Press, 1980.

Lichtman, Allan J. *Your Family History: How to use oral history, personal family archives, and public documents to discover your heritage*. New York: Random House. 1978.

Moore, Robin. *Awakening the Hidden Storyteller: How to Build a Storytelling Tradition in Your Family*. Boston: Shambhala Publications, 1991.

Preserving Our Culture

Baltuck, Naomi. *Apples from Heaven: Multicultural Folk Tales About Stories and Storytellers.* Hampden, CT: Linnet Books, 1995.

Cole, Joanna., ed. *Best-Loved Folktales of the World.* New York: Doubleday, 1992.

Curry, Lindy Soon. *A Tiger by the Tail and Other Stories from the Heart of Korea.* Englewood, CO: Teacher Ideas Press/Libraries Unlimited, 1999.

DeSpain Pleasant. *The Emerald Lizard: Fifteen Latin American Tales to Tell in English and Spanish.* Little Rock, AR: August House, 1999.

———. *Thirty-three Multicultural Tales to Tell.* Little Rock, AR: August House, 1993.

Dooley, Norah. *Everybody Cooks Rice.* Minneapolis: Carolrhoda Books, 1991.

Faulkner, W. *The days when the animals talked: Black American folktales and how they came to be.* Lawrenceville, NJ: Africa World Press, 1993.

Forest, Heather. *Wonder Tales From Around the World.* Little Rock, AR: August House, 1995.

Goss, Linda, Marion Barnes, and Henry Louis Gates Jr.., eds. *Talk That Talk: An Anthology of African American Storytelling.* New York: Simon and Schuster, 1989.

Gunn Allen, Paula., ed. *Spider Woman's Granddaughters: Traditional Tales and Contemporary Writing by Native American Women.* New York: Ballantine Books, 1989.

Hamilton, Virginia. *The people could fly: American Black folktales.* New York: Knopf, 1985.

Johnston, Tony. *The Quilt Story.* New York: G.P. Putnam's Sons, 1985.

Lester, Julius. *The Tales of Uncle Remus: The Adventures of Brer Rabbit.* New York: Dial Books, 1987.

Pijoan, Teresa. *White Wolf Woman. Native American Transformation Myths.* Little Rock, AR: August House, 1992.

Rosen, Michael. *South and North, East and West: The Oxfam Book of Children's Stories.* Cambridge, MA: Candlewick Press, 1992.

Shah, Idries. *The Subtleties of the Inimitable Nasrudin.* London: Octagon Press, 1989.

Sherman, Josepha. *Rachel The Clever and Other Jewish Tales.* Little Rock, AR: August House, 1993.

Spagnoli, Cathy. *Asian Tales and Tellers.* Little Rock, AR: August House, 1998.

———. *Jasmine and Coconuts: South Indian Tales.* Englewood, CO: Libraries Unlimited, 1999.

———. *Terrific Trickster Tales from Asia.* Fort Atkinson, WI: Highsmith Press, 2001.

———. *A Treasury of Asian Stories and Activities for Schools and Libraries.* Fort Atkinson, WI: Highsmith Press, 1998.

Vigil, Angel. *The Corn Woman: Stories and Legends of the Hispanic Southwest.* Englewood, CO: Teacher Ideas Press/Libraries Unlimited, 1995.

Webber, Desiree, and Dee Ann Corn. *Travel the Globe: Multicultural Story Times.* Englewood, CO: Teacher Ideas Press/Libraries Unlimited, 1998.

Wichman, Frederick B. *Kaua'i: Ancient Place-Names and Their Stories.* Honolulu: University of Hawaii Press, 1998.

Yolen, Jane. *Favorite Folktales from Around the World.* New York: Pantheon Books, 1988.

Resiliency

Resiliency — Story collection

Nelson, Annabelle. *Storytelling for Prevention.* Colorado: The WHEEL Council, (www.wheelcouncil.org), 1998.

Resiliency — Selected stories

Holt, David, and Bill Mooney., eds. "Little Burnt Face" in *Ready-To-Tell Tales: Sure-Fire Stories from America's Favorite Storytellers.* Little Rock, AR: August House, 1994.

McCall Smith, Alexander. "A Blind Man Catches a Bird" in *Children of Wax: African Folk Tales.* New York: Interlink Books, 1991.

Miller, Teresa, Anne Pellowski, and Norma Livo. "Freedom Bird" in *Joining In: An Anthology of Audience Participation Stories and How to Tell Them.* Cambridge MA: Yellow Moon Press, 1991.

Storm, Hyemeyohsts. "Jumping Mouse" in *Seven Arrows.* New York: Ballantine Books, 1985.

Resiliency — Additional resources

Benard, Bonnie. *Fostering Resiliency in Kids: Protective Factors in the Family, School and Community.* Portland, OR: Northwest Regional Educational Laboratory, 1991.

Garbarino, James. *Children in Danger: Coping with the Consequences of Community Violence.* San Francisco: Jossey-Bass, 1992.

Muller, Wayne. *Legacy of the Heart: The Spiritual Advantages of a Painful Childhood.* New York: Simon and Schuster, 1992.

Noddings, Nel. *The Challenge to Care in Schools: An Alternative Approach to Education.* New York: Teachers College Press, 1992.

Werner, Emily, and Ruth S. Smith. *Overcoming the Odds: High-Risk Children from Birth to Adulthood.* Ithaca, NY: Cornell University Press, 1992.

Wolin, Steve, and Sybil Wolin. *The Resilient Self: How Survivors of Troubled Families Rise Above Adversity.* New York: Villard Books, 1993.

Spiritual Healing

Spiritual healing — Story collections

Bausch, William. *Storytelling: Imagination and Faith.* Mystic, CT: Twenty-Third Publications, 1984.

de Mello, Anthony. *One Minute Wisdom.* New York: Doubleday, 1985.

———. *The Song of the Bird.* New York: Doubleday, 1982.

Forest, Heather. *Wisdom Tales from Around the World.* Little Rock, AR: August House, 1996.

Feldman, Christina, and Jack Kornfield. *Stories of the Spirit, Stories of the Heart: Parables of the Spiritual Path From Around the World.* San Francisco: HarperCollins, 1991.

Houston, Jean. *The Search for the Beloved: Journeys in Mythology and Sacred Psychology.* Los Angeles: J.P. Tarcher, 1987.

Kornfield, Jack, and Christina Feldman. *Soul Food: Stories to Nourish the Spirit and the Heart.* San Francisco: HarperSanFrancisco, 1996.

Kurtz, Ernest, and Katherine Ketcham. *The Spirituality of Imperfection: Storytelling and the Journey to Wholeness.* New York: Bantam Books, 1994. An anthology of tales for those in recovery.

Pearmain, Elisa. *Doorways to the Soul: Fifty-Two Wisdom Tales from Around the World.* Cleveland: Pilgrim Press, 1998.

Simpkinson, C., and A. Simpkinson., eds. *Sacred stories: A Celebration of the Power of Stories to*

Transform and Heal. San Francisco: HarperSanFrancisco, 1993.

Swami Prakashananda. *Don't Think of a Monkey and other Stories my Guru Told Me*. Fremont, CA: Sarasvati Productions, 1994.

Theophane the Monk. *Tales of the Magic Monastery*. New York: Crossroads, 1992.

Spiritual healing — Specific traditions
Buddhist/Hindu

The Panchatantra. Arthur W. Ryder, translator. Chicago: University of Chicago Press, 1964.

Jewish

Buxbaum, Yitzhak. *Storytelling and Spirituality in Judaism*. Northvale, NJ: Jason Aronson, 1994.

Epstein, Lawrence J. *A Treasury of Jewish Inspirational Stories*. Northvale, NJ: Jason Aronson, 1993.

Lipman, Doug. *The Forgotten Story: Tales of Wise Jewish Men*. Cambridge, MA: Yellow Moon Press, 1988. (Audiocassette)

Schram, Peninah., ed. *Chosen Tales*. Northvale, NJ: Jason Aronson, 1995.

Shamanism

Van Deusen, Kira. *Raven and the Rock: Storytelling in Chukotka*. Seattle: University of Washington Press, 1999.

———. *The Flying Tiger*. Women Shamans and Storytellers of the Amur. Montreal/Kingston: McGill-Queens University Press, 2001.

Sufi/Muslim

Downing, Charles. *Tales of the Hodja*. New York: Henry Z. Walk, 1965.

Shah, Idries. *Exploits of the Incomparable Mulla Nasrudhin*. New York: Simon and Schuster, 1966.

———. *The Way of the Sufi*. London: Octagon Press, 1980.

Merton, Thomas. *The Wisdom of the Desert: Sayings from the Desert Fathers of the Fourth Century*. Boston: Shambhala Publications, 1994.

Zen

Reps, Paul. *Zen Flesh, Zen Bones: Collection of Zen and Pre-Zen Writings*. Boston, MA: Shambhala Publications, 1994.

Martin, Rafe. *One Hand Clapping: Zen Stories for all Ages*. New York: Rizzoli International Publications, 1995.

Storytelling — How To Tell

How to tell — Teaching storytelling

Hamilton, Martha, and Mitch Weiss. *Children Tell Stories: A Teaching Guide*. Kaytona, NY: Richard C. Owens Publishers, 1990.

Holt, David, and Bill Mooney. *The Storyteller's Guide: Storytellers Share Advice*. Little Rock, AR: August House, 1996.

Kinghorn, Harriet, and Mary Helen Pelton. *Every Child a Storyteller: A Handbook of Ideas*. Greenwood Village, CO: Teacher Ideas Press, 1991.

Lipman, Doug. *Improving Your Storytelling: Beyond the Basics for All Who Tell Stories in Work or Play*. Little Rock, AR: August House, 1999.

Lipman, Doug, and Jay O'Callahan. *The Storytelling Coach: How to Listen, Praise, and Bring Out People's Best*. Little Rock, AR: August House 1995.

Lottridge, Celia Barker. *You Can Tell a Story: A Handbook for New Storytellers*. Toronto: The Parent-Child Mother Goose Program, 2002.

Mellon, Nancy. *Storytelling with Children.* England: Hawthorn Press, 2000.

How to tell — Story collections

Hamilton, Martha, and Mitch Weiss. *How and Why Stories: World Tales Kids Can Read and Tell.* Little Rock, AR: August House.

Holt, David, and Bill Mooney., eds. *Ready-To-Tell Tales: Sure-Fire Stories from America's Favorite Storytellers.* Little Rock, AR: August House, 1994.

————. *More Ready-To-Tell Tales from Around the World.* Little Rock, AR: August House, 2000.

MacDonald, Margaret Read. *The Storyteller's Start-Up Book: Finding, Learning, Performing, and Using Folktales, Including Twelve Tellable Tales.* Little Rock, AR: August House, 1993.

Pellowski, Anne. *The Story Vine: A Source Book for Unusual and Easy-to-tell Stories from Around the World.* New York: Aladdin Books/Macmillan, 1984.

Sawyer, Ruth. *The Way of the Storyteller.* New York: Penguin, 1998.

How to tell — Personal stories

Atkinson, Robert. *The Gift of Stories: Practical and Spiritual Applications of Autobiography, Life Stories and Personal Mythmaking.* Westport, CT: Bergin and Garvey, 1995.

Arthur, Stephen, and Julia Arthur. *Your Life and Times: How to Put a Life Story on Tape.* Baltimore, MD: Genealogical Publishing Company, 1987.

Davis, Donald. *Telling Your Own Stories: For Family and Classroom Storytelling, Public Speaking, and Personal Journaling.* Little Rock, AR: August House, 1993. Celebrating remembrance.

Maguire, Jack. *The Power of Personal Storytelling.*

New York: J.P. Tarcher/ Putnam, 1998.

Moore, Robin. *Awakening the Hidden Storyteller: How to Build a Storytelling Tradition in Your Family.* Boston: Shambhala Publications, 1991.

Nelson, Annabelle. *The Storytelling Project: How to tell your story to impress others and find your voice.* Colorado: The WHEEL Council, (www.wheelcouncil.org), 1999.

Stone, Elizabeth. *Black Sheep and Kissing Cousins: How Our Family Stories Shape Us.* New York: Penguin, 1989.

Taylor, Daniel. *Tell Me A Story: The Life-Shaping Power of Our Stories.* St Paul MN: Bog Walk Press, 2001.

Storytelling For Parents

Storytelling for parents — Collections

Baltuck, Naomi. *Crazy Gibberish and other story hour stretches from a storyteller's bag of tricks.* Hampden, CT: Linnet Books, 1993.

DeSpain, Pleasant. *Twenty-Two Splendid Tales to Tell* (Volumes 1 and 2). Little Rock, AR: August House, 1990.

Forest, Heather. *Wisdom Tales From Around the World.* Little Rock, AR: August House, 1996.

Fujita, Hiroko and Fran Stallings. *Stories to Play With: Kids' Tales Told With Puppets, Paper, Toys and Imagination.* Little Rock, AR: August House Little Folk, 1996.

Lottridge, Celia Barker. *Ten Small Tales.* Toronto: Groundwood, 1993.

MacDonald, Margaret Read, Jen Whitman, Nat Whitman, and Wajuppa Tossa. *Shake-It-Up Tales! Stories to Sing, Dance, Drum, and Act Out.* Little Rock, AR: August House, 2000.

MacDonald, Margaret Read. *Tuck-Me-In Tales: Bedtime Stories from Around the World*. Little Rock, AR: August House Little Folk, 1996.

———. *Twenty Tellable Tales: Audience Participation Folktales for the Beginning Storyteller*. New York: H.W. Wilson, 1986.

Mayo, Margaret. *The Book of Magical Tales*. New York: Doubleday, 1988.

Rockwell, Anne. F. *The Three Bears and 15 Other Stories*. New York: Crowell, 1975.

Sierra, Judy. *Multicultural Folktales: Stories to Tell Young Children*. Phoenix, AZ: Oryx Press, 1991.

Sierra, Judy, and Bob Kaminski. *Mother Goose's Playhouse: Toddler Tales and Nursery Rhymes, with Patterns for Puppets and Feltboards*. Ashland, OR: Bob Kaminski Media Arts, 1994.

Storytelling for parents — Selected stories

Ata, Te, and Lynn Moroney. *Baby Rattlesnake*. San Francisco: Children's Book Press, 1993.

MacDonald, Margaret Read."Let's Go On A Bear Hunt" in *The Parent's Guide to Storytelling: How to Make Up New Stories and Retell Old Favorites*. Little Rock, AR: August House, 2001.

McGovern, Ann. *Too Much Noise*. Boston: Houghton Mifflin 1967.

Substance Abuse Issues

Substance abuse issues — Story collections

Kurtz, Ernest, and Katherine Ketcham. *The Spirituality of Imperfection: Storytelling and the Journey to Wholeness*. New York: Bantam Books, 1994. An anthology of tales for those in recovery.

Nelson, Annabelle. *Storytelling Powerbook*. Arizona: The WHEEL Council, (www.wheelcouncil.org), 1997

Substance abuse issues — Selected stories

Bennett, William J. ., ed."The Magic Thread" in *The Book of Virtues: A Treasury of Great Moral Stories*. New York: Simon and Schuster, 1993.

Caduto, Michael, and Joseph Bruchac. "The Boy and the Rattlesnake" in *Keepers of the Animals: Native American Stories and Wildlife Activities for Children*. Golden, CO: Fulcrum Publishing, 1991.

Cole, Joanna., ed."The Fisherman and His Wife" in *Best-Loved Folktales of the World*. New York: Doubleday, 1992.

Dutton, Cheryl. *Not In Here, Dad!* Hutchinson, London: Children's Books, 1992. A story with an anti-smoking message. Have the audience join in on"Not in here, Dad!"

Ellis, Rex."Bennie" and "Cocaine" in *The Ups And Downs of Being Brown: Traditional and Contemporary African-American Stories*. Little Rock, AR: August House, 1997. (Audio recording)

Kronberg, Ruthilde, and Patricia McKissack. "Bundles of Troubles and Bundles of Blessings" in *A Piece of the Wind and Other Stories to Tell*. San Francisco: HarperCollins, 1990.

Ransome, Arthur. "Misery" in *Old Peter's Russian Tales*. Toronto: Thomas Nelson and Sons, 1967.

Rylant, Cynthia. "Drying Out" in *Every Living Thing*. New York: Aladdin Books/Macmillan, 1985. This book contains 12 short stories about changing perspective through the inspiration of animals.

Smith, Mary Carter. "Two Little Birds" in *Mary Carter Smith...Nearing Seventy-five*. Baltimore: Aframa Agency, 1993. (Audio recording)

Taylor, Clark. *The House That Crack Built*. San Francisco: Chronicle Books, 1992.

Van Der Post, Laurens. "The Man Who Had Black And White Cows" in *The Heart of the Hunter*. New York/San Diego: Harcourt Brace (Harvest Books), 1980. Breaking Trust.

Teach Your Children Values

Teach your children values — Story collections

Barchers, Suzanne. *Fifty Fabulous Fables*. Greenwood Village, CO: Teacher Ideas Press, 1997.

Campbell, Joseph. *Myths to Live By*. New York: Viking, 1972.

Creeden, Sharon. *Fair as Fair: World Folktales of Justice*. Little Rock, AR: August House, 1997.

DeSpain, Pleasant. *The Books of Nine Lives: Tales of Wisdom and Justice*. Little Rock, AR: August House Little Folk. 2001.

Forest, Heather. *Wonder Tales From Around the World*. Little Rock, AR: August House, 1995.

Gellman, Rabbi Marc, and Monsignor Thomas Hartman. *How Do You Spell God? Answers to the Big Questions From Around the World*. New York: William Morrow/Junior Books, 1995.

Flack, Jerry. *From the Land of Enchantment: Creative Teaching with Fairy Tales*. Greenwood Village, CO: Teacher Ideas Press, 1997.

Kraus, Anne Marie. *Folktale Themes and Activities for Children: Trickster and Transformation Tales*. Greenwood Village, CO: Teacher Ideas Press, 1995.

Norfolk, Bobby, and Sherry Norfolk. *The Moral of the Story: Folktales for Character Development*. Little Rock, AR: August House, 1999.

Smith, Charles. *From Wonder to Wisdom: Using Stories to Help People Grow*. New York: Penguin, 1989.

Stotter, Ruth. *The Golden Axe and Other Folk Tales of Compassion and Greed*. Stinson Beach, CA: Stotter Press, 1998.

Teach your children values — Selected stories

Bennett, William J.., ed. "The Bundle of Sticks" and "The King and His Hawk" in *The Book of Virtues*. New York: Simon and Schuster, 1993.

Cole, Joanna., ed. "The Fisherman and His Wife" in *Best-Loved Folktales of the World*. New York: Doubleday, 1992.

Evetts-Secker, Josephine. "The Waterfall of White Hair" in *Mother and Daughter Tales*. New York: Abbeville Press, 1996.

Rodanas, Kristina. *Dragonfly's Tale*. New York: Clarion Books, 1992.

Yolen, Jane., ed. "The Old Woman Who Lived in a Vinegar Bottle" in *Favorite Folktales from Around the World*. New York: Pantheon Books, 1988.

Therapeutic Storytelling

Bettelheim, Bruno. *The Uses of Enchantment: The Meaning and Importance of Fairy Tales*. New York: Vintage, 1989.

Brett, Doris. *Annie Stories*. New York: Workman Publishing, 1986. Design stories to aid children in coping with fears, loss, pain, siblings, and other challenges.

Brun, Brigitte, Ernst Pedersen, and Marianne Runberg., eds. *Symbols of the Soul: Therapy and Guidance Through Fairy Tales*.

London/Philadelphia: Jessica L. Kingsley Publishers, 1993.

Dieckmann, Hans. *Twice Told Tales: The Psychological Uses of Fairy Tales.* Wilmette, IL: Chiron Publications, 1986.

Estes, Clarissa Pinkola. *Women Who Run With The Wolves.* New York: Ballantine Books, 1992.

Feinstein, David, and Stanley Krippner. *Personal Mythology: The Psychology of Your Evolving Self.* Los Angeles: Tarcher, 1988.

Frank, Arthur W. *The Wounded Storyteller.* Chicago: University of Chicago Press, 1995.

Franzke, Erich. *Fairy Tales in Psychotherapy: The Creative Use of Old and New Tales.* Lewiston, NY: Hans Huber, 1989.

Gersie, Alida. *Reflections on Therapeutic Storymaking: The Use of Stories in Groups.* London: Jessica L. Kingsley Publishers, 1997.

Gersie, Alida, and Nancy King. *Storymaking in Education and Therapy.* London: Jessica L. Kingsley Publishers, 1990. Therapeutic work with folktales and myth.

Gordon, David. *Therapeutic Metaphors: Helping Others Through the Looking Glass.* Cupertino, CA: META Publishers, 1978.

Heuscher, Julius E. *A Psychiatric Study of Myths and Fairytales: Their Origin, Meaning and Usefulness.* Springfield, IL: Charles Thomas, 1974.

Houston, Jean. *The Search for the Beloved: Journeys in Mythology and Sacred Psychology.* Los Angeles: Tarcher, 1987.

Kast, Verena. *Folktales as Therapy.* New York: Fromm International Publishing Corporation, 1995.

Keen, Sam, and Anne Valley-Fox. *Your Mythic Journey: Finding Meaning in Your Life through Writing and Storytelling.* New York: G.P. Putnam's Sons, 1989.

Larsen, Stephen. *The Mythic Imagination: Your Quest for Meaning Through Personal Mythology.* New York: Bantam, 1990.

Meade, Erica Helm. *Tell It by Heart: Women and the Healing Power of Story.* Chicago: Open Court, 1995. Combines myth and personal story with therapeutic examples.

Meade, Erica Helm. *The Moon in the Well.* Chicago: Open Court, 2001. 63 wisdom tales along with reflections and therapeutic applications

Mills, Joyce C., and Richard J. Crowley. *Therapeutic Metaphors For Children and The Child Within.* New York: Bruner/Mazel, 1986.

Simpkinson, C., and A. Simpkinson., eds. *Sacred stories: A Celebration of the Power of Stories to Transform and Heal.* San Francisco: HarperSanFrancisco, 1993.

Stone, Richard. *The Healing Art of Storytelling: A Sacred Journey of Personal Discovery.* New York: Hyperion, 1996. How personal stories heal through the telling.

Von Franz, Marie-Louise. *The Psychological Meaning of Redemption Motifs in Fairytales.* Toronto: Inner City Books, 1980.

———. *The Interpretation of Fairy Tales.* Dallas: Spring Publications, 1970.

———. *Shadow and Evil in Fairytales.* Zurich, Switzerland: Spring Publications, 1974.

Wallas, Lee. *Stories for the Third Ear.* New York: W.W. Norton and Company, 1985.

Violence Prevention/Peace Initiatives

Violence prevention/Peace initiatives — Story collections

Bauman, Elizabeth Hershberger. *Coals of Fire.* Scottdale, PA: Herald Press, 1982. True stories of people who returned good for evil.

Brody, Ed, Jay Goldspinner, Katie Green, Rona Leventhal, and John Porcino., eds. *Spinning Tales, Weaving Hope: Stories, Storytelling, and Activities for Peace, Justice and the Environment.* Gabriola Island, BC: New Society Publishers, 2002.

Dass, Ram, and Paul Gorman. *How Can I Help? Stories and Reflections on Service.* New York: Knopf, 1990. Stories about compassion, suffering, listening, anger, conflict, burnout, and healing.

Durrell, Ann, and Marylin Sachs., eds. *The Big Book of Peace.* New York: Dutton, 1990.

Lehn, Cornelia. *Peace Be With You.* Newton, KS: Faith and Life Press, 1980. Fifty-nine stories of peace heroes throughout the ages.

Simms, Laura. *Stories To Nourish the Hearts of Our Children In a Time of Crisis.* New York: Holland and Knight, 2001.

Stotter, Ruth. *The Golden Axe and Other Folk Tales of Compassion and Greed.* Stinson Beach, CA: Stotter Press, 1998.

Violence prevention/Peace initiatives — Selected stories

Collier, Kenneth W. "How Coyote Lost His Songs, Music and Dance" in *Our Seven Principles in Story and Verse.* Boston: Skinner House Books, 1997.

Davar, Ashok. *The Wheel of King Asoka.* Chicago: Follett Publishing, 1977. True story of an Indian ruler who abandoned war for peace.

DeSpain, Pleasant. "All Things Are Connected" in *Eleven Nature Tales: A Multicultural Journey.* Little Rock, AR: August House, 1996.

Kronberg, Ruthilde, and Patricia McKissack. "The Rabbit And The Elephant" in *A Piece of the Wind and Other Stories to Tell.* San Francisco: HarperCollins, 1990. Dealing with a bully.

Leichman, Seymour. *The Boy Who Could Sing Pictures.* New York: Holt Rhinehart and Winston: 1973. A king realizes how war hurts his people when a boy sings of the sadness he sees.

MacDonald, Margaret Read. "War Between the Sandpipers and the Whales" and "Holding Up the Sky" in *Peace Tales: World Folktales to Talk About.* Hampden, CT: Linnet Books, 1992.

Maruki, Toshi. *Hiroshima No Pika.* New York: Lothrop, Lee and Shepard, 1980. The effects of the bombing of Hiroshima on one family.

Pomerantz, Charlotte. *The Princess and the Admiral.* New York: Feminist Press; 1992.

Zolotow, Charlotte. *The Hating Book.* New York: Harper Trophy, 1989.

———. *The Quarreling Book.* New York: HarperTrophy, 1982.

Violence prevention/Peace initiatives — Additional resources

Credle, Ellis. "How To Grow Hot Peppers" in *Tall Tales From The High Hills.* New York: Nelson, 1957. Good for discussions about anger.

Fredericks, Linda, and the Colorado School Mediation Project. *Using Stories to Prevent Violence and Promote Cooperation.* Boulder: Colorado School Mediation Project, 1996.

———. *Healing Wounds with Words: A Guide to Conflict Resolution Through Storytelling.* Boulder: Colorado School Mediation Project, 2000.

Frum, Thomas F. *The Magic of Conflict.* New York: Simon and Schuster, 1987. Stress reduction and conflict resolution based on Aikido. The book contains non-fiction stories and traditional tales.

Fry, A. Ruth. *Victories Without Violence*. Santa Fe, NM: Ocean Tree Books, 1986.

Glassman, Bernie. *Bearing Witness: A Zen Master's Lessons in Making Peace*. New York: Bell Tower, 1998.

Women's Issues

Carter, Angela., ed. *The Old Wives' Fairy Tale Book*. New York: Pantheon Books, 1990.

Chinen, Allan B. *Once Upon a Midlife: Classic Stories and Mythic Tales to Illuminate the Mythic Years*. New York: Putnam, 1992.

———. *Waking the World: Classic Tales of Women and the Heroic Feminine*. New York: Putnam, 1996.

Creedon, Sharon. *In Full Bloom: Tales of Women in Their Prime*. Little Rock, AR: August House, 1999.

Estes, Clarissa Pinkola. *Women Who Run With The Wolves*. New York: Ballantine Books, 1992.

Evetts-Secker, Josephine. *Mother and Daughter Tales*. New York: Abbeville Press, 1996.

Gunn Allen, Paula., ed. *Spider Woman's Granddaughters: Traditional Tales and Contemporary Writing by Native American Women*. New York: Ballantine Books, 1989.

Hastings, Selina. *Sir Gawain and the Loathly Lady*. Lothrop, Lee and Shepard, 1985.

Haven, Kendall. *Amazing American Women: 40 Fascinating 5-Minute Reads*. Greenwood Village, CO: Teacher Ideas Press, 1995.

Holmes, Kenneth L., ed. *Covered Wagon Women: Diaries and Letters From the Western Trails, 1852, The California Trail*. Lincoln, NE: University of Nebraska Press, 1985.

McVickar Edwards, Carolyn. *The Storyteller's Goddess: Tales of the Goddess and Her Wisdom from Around the World*. San Francisco: HarperSanFrancisco, 1991.

Meade, Erica Helm. *Tell It by Heart: Women and the Healing Power of Story*. Chicago: Open Court, 1995.

Monaghan, Patricia. *Wild Girls: The Path of the Young Goddess*. St. Paul, MN: Llewellyn Publications, 2001.

Phelps, Ethel Johnston. *Tatterhood And Other Tales*. New York: The Feminist Press, 1978.

———. *The Maid Of The North: Feminist Folktales from Around The World*. New York: Holt, Rhinehart and Winston, 1982.

Ragan, Kathleen., ed. *Fearless Girls, Wise Women, and Beloved Sisters: Heroines in Folktales from Around the World*. New York: W.W. Norton and Company, 1998.

San Souci, Robert, and Brian Pinkney. *Cut From The Same Cloth: American Women Of Myth, Legend and Tall Tale*. New York: Philomel Books, 1993.

Seagraves, Anne. *Soiled Doves: Prostitution in the Early West*. Hayden Lake, ID: Wesanne Publications, 1994.

Simms, Laura. *Moon On Fire: Calling Forth The Power Of The Feminine*. Cambridge, MA: Yellow Moon Press, 1987.

———. *Women and Wild Animals: Howl the Morning Welcome*. Minocqua, WI: Northword Press, 1992 (available from the author at www.laurasimms.com).

Stanley, Jo., ed. *Bold in Her Breeches: Women Pirates Across the Ages*. San Francisco: Pandora Books, 1995.

Zipes, Jack. *Don't Bet On the Prince: Contemporary Feminist Tales in North America and England*. New York: Routledge, 1989.

Youth On The Edge

Youth on the edge — Story collections

Czarnota, Lorna. *Crossroads*. New York: Self published, 1999. Phone: 716-837-0551.

Meade, Erica Helm. *The Moon in the Well: Wisdom Tales to Transform Your Life, Family, and Community*. Chicago: Open Court, 2001.

Meyers, Walter Dean. *Sweet Illusions*. New York: Teachers and Writers Collaborative, 1986.

Simon, Solomon. *The Wise Men of Helm and their Merry Tales*. Springfield, NJ: Behrman House, 1996. Coping through humour.

Youth on the edge — Selected stories

Barchers, Suzanne. "The Stolen Bairn and the Sìdh" in *Wise Women: Folk and Fairy Tales from Around the World*. Englewood, CO: Libraries Unlimited, 1990. Excellent story for teen mothers.

Chinen, Allan B. "The King has Goats Ears," in *Beyond the Hero*. New York: Tarcher/Putnam, 1993. The power of secrets.

Colum, Padraic. *The Girl Who Sat By the Ashes*. New York: Macmillan, 1968.

Hastings, Selina. *Sir Gawain and the Loathly Lady*. New York: Lothrop, Lee and Shepard, 1985.

Holt, David, and Bill Mooney., eds. "The Black Prince" in *Ready-To-Tell Tales: Sure-Fire Stories from America's Favorite Storytellers*. Little Rock, AR: August House, 1994.

Kimmel, Eric A., and Leonard Fisher. *The Three Princes*. New York: Holiday House, 2000.

MacDonald, Margaret Read. "The Lion's Whisker" in *Peace Tales: World Folktales to Talk About*. Hampden, CT: Linnet Books, 1992.

McDermott, Gerald. *Musicians of the Sun*. New York: Aladdin Books, 2000.

Meade, Michael. "The Half-Boy" from Throw Yourself Like Seed. Pacific Grove, CA: Oral Tradition Archives, 1996. (audio cassette).

Storm, Hyemeyohsts. "Jumping Mouse" in *Seven Arrows*. New York: Ballantine Books, 1985.

Wolkstein, Diane. "I'm Tipingee, She's Tipingee, We're Tipingee Too" in *The Magic Orange Tree and other Haitian Folktales*. New York: Schocken Books/Random House, 1997.

Zeman, Ludmilla. *Gilgamesh The King*. Minneapolis, MN: Econo-Clad Books, 1999. Destructive power is tamed by friendship and reconciliation with an enemy.

Youth on the edge — Additional resource

Hillman, James, Michael Meade and Malidoma Some. *Images of initiation*. Pacific Grove, CA: Oral Tradition Archives, 1992. (audio cassette).

Mahdi, Louise Carus, Nancy Geyer Christopher and Michael Meade. *Crossroads: The quest for contemporary rites of passage*. Chicago: OPen Court, 1996.

Mahdi, Louise, Steven Foster, and Meredith Little, eds. *Betwixt and Between: Patterns of Male and Female Initiation*. Peru, IL: Open Court Publishing, 1987. Rites of passage.

Author Biographies and Contact Information

David H. Albert (Editor) holds degrees from Williams College, Oxford University, and the Committee on Social Thought, University of Chicago, but says, "the best education he ever received he gets from his kids." He writes a regular column — "My Word!" — for *Home Education Magazine*. He is author of two books on homeschooling — *And the Skylark Sings with Me: Adventures in Homeschooling and Community-Based Education* (New Society Publishers, 1999) and *Homeschooling and the Voyage of Self-Discovery: A Journey of Original Seeking* (Common Courage Press, 2003). As founder of New Society Publishers, he was also publisher of *Spinning Tales, Weaving Hope: Stories of Peace, Justice, and the Environment*, to which he contributed, and which has recently been reissued in a 10th anniversary edition. David lives in Olympia, Washington with his partner Ellen and two wonderful daughters, Aliyah (age 15) and Meera (12). When he is not learning with and from his kids, writing or telling stories, making music, or raising funds for child welfare or community development projects in India, he serves as senior planning and policy analyst for the Washington State Division of Alcohol and Substance Abuse. David is also an active member of the Religious Society of Friends (Quakers).

1717 18th Ct., N.E., Olympia, WA 98506 USA
Phone: (360) 352-0506
E-mail: shantinik@earthlink.net
Website: www.skylarksings.com

Allison Cox (Editor) has a Masters degree in counseling psychology and a graduate certificate in public health. She has worked as a mental health therapist, social worker, health educator, health promotion specialist, and prevention specialist —and for the past 20 years, storytelling has accompanied her along these many paths. Allison's health-related storytelling projects have included parent/baby groups, the Adolescent Pregnancy Prevention Project, substance abuse prevention/intervention efforts, training volunteers for the Asthma and Allergy Prevention Project, women's health issues, the Ethnic Elder Health Promotion program, and using story in community assessment and development in her work for the Tacoma Pierce County Health Department. She was the chair for the Storytelling for Prevention Conference in Fife, Washington, in 1998 and is the vice chair and a founding board member of the Healing Story Alliance Special Interest Group of the National Storytelling Network. She is the editor and graphic artist for the Healing Story Alliance journal, *Diving In The Moon: Honoring Story, Facilitating Healing*. Allison has performed as a professional storyteller across Canada and the U.S., offering concerts and workshops on storytelling as a healing art, and also performs storytelling concerts just for the fun of it! She lives on Vashon Island in Puget Sound with her family and her gardens in the woods.

25714 Wax Orchard Rd., SW,
Vashon Island, WA 98070 USA
Phone: (206) 463-3844
Fax: (206) 463-2026
E-mail: allison@dancingleaves.com
Website: http://www.dancingleaves/allison

W. Kirk Avery likes to describe himself as one of the last dinosaurs, a gentle warrior, still open to the magic of life unfolding. A Korean War trauma survivor (USMC, 1952), he started telling and writing much later in life than most. Honored for his teaching, hospice volunteering, and domestic violence/sexual assault survivor support, he is committed to storytelling as a healing art. His is a quieter voice, a human reminder that even darker memories might yet be transformed into life, renewal, hope.

PO Box 411
Bridgewater, MA 02324 USA
Phone: (508) 697-1984 or (508) 472-8703
E-mail: kavery@bridgew.edu

Susan Charters is a writer, teacher, and mother of four. One day, she heard a story that revealed how stories broaden, challenge, and change lives when passed from person to person. She responded by becoming a storyteller. Susan tells traditional tales (chiefly from the British Isles), biblical stories, women's stories, and stories from her collection of world wolf tales. She adds song to many tales, at times working with a musician, in parenting programs, schools, churches, at conventions, and at festivals.

Phone: (705) 325-8463
Fax: (705) 325-5596
E-mail: skcharters@rogers.com

Mary Louise Chown performs at festivals across Canada and at schools in rural and northern Manitoba through the Manitoba Arts Council. She has also been storyteller-in residence at the Winnipeg Public Library. She is a trained shamanic practitioner who has studied mediation and conflict resolution. Mary Louise plays hammered dulcimer and percussion with two Winnipeg bands. Encouraging people to share their stories is an important part of her work and has taken her most recently into working at a local hospital.

35 Cordova St.,
Winnipeg, MB
R3N 0Z9 Canada
Phone: (204) 489-6994
Fax: (204) 489-5460
E-mail: chown@ilos.net

Teresa Clark once heard someone say, "If we forget the ways of the forest — we get lost in the woods; if we forget the stories — we forget who we are." Since then she has dedicated her life to preventing our forgetfulness. Teresa is the executive director of the Storytelling Guild of Eastern Idaho and a 1998 National Storytelling Association Service Award recipient. She is also a 2000 National Storytelling Network research grant recipient for her project with hospice, "Passing On — Their Stories."

380 Ladino Dr.,
Idaho Falls, ID 83401-3834 USA
Phone: (208) 529-3276
E-mail: tclark@idahofallsarts.org
Website: www.teresaclark.com

Kevin Cotter is a registered nurse who specializes in mental health services and uses stories to help people see life in a different perspective. Kevin, a resident of Seattle, has been telling stories for over 25 years and often draws material for his tales from his New Zealand homeland and Irish heritage. Kevin has appeared in festivals and conferences throughout the northwestern United States and overseas.

2329 10th Ave E., Apt. 305,
Seattle, WA 98102-4057 USA
Phone: (206) 860-2021
E-mail: kcotter@u.washington.edu

Lorna Czarnota is a professional storyteller, award-winning author, educator, co-director of the Western New York Storytelling Institute, and president of Crossroads Story Center Inc., a not-for-profit reaching at-risk youth through story, music, and art. She specializes in healing stories and rites of passage for women and youth at-risk, medieval and colonial American historical programs, Celtic culture, and the use of metaphor in story.

PO Box 1641,
Buffalo, NY 14215 USA
Phone: (716) 837-0551
E-mail: Lczarnota@aol.com
Website: www.sff.net/people/lorna

Jana Dean lives in Olympia, WA, where she tells stories to her middle school students and to her own children. Prior to teacherhood and motherhood, she worked as a storyteller, waitress, farm laborer, naturalist, and writer. The story in her contribution to this book came from an environmental education project in which she sought to learn and tell the stories of her neighborhood. She has taught storytelling to both children and adults and is active in her local storytelling guild.

Phone: (360) 754-5869

Mary Dessein has been working in the chemical dependency field for over 13 years and started exploring the use of story and folklore in the adult treatment setting six years ago. She currently works with the drug court of Snohomish County. Mary hosts *Global Griot*, a public radio program of stories and music from around the world, broadcast in northwestern Washington State, including emceeing live broadcasts of storytellers. She includes her harp playing and other instruments in her performances.

1918 Everett Ave.,
Everett, WA 98201 USA
Phone (888) 240-8572, X3327
E-mail: marystoriesmusic@excite.com

Dennis Freeman, a professional storyteller since 1983, is a senior roster artist with the Arizona Commission on the Arts and has toured extensively throughout the Southwest. Dennis is a collector of oral histories, a folksinger, scriptwriter, and playwright. He draws from varied experiences as a Vietnam helicopter pilot, a sailor on the open sea, and an expatriate living in the jungles of Ecuador. Dennis now lives in the Sonoran Desert with his wife, horses, dog, cat, and assorted chickens.

Autumn Joy Productions, Inc.,
PMB 377, PO Box 42036,
Phoenix, AZ 85080-2036 USA
Phone: (623) 465-7791
E-mail: cuento@earthlink.net

Joseph Andrejchak Galata served on the Social Economic Council of the United Nations for the international Rom (Gypsy) population. Galata's television/video productions have been broadcast around the world and include *My Father Was A Junkman: Stories Of The Gypsies* and *The Shuffle of Shoes Left Behind* (personal stories of WW II

232 THE HEALING HEART ~ Communities

concentration camps). Galata is a former dancer with Gypsy, Russian, Ukrainian, Spanish, Turkish, and Israeli companies. He is an international lecturer and workshop facilitator on the creative arts.

1193 Wagon Wheel,
Reno, NV 89503 USA
Phone: (775) 677-3560
E-mail: JGalata@aol.com

Margaret Jones, MEd, is the director of prevention services for Day One, an adolescent substance abuse agency that is currently in the fifth year of a storytelling grant. She has trained hundreds of professionals, both locally and nationally, to use storytelling in their work and has led storytelling groups with youth.

Day One, 188 State St., Suite 400,
Portland, ME 04101 USA
Phone: (207) 842-2995
E-mail: margaretj@day-one.org

Bob Kanegis is the founder of Tales & Trails. He outfits schools, libraries, camps, and conferences with stories that celebrate the power of imagination and reverence for life. As the director of Future WAVE (Working for Alternatives to Violence Through Entertainment) he works to find ways to use the power of story and storytelling in service of positive communication and healthy relationships.

Tales & Trails
PO Box 6460
Santa Fe NM 87502 USA
Phone: (505) 982-8882
Fax: (505) 955-9585.
E-mail: stories@peacepath.org

Dan Keding has been entertaining audiences for almost 30 years, traveling internationally and performing at some of the most prestigious festivals in the world including the National Storytelling Festival in Jonesborough, Tennessee, and the Sidmouth Folk Arts Festival in England. Dan was inducted into the National Storytelling Network's Circle of Excellence in 2000, and his recordings have won numerous awards. Dan tells traditional folktales, original stories, and personal tales and sings ballads and folk songs, accompanying himself on guitar, banjo, and spoons.

203 G.H. Baker Drive,
Urbana, IL 61801 USA
Phone: (217) 344-8460
Fax: (217) 344-8476
E-mail: dantale@earthlink.net

Erica Lann-Clark is one of America's feminist Jewish folktellers, an internationally known storyteller, and an award-winning playwright who makes you laugh, think, and laugh about thinking. An educator and grant recipient, Erica was storyteller-in-residence for the Monterey Bay Aquarium and presents exemplary Arts-in-Education programs/residencies. Her radio show, *The Storytellers* (KKUP 91.5 FM) brings stories from Tellers Across America to eager listeners in the Silicon Valley. Erica's story can be heard on her audiotape of folktales and personal stories — *The Goats Know The Way: Stories From Lore, Stories From Life.*

132 Alturas Way
Soquel, CA 95073 USA
Phone: (831) 479-1874
E-mail: lanntell@cruzio.com

Cheryl L'Hirondelle Waynohtêw is an Alberta-born, First Nation/Kikino Métis, and currently a Saskatchewan-based interdisciplinary artist. She has created, performed, programmed, and collaborated in a variety of media: performance art, music, theatre, poetry, storytelling, video, and multimedia. Since the early 1990s, Cheryl has also been actively involved as an arts programmer, cultural strategist, activist, and arts consultant. She works as a producer independently and in the artist network, with First Nation's bands and tribal councils and with Canadian government agencies.

Website: www.ndnnrkey.net

Doug Lipman became aware of the healing power of storytelling one day in 1970, when he accidentally entranced 70 "emotionally disturbed" children in the school where he taught. Since then he has told stories and coached on four continents, using the power of storytelling to teach, empower, and connect. He specializes in supportive coaching — and in training corporate executives to use storytelling for personal and organizational transformation. He offers a free e-mail newsletter, "eTips from the Storytelling Coach," via his website.

PO Box 441195
West Somerville, MA 02144 USA
Phone: (781) 391-3672
Fax: (781) 391-6341
Toll-free: (888) 446-4738
E-mail: healingstory@storydynamics.com
Web page: http://www.storydynamics.com

Olga Loya uses a dramatic mix of Spanish and English to tell family stories and Latin American folklore. She also tells She-ro stories, world tales, and healing stories. Loya is a recording artist with seven videos and five cassettes of stories and is the award-winning author of *Momentos Magicos, Magic Moments* (Aesop Accolade, International Reading Association Award, Americas Award). Loya offers adult storytelling concerts such as "Jumping through Flames" and "The Dark and Light in Us All." Loya has been featured at the first Latin American Storytelling Festival in Guadalajara, 1993 National Storytelling Festival, and other festivals around the country and beyond.

PO Box 6482
San Jose, CA 95150 USA
Phone/Fax: (408) 297-3550
E-Mail: oloya1@mindspring.com

Margaret Read MacDonald works as a children's librarian at the Bothell branch of the King County Library in Seattle, WA, where she shares her tales with over 15,000 listeners every year. She has told stories and offered workshops in storytelling around the world. Margaret holds a PhD in folklore and is the author of over 30 books — many of which have become the favorite story collections of veteran storytellers. Margaret has pulled her repertoire from folktales around the world and encouraged many to give storytelling a try.

11507 NE 104th Street
Kirkland, WA 98033 USA
Phone/Fax: (425) 827-6430
E-mail: margmacd@kcls.org

Joseph Naytowhow, a Woodland Cree, was born in the 1950s at Sturgeon Lake First Nation. Stories that he heard as a child came from ceremonial, hunting, gathering, and family get-together circles. By age 25 he was spinning yarns at the university in Saskatoon. Mary Lee and George Mantee were two of many Elders who inspired Joseph as a storyteller. For 10 years now,

Joseph has been appearing professionally, telling trickster tales, legends, creation myths, value-based, supernatural, and humorous stories.

PO Box 673
Dundurn, SK
S0K 1K0 Canada
Phone: (306) 492-4625
E-mail: josephnaytowhow@hotmail.com

Steve Otto is a full-time professional storyteller who tells nationally. His love of telling stories is exceeded only by the joy of having his audience absorb the wonder of storytelling. His repertoire of over 450 stories has something for all ages and audiences. His programs for intergenerational storytelling span the generations to bring families together. His workshops and in-service training programs stress the use of storytelling techniques as learning tools for schools and business.

3606 N.E. 62nd Terrace,
Kansas City, MO 64119 USA
Phone/Fax: (816) 454-7262 or (888) 29i-tell
E-mail: i-tell@juno.com
Website: www.storynet.org/tellers/steveotto

Leticia Pizzino is a freelance storyteller and musician who lives in Vista, CA, with her husband, Jeff, and their four children. She tells for both young and old, with her favorite audiences being families. Leticia performs at festivals, libraries, schools, conferences, and other venues. She is also an artist-in-residence for schools, Community Nursing Services, Utah Art Council/Arts in Education, Art Access, and other organizations. Her belief is that storytelling is intertwined with the very essence of humanity.

PO Box 475, Vista, CA 92085-0475 USA
Phone: (800) 669-7533
E-mail: leticia@imtellinginc.com
Website: imtellinginc.com

John Porcino writes: In the fall of 1980, at a stunning old Adirondack Mountain lodge, John Porcino accidentally stumbled into a class on storytelling. A few years later, somehow, John's love for this simple art form led him to hang up a shingle to the world saying "Storyteller Musician." Thousands of performances and workshops later, and that love has only deepened. His publications include the book *Spinning Tales, Weaving Hope*, feature articles in *Family Fun* magazine, and the recording *A Heck of a Way to Stay Warm*.

120 Pulpit Hill Rd. #10
Amherst, MA 01002 USA
Phone: (413) 549-5448
E-mail: john.porcino@cohousing.com
Website: www.johnporcino.com

Robert Reiser performs his original work and tales from around the world at major festivals like the annual Clearwater Revival, 3 Apples Festival, and the National Storytelling Network conference. Bob is listed as one of the 120 best living English-speaking storytellers in *Storytellers* by McFarland Press. His books with Pete Seeger, *Carry it On* and *Everybody Says Freedom*, are read across the country. His new children's book, *David Gets His Drum*, co-written with jazz drummer Panama Francis, was published in fall 2002 by Marshall Cavendish.

15 Oak Ave.,
Tarrytown, NY 10591
Phone: (914) 422-1156
E-mail: RSReiser@aol.com

Cathy Spagnoli has been a professional storyteller for over 20 years, giving numerous programs in the U.S. and Asia. Funding from national and international sponsors has allowed her to research Asian storytelling and to collect stories from refugees in the U.S. Her tales are also shared through her many books, tapes, and articles. Cathy lives with her husband, Indian sculptor Paramasivam, and their son, Manu, on Vashon Island, in a home they built themselves, and in Cholamandal Artists' Colony in South India.

27225 97th Avenue SW
Vashon, WA 98070 USA
Phone/Fax: (206) 463-4054
E-mail: spagnoli@nwlink.com
Website: http://wwwcathyspagnoli.com

Susan Strauss has engaged audiences across the U.S. and Europe for over 20 years with stories from diverse cultures and often with themes of the natural world. She frequently performs for the National Park and Forest Service and for museums. She has written three children's books and *The Passionate Fact: Storytelling in Natural History & Cultural Interpretation*. Susan is an affiliate faculty member for the University of Idaho and teaches "The Passionate Fact" workshop for natural history storytelling several times a year.

PO Box 1141
Bend, OR 97709 USA
Phone: (541) 382-2888
Website: www.straussstoryteller.com

Terry Tafoya is a Native American of the Taos Pueblo and Warm Springs Nations, a clinical psychologist, and a traditional storyteller. He is the executive director of Tamanawit Unltd., an international multicultural consulting company that specializes in bilingual education, cross-cultural competence and communication, gender and sexuality, grief and loss, Native American heritage, and spiritual healing. Dr. Tafoya has directed the training efforts of a national program for AIDS awareness and prevention, and he serves as a national consultant for the U.S.

Center for Substance Abuse Prevention Project. His work in the areas of cultural diversity, educational methodology and philosophy, community healing, and cross-cultural communication is professionally recognized worldwide.

Tamanawit Unlimited,
1122 E. Pike Street, Suite 575
Seattle, WA 98122 USA
Phone: (206) 632-8124
Fax: (509) 463-4983
E-mail: Tamanawit@aol.com

Bruce Taylor writes magic realism. His book *The Final Trick of Funnyman and Other Stories*, was published in 1997. Now reprinted, it is available through print on demand (Fairwoodpress.com). He is founder and director of the Magic Realist Writers International Network (www.pantarbe.com), president of the Seattle Writers Association, and co-director of the Wellness Program at Harborview Medical Center. He has written over 1000 short stories and teaches novel writing and dealing with creative blocks at North Seattle Community College.

PO Box 9599
Seattle, WA 98109 USA
Phone: (206) 323-5483
E-mail: brucebtaylor@aol.com
Website:
http://www.pantarbe.com/mrmagicrealism

Kira Van Deusen has spent parts of the last ten years traveling in Siberia, learning about storytelling and spiritual traditions from indigenous people. She has performed stories and music extensively in Canada and the U.S. and also arranged cultural exchanges between Siberia and Canada. Much of Kira's work focuses on women's traditions — both as tellers and as lively, intelligent heroines. She is helping develop learning materials for native language programs in Russia.

307-1738 Frances St.,
Vancouver, BC
V5L 1Z6 Canada
Phone/Fax: (604) 255-8366
E-mail: kiravan@imag.net

Liz Weir is a storyteller, based in County Antrim, Northern Ireland, who travels the world promoting the art for which the Irish are world famous. She has been a featured teller at the National Storytelling Conference in Jonesborough, Tennessee, as well as at many prestigious festivals through the United States and Canada. Liz has told stories in Israel, Russia, Australia, and in many parts of Europe and is the director of the annual Ulster Storytelling Festival. Formerly children's librarian for the city of Belfast, she actively works for peace in her native country and in 2002 was the first recipient of the National Storytelling Network's International Storybridge Award.

127 Ballyemon Road,
Cushendall, Co.
Antrim, Northern Ireland
Phone: +44 28 2175 8451
E-mail: liz@taleteam.demon.co.uk
Website: www.taleteam.demon.co.uk

Wendy Welch tells stories as second nature. She writes a newspaper column on folklore and storytelling, is founder of the American Folklore Society's Storytelling Section, has written numerous articles on the art and study of storytelling, and teaches college classes on folklore and telling techniques. Her repertoire comes from her native Appalachia, studies in Newfoundland, and current home in Scotland. Wendy infuses her tales with depth and meaning. Her listeners never fail to enjoy themselves and learn something new.

The Old Schoolhouse,
New Gilston, Fife
KY8 5TF United Kingdom
Phone: 01144 1334 840234
E-mail: jbeck69087@aol.com

Cathryn Wellner has been traveling the storyteller's path for two decades and now performs primarily with her husband, Richard Wright. Storytelling is an integral part of their consulting practice, GrassRoots Consulting Group Inc., which focuses on communications, research, publishing, and community development. Whether addressing a business group, teaching seminars or workshops, keynoting a conference, or performing at a festival, stories are at the heart of their work.

Miocene Box 15,
4030 Horsefly Road
Williams Lake, BC
V2G 2P3 Canada
Phone: (250) 296-4432
Fax: (250) 296-4429
E-mail: cwellner@grassrootsgroup.com
Website: http://grassrootsgroup.com

Laurel Wells writes: Of her many hats, storyteller is one of Laurel's favorites. She lives "so happy together" in a cottage in the woods with her storyteller husband, David Novak, her twin 11 year olds, and her newborn son in the mountains of North Carolina.

E-mail: Lstory2000@aol.com

Diane F. Wyzga is a nurse-attorney, former healthcare business executive, and founder of Tell It By Heart and StrategicStorytelling story companies. An active professional member of the

National Speakers Association and the National Storytelling Network, she is widely sought as a keynote speaker, workshop leader, and storyteller with the ability to educate, inspire, enchant, and delight. Diane also trains attorneys in the use of storytelling techniques to craft a persuasive legal story understandable to a jury. Diane volunteers her speaking and storytelling skills to environmental and domestic abuse cases.

Tell It By Heart,
PO Box 1213
San Clemente, CA 92674 USA
E-mail: dfwyzga@attglobal.net

Dan Yashinsky is the founder of the Toronto Festival of Storytelling. He is the author of *The Storyteller at Fault* and the editor of four collections of Canadian storytelling. He also wrote *Suddenly They Heard Footsteps: A Storyteller's Logbook* (forthcoming).

19 Kenwood Avenue,
Toronto, ON
M6C 2R8 Canada
Phone: (416) 654-1542
E-mail: Dan_Yashinsky@swiftnet.org

If you have enjoyed *The Healing Heart*, You may also enjoy the following title from New Society Publishers

SPINNING TALES WEAVING HOPE

Stories, Storytelling and Activities for Peace, Justice and the Environment

Edited by Ed Brody, Jay Goldspinner, Katie Green, Rona Leventhal and John Porcino
Foreword by Holly Near

The second edition of this much-loved storytelling sourcebook features 29 wondrous children's stories from around the world. From the mythic and the fantastic, to the silly and the serious, these timeless tales encourage conflict resolution, compassion, and sensitivity to the Earth and all living things. An incredible sourcebook for storytellers, teachers, parents and healers, each story is followed by suggested activities and exercises, storytelling tips, and resources, all designed to deepen the storytelling experience. Includes an Age Suitability Index, a Thematic Index, and a Directory of Contributors. A new introduction focuses on storytelling in education.

The editors are all dedicated storytellers and members of the Stories for World Change Network, founded by Ed Brody. They all live in Massachusetts.

296 pages 8.5 x 11"

Education & Teaching / Folklore / Fiction Anthology

ISBN 0-86571-447-9

US$24.95 / Can$33.95

If you have enjoyed *The Healing Heart ~ Communities* you might also enjoy other

BOOKS TO BUILD A NEW SOCIETY

New Society Publishers' mission is to publish books that contribute in fundamental ways to building an ecologically sustainable and just society, and to do so with the least possible impact on the environment, in a manner that models this vision.

Our books provide positive solutions for people who want to make a difference.
We specialize in:

• Sustainable Living • Ecological Design and Planning •
• Natural Building & Appropriate Technology • Environment and Justice •
• New Forestry • Conscientious Commerce • Resistance and Community •
• Nonviolence • Progressive Leadership • Educational and Parenting Resources •

For a full list of NSP's titles, please call 1-800-567-6772 or check out our web site at:
www.newsociety.com

New Society Publishers

ENVIRONMENTAL BENEFITS STATEMENT

New Society Publishers has chosen to produce this book
on New Leaf EcoBook 100, recycled paper made with 100% post
consumer waste, processed chlorine free, and old growth free.

For every 5,000 books printed, New Society saves the following resources:[1]

37	Trees
3,370	Pounds of Solid Waste
3,708	Gallons of Water
4,836	Kilowatt Hours of Electricity
6,126	Pounds of Greenhouse Gases
26	Pounds of HAPs, VOCs, and AOX Combined
9	Cubic Yards of Landfill Space

[1] Environmental benefits are calculated based on research done by the Environmental Defense Fund and other members of the Paper Task Force who study the environmental impacts of the paper industry.

For more information on this environmental benefits statement, or to inquire about environmentally friendly papers, please contact New Leaf Paper – info@newleafpaper.com – 888•989•5323.

NEW SOCIETY PUBLISHERS